Corporate Lending

ifs **School of Finance**
Incorporated by Royal Charter

Corporate Lending

Peter Lyons

The **ifs** School of Finance is a registered charity, incorporated by Royal Charter.

ifs School of Finance
IFS House
4–9 Burgate Lane
Canterbury
Kent
CT1 2XJ

T   01227 818649
F   01227 784331
E   editorial@ifslearning.ac.uk
W www.ifslearning.ac.uk

Typeset by John Smith

Printed by Antony Rowe Ltd, Wiltshire

© *ifs* School of Finance 2004

Reprinted 2007, 2008

ISBN 1-84516-066-5

ifs School of Finance
Incorporated by Royal Charter

Contents

Corporate Lending

Introduction

The traditional base activities of a bank are to accumulate deposits, lend money (and subsequently get the loans repaid) and to transmit customer funds. Lending may not now be the most profitable service the bank provides, depending on the definition of profitable, but it offers regularity of income in a relatively risk free environment. It is the elimination of risk that bankers should always strive to attain.

To take a simple example, if a bank lends £100 and expects to make a net profit of 2.5% pa from the arrangement but the debt proves irrecoverable, the loss of £100 for the bank will mean that 40 similar deals will have to be placed during that year to recover the lost funds. It is important for each bank to apply a balanced approach to its lending portfolio so as to spread the risks as much as possible and to safeguard against undue losses arising in any one market.

The rewards accruing to a bank from lending will depend on the particular mix of facilities offered that are taken up and on the profit margin that can be enjoyed by the bank in what has now become a very legislative and competitive lending environment. Rewards can be measured against the bank's capital requirement for investing in different types of lending. The income may be received immediately, as through an arrangement fee, as well as being spread over the period of the loan by way of renewal fees and the profit 'turn' achieved on the funds lent.

The type of lending portfolio built up will determine how much reward will accrue to the bank. Participation in a loan syndicated by other banks will be counted in terms of a small number of basis points (hundredths of one percent) of earnings, whereas a small commercial loan may be agreed at a margin of several whole percentages. The importance of choosing the most efficient type of loan for the bank that will also suit the client may be judged by the following hypothetical example.

The client has an overdraft facility that may be described as a hardcore (ie more or less permanent) borrowing need. The business is profitable and the request for additional support from a worthwhile client is reasonable. As banker to the business, you are asked to look at the request for an increase in the overdraft limit of £10,000 but you would prefer not to have the extra funds extend the hardcore element of the facility. It is decided to look into the option of offering a programmed loan.

The interest rate on a three-year loan for the client is assumed 7% pa, payable quarterly, and the cost of funds assumed taken from the money market is 4% pa, giving the bank a gross profit margin of 3% pa. Assuming all other client fees and bank expenses are identical for both facilities, the reward to the bank of the two lending alternatives may be calculated in broad terms as follows.

Overdraft

Quarters	Balance brought forward	Interest at 7% per annum	Balance carried forward	Repayment	Interest present value
1	10,000.00	175.00	10,000.00	Nil	173.25
2	10,000.00	175.00	10,000.00	Nil	171.50
3	10,000.00	175.00	10,000.00	Nil	169.75
4	10,000.00	175.00	10,000.00	Nil	168.00
5	10,000.00	175.00	10,000.00	Nil	166.25
6	10,000.00	175.00	10,000.00	Nil	164.50
7	10,000.00	175.00	10,000.00	Nil	162.75
8	10,000.00	175.00	10,000.00	Nil	161.00
9	10,000.00	175.00	10,000.00	Nil	159.25
10	10,000.00	175.00	10,000.00	Nil	157.50
11	10,000.00	175.00	10,000.00	Nil	155.75
12	10,000.00	175.00	10,000.00	Nil	154.00
Total		2,100.00			1,963.50

Programmed loan

Quarters	Balance brought forward	Interest at 7% per annum	Repaid quarterly	Principal element	Cumulative interest at 4% per annum	Total interest	Interest present value
1	10,000.00	175.00	931.14	756.14	7.56	182.56	180.74
2	9,243.86	161.77	931.14	769.37	15.26	177.02	173.48
3	8,474.49	148.30	931.14	782.83	23.08	171.39	166.25
4	7,691.66	134.60	931.14	796.53	31.05	165.65	159.03
5	6,895.12	120.66	931.14	810.47	39.15	159.82	151.83
6	6,084.65	106.48	931.14	824.66	47.40	153.88	144.65
7	5,259.99	92.05	931.14	839.09	55.79	147.84	137.49
8	4,420.91	77.37	931.14	853.77	64.33	141.69	130.36
9	3,567.13	62.42	931.14	868.71	73.02	135.44	123.25
10	2,698.42	47.22	931.14	883.92	81.85	129.08	116.17
11	1,814.50	31.75	931.14	899.38	90.85	122.60	109.12
12	915.12	16.01	931.14	915.12	100.00	116.01	102.09
Total		1,173.65	11,173.65		629.34	1,802.99	1,694.45

The repayments of principal arising from the programmed loan have earned only 4% pa and the return to the bank is improved through increasing the overdraft limit. The conclusion would reverse, however, if the interest return on the programmed loan were higher than 6.4732% pa.

Many factors other than the empirical return on funds lent must be considered in corporate lending, as Section 1 on Corporate Strategy reveals.

One

Corporate strategy

1.1 Introduction

If a company is commencing a business it should have researched and adopted in advance a strategy for trading. This can be broken down into four basic components.

- An **internal strategy** that the company can manipulate: the internal strategy will decide answers to questions such as: what products will be promoted; in what markets and locations will they be traded; at what selling prices; what customers will be targeted and for what profit?
- An **external strategy**, to which the company can react: the internal strategy can then be married to external situations: what is the competition and how is it likely to affect business; how will customers react to the products on sale and their pricing?
- There will be a **strategy of timing**: over what future time period will the company assess the success or otherwise of its current trading decisions?
- Finally, there is a **recognition strategy**: what aspects of trading, whether internal or external, may change in the future? Will the typewriter be replaced by the computer keyboard and, if so, should the company recognise the advent of this new technology in advance?

The bank will perceive its lending risk in accordance with the trading strategy adopted by the borrowing company.

1.2 Examples why a strategy should be adopted

A strategic overview must always be present regardless of the size of a business. The aim will be to keep the objectives of the business constantly in mind and to prepare for changing circumstances should they arise. Consider two examples.

> Eastman Kodak, the American photography company and a giant in its industry, announced early in 2004 further sweeping job cuts of up to 15,000 employees (equivalent to 24% of an already reduced workforce) as digital technology replaced film cameras worldwide. The company reported that the cost of its re-focusing would be up to US$ 1.7 billion, but that the new strategy would generate savings in operating costs by 2007 of an estimated US$ 1 billion. Digital cameras were virtually unknown in 1996 but sales are expected to overtake film cameras by 2007. The company commenced strategic acquisitions of digital technology companies from the latter half of 2003. Had Eastman Kodak prepared early enough for this quantum change in the market?

> Lastminute.com floated on the Stock Market near the end of the so-called 'Dot Com' boom in companies offering their services on the World Wide Web. The money raised gave the business several years lifeline to build up its presence and to transform the company from loss with little income to a tangible asset base earning a profit. Lastminute is now established in 18 countries and is trading profitably through the astute acquisition, for cash and shares, of other company businesses ancillary to its own specialization in the consumer leisure field. The strategy of building up value through bolting on established businesses, while at the same time continuing to market its own trading brand, has led to this growth and was a prime objective at the time of floatation.

Private companies of very modest size should also hold a strategic overview of their trading options. Take the case of a small manufacturing business operating in a very competitive environment whose two principal customers account for the majority of turnover. On the one hand, so long as these strategic customers remain, the business has a firm turnover foundation. Should either or both customers change their buying preferences to a competitor supplier, the fixed cost base of the company will be undermined and there will be little time to replace the lost business. The company objective should be to rely less on these customers, so that if circumstances change adversely, the business can remain a viable unit.

As can be seen from the examples highlighted, both external market (Eastman Kodak) and internal strategic (Lastminute) changes affect the businesses concerned. Eastman Kodak was affected by industry change and the threat of competition posed by new entrants (and their products) into the market. As a result, the group's profitability suffered as the general public, the buyers, increasingly accepted the new technology. The group has adopted a changed strategy of acquiring existing suppliers of related digital technology products. It has had to invest capital in this new technology.

1.3 What are the strategic variables?

An optimum corporate strategy embodies several variables:

- ◆ the perceived needs of the owners (shareholders);
- ◆ the directorate's need to underline the worth of the business;
- ◆ the continuing success of the business itself;
- ◆ the time period(s) over which all variables are evaluated.

The shareholders will judge their investment by the income (dividends) and capital (share value) that is achieved. The directorate may have incentives to provide successful management (share options; salary progression and reputation) and will be judged on how they react to changing operating circumstances. The company itself must show added value in its marketplace through higher earnings and greater market share. It should be noted that higher earnings is not the same as higher dividends: the former does not necessarily lead to the latter (refer to the very profitable company Microsoft that has only now commenced a dividend distribution policy).

1.4 Batelle's six inputs

How should these variables be evaluated in practice? Dr Stephen Millett (Batelle) identified six inputs, each of which may be declining, staying constant, or expanding at any one point in time.

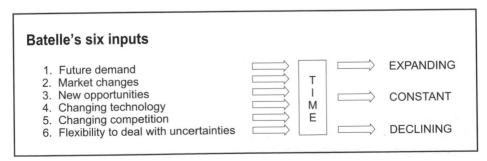

Batelle's six inputs

1. Future demand
2. Market changes
3. New opportunities
4. Changing technology
5. Changing competition
6. Flexibility to deal with uncertainties

TIME

EXPANDING

CONSTANT

DECLINING

To draw an analogy with bank lending, interest rates (input 2) may be increasing and this is likely to lead to a reduced lending demand (1). New services (3) are being offered via the internet (4) but will take time to become established (6). Meanwhile, other banks may be quicker to adapt to these circumstances (5). By how much will these factors affect the future earnings of the bank relative to its peer group?

1.5 Porter's Five Forces

A simplified and earlier analysis of this type of external corporate strategy was undertaken by Porter, to determine the profitability of an industry relative to its cost of capital, through the interaction of five principal sources of competitive pressure. This is usually demonstrated as follows.

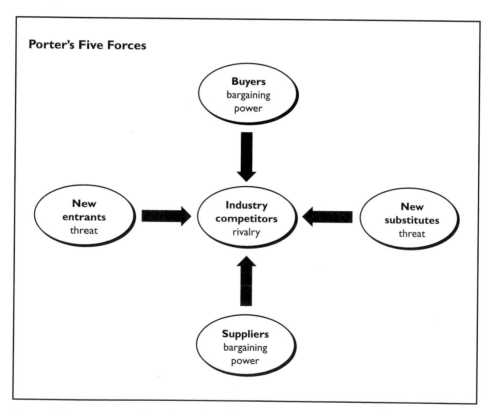

Buyers' (ie customers) and suppliers' bargaining powers will affect the pricing structure of the products and the pricing policy of the company. Their relative bargaining strengths will determine the profitability of the company: if there is dependence on one major supplier, the bargaining power (or choice) of the buyers will affect the profit margin attainable on the product. If the company relies on one major buyer, its profitability will rely on the bargaining (pricing) power of the supplier(s).

Buyers potentially have the power to substitute their choice of provider or there may arise the threat of a choice of substitute products. New entrants may have excess production capacity and/or more modern equipment, enabling them to reap the benefit of economies of scale that give them cost advantages leading to a more competitive pricing structure. All these factors will determine the extent of competition in the industry and how it will affect individual companies.

The aim for the company will be to compute in financial terms its own strengths (Porter's Five Forces) relative to its competitors and to translate that into a strategy to enhance its own return and to counteract the effect of the competition. There are some omissions in the analysis: the reading is usually at one point in time and must be repeated for any underlying changes. Also, it does not take into account the time required to effect a strategic change in direction. Eastman Kodak is suggesting a time period of three years for the full results of its new strategy to be felt.

1.6 Evaluating the strategic variables

How is an evaluation done? Multinational companies assess the scenario through the following steps (Batelle).

1. Defining the issue (time frame/measuring unit/scope/key drivers)

2. Identifying the areas of influence (the impacting events)

3. Analysing the environmental factors (calculating probabilities)

4. Estimating the cross-impacts (and running the model)

5. Analysing the results (for further study)

6. Introducing sensitivity analysis ('what if' changes to the variables)

7. Preparing forecasts (and studying the implications)

Small companies have to rely on a simpler analysis of the variables affecting trading and consider a much shorter time scale. An example might be the situation of a corner shop business that has just been made aware of a planning application by a supermarket chain to build a new superstore close by. The steps shown above might be interpreted along the following lines.

Steps	Assessment examples
Defining issues	How will profits be affected by the new store opening
Influential areas	Selling prices; turnover; loss of customers; products
Calculate factors	What drop in selling prices is needed to retain sales etc
Cross-impacts	Can product emphasis be changed to maintain margins
Analysing results	What are the best practical options to adopt
Sensitivities	Re-assess the options and choose the best one to adopt
Forecasting	Calculate the revised turnover and profit forecast

1.7 The Boston measurement matrix

The measurement of company profitability relative to its investment requirement led to the Directional Policy (Business Portfolio) Matrix (shown hereafter) as drawn up by the Boston Consulting Group. This model compared the market growth (by value) to the market share held by a business.

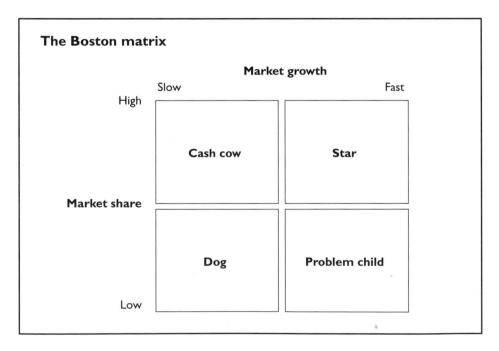

We can compare a company increasing its grocery market share when the value of the market as a whole is growing slowly (a cash cow) with a competitor that is losing market share and showing slower growth (a dog). When considering the major supermarket chains, an example of the former would be Tesco – the market leader – and an example of the latter would be Safeway prior to its 2004 takeover by William Morrison. Morrison's has shown steady growth over many years but from a relatively low market share (a problem child), and a major factor in William Morrison's decision to acquire Safeway was undoubtedly a desire to boost its market share and consequently approach cash cow status.

Lastminute.com is an example of star company within the fast-growing consumer leisure sector, holding a dominant market share of the major quoted company players in late travel and ancillary services bookings. There are, however, inherent factors that can affect a matrix definition when converting perceived market growth into market value, and it can be seen that Lastminute.com has yet to become a profit-earning cash cow, while Tesco is basing its current market value partially on growth in overseas markets and partially from supplementary – non-grocery – trading interests.

1.8 Benchmarking

Benchmarking is becoming increasingly popular to evaluate whether the correct business strategy is being applied to the operations of a company when returns cannot necessarily, or wholly, be calculated in straight financial values. It can show management those parts of the business that are operating below target and it can indicate trends when assessed on a regular basis. It can be useful both as an internal company measurement guide, when assessing a business through its separate accounting centres, or when evaluating non profit-making entities. When adopted externally, individual corporate returns may be compared with the benchmark aggregate returns from a number of similar businesses and any significant deviations may be queried.

Usually up to five internal key performance indicators (KPIs) are chosen according to the characteristics of the company. Four indicators are shown in the example. A weighting will be applied as a percentage to each indicator, adding up to 100%. Key ratios are then chosen within each measure and sub-weighting applied to each, again adding up to 100%. All the sub-weightings are converted to an overall percentage +/- to 100% (or to '1' if preferred) to obtain a final reading for the company. This is compared with a pre-set target of where the company wishes to be in the future. The percentage change required for each key performance indicator to reach its set target will provide the company where, and to what degree, an improvement is needed. Regular comparisons at set intervals (eg annually) will show the progress made.

As a notional example, a supermarket company may wish to measure the following:

Measures	Weighting	Assessments	Sub-weight
Financial	35%	Turnover per sq ft	30%
		Profit margin %	30%
		Return on capital employed % pa	40%
Customers	25%	Number of till transactions	30%
		Additional services taken up	20%
		Number of complaints	50%
Suppliers	20%	Deliveries on time (proportion)	20%
		Quality of goods (rejections)	50%
		Pricing competitiveness	30%
Staff	20%	Proportion of leavers	40%
		Absenteeism	30%
		Vacancy level	30%

1.9 McKinsey's 7-S framework

The McKinsey model applies a 7-S framework to analyse a company's internal strategy as follows.

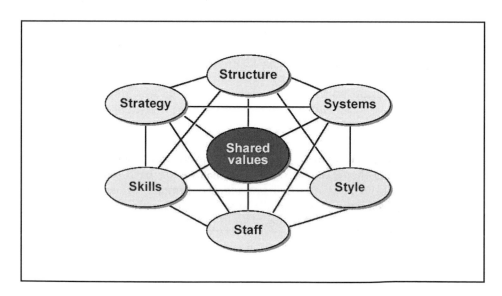

1. **Strategy**   the allocation of the business's resources
2. **Structure**   an organization chart how departments are related
3. **Systems**   the adoption of routine processes and reports
4. **Staffing**   the categories of personnel and their qualifications
5. **Style**   how the managers perform to achieve their goals
6. **Shared values** relationship of the organization to its members
7. **Skills**   the capabilities of staff and the business as a whole

It was discovered that companies performing well had a bias for action: there was autonomy and entrepreneurship shown by the staff who could identify themselves with the company; there was a belief in productivity; the working approach was hands on and value driven; the business had a simple operational structure, was efficiently staffed in numbers and could operate flexibly.

Another theme leading to corporate success was termed 'thriving on chaos'. It employed constant innovation; a partnership between all sections of the workforce with a leadership built on change and vision; an obsession to be responsive to customers' demands and with proper control of the business through its support systems measuring the right operating factors.

1.10 PEST analysis

PEST analysis defines and measures the effects of external variables outside the control of a company in order to reduce the operating risks. A weighting is given to each variable similar to benchmarking. Probabilities are assigned to each according to the likelihood of their occurrence and its quantitative effect on business operations. They are then ranked according to their expected individual impact on the business. Low rankings are discarded, leaving the company to concentrate its strategy on reducing its vulnerability on the remaining factors. There are four principal variables.

- **P**olitical
- **E**conomic
- **S**ocial
- **T**echnological

Political intervention at both national and international levels can be frequent and the effects severe. Banks may be nationalized or have exchange controls imposed. The lending environment may be restricted and there may be political preference given to indigenous lenders.

Economic risks relate to fiscal and monetary policy of the central authorities. They range from control on interest rates, money supply and taxation to more indirect influences as on disposable incomes of the population and the imposition of means to stimulate competition.

Social influences may concern the ethical grounds of corporate operations. Examples are the outsourcing of jobs overseas, social attitudes to established practices (such as 'unacceptably high' lending rates), demographic changes, the propensity to save or spend since this affects bank lending, and overseas nationalism against foreign businesses.

Technological change can have a big impact on businesses that have had a large reliance on staffing branch networks (eg banks) but can now adopt the latest computer systems and offer programmed (lending) products.

The addition of **environmental/ethical factors**, particularly relevant in issues of corporate social responsibility, and of **legislative changes** including those that arise as a consequence of EU directives, has led to PEST analysis now more commonly being approached as **PESTLE**, **LEPEST** or **PESTEL**.

Measurements of any strategy are only as good as the accurate recording of inputs and the underlying assumptions on which they are based. The misstatement of oil and gas reserves held by the Shell group of companies that was published early in 2004 would be significant enough, if substantiated, to change the strategy of the group in reallocating resources to boost exploration to find or purchase more reserves in future years.

Business strategy

1.11 The objectives of a business strategy

Strictly speaking, a business strategy should precede a financial strategy. The former sets out the business objectives of the company and the latter implements them. The business objectives should not be confused with a company's 'mission statement'. The mission statement establishes the general aspirations of the company while the business strategy specifies current thinking on how this will be achieved. Consider the following mission statement:

> the group remains totally committed to maximizing shareholder value over time and our business units continue to be focused on the group's three strategic aims: to be a leader in our chosen markets; to be first choice for our customers; and to drive down day-to-day operational costs to enable us to further invest in our business franchise.

There are unlikely to be major changes to these objectives from year to year. Examining the company's report further, one reads that the strategic business objectives achieved in the past year have been: a strengthened market share in three (stated) key product areas; a strong recruitment of new customers with greater cross-selling of products; and a reduction in staff numbers. The example taken is that of a major bank.

For a trading company the owners (or delegated directors and/or managers) of a business should have a continuous idea of where they wish their business to be placed within the market(s) in which they are trading; how profitable they wish the business to be; and how they are best able to achieve these objectives. This concept has to be ongoing and responsive to changing circumstances.

The strategy established to meet these objectives may embody a number of options and the examples given below are not exhaustive:

- to grow to a strategic size for better control of trading in the company's chosen markets;
- to grow and become a public quoted company for ease of raising (cheaper) finance;
- to expand into new markets overseas to gain advantage of better trading margins;
- to expand into new markets to dilute the risk of a trading downturn in one area of the business;
- to diversify into other products for the same reason;
- to gain better reward for the owners of the business, whether in higher dividends, greater remuneration or capital value improvement;
- to remain at the forefront of technological change and thereby safeguard the company's future trading interests.

1.12 Where is the business to be placed in its trading market(s)?

In order to answer this question it should be established where the business is in its life cycle.

1. At the embryo or start-up stage

2. At the survival stage

3. At the expansion stage

4. At the mature life stage

5. At the declining end of life stage

The embryo/start-up stage

It should be determined whether or not the business is a 'niche' player, where competition is modest and the skills of management are sufficient to exploit the product(s) or services offered. The business may otherwise be about to trade in a very competitive environment where the marketing prowess or existing contacts of the management will be relied on heavily to ensure success. The business strategy for each case will be different: the former example will have the characteristic of an aversion to risk while the latter will be relying more on marketing and a wish to trade out of poor demand.

With the former case, the lending banker will be asking whether it is likely that competition will materialise in future; whether there is a risk that the business will not achieve the results expected due to a lack of demand or failings in the product when it is produced; or whether the goods or services are likely to be copied. With the latter case, the strength of the competition must be assessed. For example, how many similar service companies are offering an identical product within the company's trading area relative to the demand expected for the service? The answer will affect the degree of profitability expected.

The survival stage

The great majority of small start-up businesses fail within the first two years. The business strategy in most cases has not been properly planned and the entrepreneur is relying on the three 'H's:

+ **happiness** in their chosen occupation;
+ **hard work** to establish the business;
+ **hope** that it will be a success.

It is critical that a proper business strategy is employed to make the most of the (probably) limited capital invested in the venture and that this capital is both adequate and spent wisely.

Survival may be the requirement of the established business that is suffering from poor trading. In this case there will be an immediate need to conserve cash and extend the time that the company can remain trading without becoming insolvent. The strategy will be to cut costs and concentrate on those products or services that are selling well and to offer the best financial returns. There may also be scope to raise additional capital to help trade out of the difficulty and, over a longer time period, to sell some peripheral activities to release capital for investment elsewhere. The lending banker will frequently be asked to assist with this reorganization and it will be necessary to examine closely the business strategy offered in order to determine whether this will achieve a recovery in the fortunes of the company.

The expansion stage

Many businesses look upon the lending service of a bank as being akin to providers of permanent capital. It is a flawed strategy on which to base and run a company and sympathy must go to an overworked lending officer who will, in effect, be monitoring the account and, ipso facto, acting as the company's strategist. This may, or may not, be related to the question of borrowing to expand the business. Care must be taken to ensure that the debt can be repaid within the agreed period.

Management can plan expansion internally or it may arise through external factors occurring independent of the business. By definition, planning expansion organically will mean the company will have faced the questions that their banker will want to ask: are there sound reasons behind the strategy; have all probable trading scenarios been assessed correctly; are the financial projections reasonable? External factors may have a positive or negative impact on expansion plans, such as changes in fiscal regulations or natural supply and demand within the national economy, a major competitor closing down or marketing a new product, or a price war.

The mature life stage

This is generally the most lucrative period in a product or service life for the company. No further investment should be needed in plant or specific marketing for expansion. The company should be mindful to maintain its overall profit margin and market share. Strategy will be largely defensive and ready to combat any trading moves by any competitor. The bank should be looking to the company to reduce gradually any outstanding loans specific to the product or service over this period out of the profits being earned. The bank has its own strategy to consider: as the customer is a good credit risk, should it be looking to increase its exposure?

The end of life stage

At this point in the development of a product or service there will be an established customer following and perhaps even an aversion to change. The strategy should be to concentrate on promoting the brand name to retain sales and to use the now greater profitability on the product(s) sold to invest in research and development of the next generation of goods, thereby stimulating a continuing growth in turnover. This will occur after having written off the initial marketing costs and depreciated fully the plant and machinery necessary for production, thus lowering the current cost of manufacture per item. The lender will be wishing to assess how long existing product sales can remain, at what level, and whether there will be a gap before new product(s) make an impact after this expected rundown.

1.13 How profitable should be the business?

Many small and medium-size businesses fail to address this operational area properly. Ideally, a target net profit after taxation should be set sufficient to reward the proprietor(s)/shareholders(s) and shall leave adequate capital in the business to finance future operations. Working back from this base, allowance should be made for the indirect costs attributable to the business and this, in turn, will set a gross profit target figure. The turnover target will be calculated by taking the gross profit percentage margin available when trading.

Example

	£'000
Profit after tax target	600
Indirect fixed costs of the business	1,200
Resultant gross profit	1,800
Average gross profit margin assumed on sales	60%
Turnover target	**3,000**

The management now have a yardstick by which to plan their trading strategy. Can the business earn sales of £3 million? What is its present capability? In order to earn £3 million what changes have to be made operationally? Will a reduction in costs be sufficient? If not, what else must be done? If the answer is to increase production this may lead to higher indirect costs and the whole example will have to be calculated afresh. In all probability, part of the optimum solution will devolve around the interaction of average selling prices between products or services and the relationship between selling prices and turnover. This is a very important business strategy that constantly arises for companies.

Example

	Product A	Product B	Combined
No of products expected to be sold	I million	I million	2 million
Selling price per product	£1.30	£1.56	
Turnover (£ '000)	1,300	1,560	2,860
Direct costs (£ '000)	520	780	1,300
Gross profit earned (£ '000)	780	780	1,560
Gross profit margin on sales	60%	50%	

Problem

The company wishes to earn a gross profit of at least £1.69 million to achieve the required shareholder reward after tax.

One solution

	Product A	Product B	Combined
Increase the price per product by	10%		
Reduce the price per product by		7%	
The selling price becomes	£1.43	£1.45	
Expected sales are now forecast at	0.9 million	1.3 million	2.2 million
Turnover (£ '000)	1,287	1,885	3,172
Direct costs (£' 000)	468	1,014	1,482
Gross profit earned (£ '000)	819	871	1,690
Gross profit margin on sales	63.6%	46.2%	

The pricing changes may have a more limiting effect if costs can be pared. The direct costs will change in proportion to the number of products sold. Many other strategies can be worked to obtain a similar end result, always bearing in mind that they must be achievable.

1.14 How is the business best able to achieve its objective(s)?

Management must examine each part of the business critically for acceptable performance. The bank, in the event of the company applying for a borrowing facility, will apply the same tests in its credit assessment.

The list following is not exhaustive but provides some idea of the questions to answer.

- ◆ Sales: are sales regularly analysed by source?
  is it known which are the most popular products?
  what is the relative profitability of different products?

- ◆ Production: is the existing plant efficient and adequate?
  can any production beneficially be outsourced?
  is there spare production capacity and is it needed?

- ◆ Labour: is the work force under/over-manned?
what percentage of productive time is charged out?
are there adequate training programmes in place?

- ◆ Selling: what is the track record of the marketing team?
how are they controlled and monitored?
what is the proportion of repeat to new business?
are selling incentives doing their work?

- ◆ Development: how much R & D is being done?
are the projects realizable?
when are projects likely to be marketed?
how much additional finance is required?

- ◆ Financial: is the current level of working capital sufficient?
are existing borrowings appropriately structured?
are debtors being collected promptly?

The bank will be looking overall to assess the following internal characteristics of its lending and the mnemonic is the word 'PREMIER':

- ◆ **P**rofitability of the lending;
- ◆ **R**egulatory procedures to uphold and their cost;
- ◆ **E**conomics of the trading outlook affecting the company and the lending;
- ◆ **M**onitoring of the individual loan and the bank's portfolio generally;
- ◆ **I**nternal management of banking ratios, staffing and public relations;
- ◆ **E**xternal exposure to competition and any offsetting marketing costs;
- ◆ **R**isk analysis of the lending portfolio as a whole (refer section 7).

Financial strategy

In its broadest sense, the financial strategy of a business will be aimed to keep the business operating in the way that its management has laid down. This may mean adopting a borrowing policy both on a short- and long-term view and to ensure that the business does not run out of funds. The financial strategy must be flexible and adaptive to changes in internal policy and external events. It must also embody a risk scenario in case the unexpected occurs. It is inter-related to the business strategy.

1.15 To whom is a financial strategy designed?

The **management** of the company (the board of directors for a limited company and the principals/owners/trustees for non-corporate entities) will have adopted an annual business plan (referred to in paragraph 1.16.1). This plan will indicate a monetary requirement for the business to achieve the operating goals that have been laid down, such as a certain growth in turnover and profits. The monetary requirement will be sub-divided into what is generally termed 'working capital' (but more accurately defined as the net total of current assets less current liabilities of the company, rather than capital that is required to be permanently employed in the business for it to trade) and 'fixed capital' (the capital that is invested in more permanent assets of the business necessary for it to trade). The financial strategy will lay down how these different requirements are to be satisfied.

The **staffing** of the company will be critical and will have a large bearing on the financial strategy finally adopted by management. Their cost is usually a large component of overall expenditure and will comprise a mixture of direct and indirect expenditure: direct wages will relate to the staff needed to produce the company's end products; indirect wages relate to the support staff employed in administration, marketing and central overhead divisions. The number of staff employed to achieve productivity will determine the efficiency of the business. The skills of the workforce will affect quality of the product(s) or service(s) offered.

Depending on the type of business, on-going staff costs may be considerable as will their accruing pension entitlement. The company may operate its own defined benefit scheme or offer employees a defined contribution scheme. The former is an open-ended cost to the company whereas the latter is not. Finally, if staff have to be made compulsorily redundant or laid off for whatever reason, the costs can be significant, so that this should never be the first remedy to choose to improve profits.

The **shareholders** of the company are its owners and, legally speaking, the company should be run by the directors for the shareholders' sole benefit. In practice, the myriad shareholders of a public company have to delegate operating responsibilities to the directors they appoint. Nevertheless, the shareholders have rights to vote at the company's Annual General Meeting (AGM) on adoption of the financial statements and what dividends will be paid out. The financial strategy of the company should be to provide on-going enhancement of shareholder value in the company through a mixture of declared dividends and by capital growth of net worth (as shown for public companies through their share value).

1.16 How is a financial strategy laid down?

The steps to complete a financial strategy are suggested below. Thereafter each step will be considered in greater detail.

1.16.1   Adopt the company's business plan for implementation

1.16.2   Project the trading results based on approved assumptions

1.16.3   Forecast future profit & loss accounts and balance sheets

1.16.4   Calculate a cash flow picture from the forecasts

1.16.5   Re-appraise the assumptions and compare with target returns

1.16.6   Revise any forecasts, as necessary

1.16.7   Review the future cash requirement to attain these forecasts

1.16.8   Decide how the cash requirement is to be met

1.16.9   Provide a sensitivity analysis of the final model

1.16.10   Incorporate a risk assessment to account for the unexpected

1.16.11   Consider reducing risks through derivatives (refer section 7)

1.16.12   Finalize the cash amount to be raised and the timing.

1.16.1 The business plan

The business plan will set out how the company operates, what its resources are, what its objectives are and how these objectives are to be met. Although every business plan is tailored to the particular circumstances of each company there are a number of general headings common to all. These have been listed in brief below.

- ♦ An **executive summary** highlights the main conclusions arising out of the business plan and what action(s) must be implemented to achieve the company's objectives.
- ♦ An **overview of the business** is by way of introduction. This will briefly describe the business and sets out aspects of the business that have been considered when creating the business plan.
- ♦ The **management** and their responsibilities will be listed, including features of their experience and track record, although a detailed curriculum vitae of each is usually shown in an appendix.
- ♦ A **track record** of past trading of the business will be disclosed. It should include both positive and negative highlights, including why the negative results were incurred and what remedial measures were taken at the time to rectify the situation.

- The principal **products** or **services** offered by the business will be described, together with some past financial record of each to display their relative importance to the overall trading result.
- The principal **markets** traded in will similarly be described and analysed.
- The **operational structure** of the business will be explained. This will include: how the business operates; which division is responsible for what; how the business is structured legally; an outline of important operating contracts; the financial terms of trading; and any other important factors relevant to current operations.
- The **business resources** will be detailed. Separate sections will cover **human resources** and **asset resources**. The former will analyse the staff by their responsibilities and the latter will comment on the properties occupied and plant and machinery employed. It will be relevant to discern, for instance, whether the business relies heavily on short-term leaseholds or freeholds, and what is the age and condition of plant that is maintained.
- The method(s) of **production** should be explained. This may, or may not, show a dependence on outsourcing. A key calculation will be the average actual production accomplished during past years compared with the theoretical maximum possible. Production should be measured against the average number of workers employed to judge whether excess capacity is evident.
- The emphasis on **marketing** should be specified: how much is the annual budget; for what products; how are they to be promoted?
- The current **financial** obligations of the business must be listed, including the types of borrowing, their terms and repayment details
- Any new or pending **projects** should be described together with their expected effect on trading results, profitability and required capital resources. Operations being discontinued should be stated.
- The **trading outlook** needs to be analysed and to incorporate both a short and long term view of prospects, with reasons. Any options for the company when adopting a future trading strategy, such as choosing markets or products or services, should be set out.
- The **capital requirements** of the business will be summarized and the decision on how it is all to be financed will be outlined.
- A suggested **action plan** will be drafted, highlighting any operational weaknesses shown by the business plan that require resolution, and setting out what the business may be expected to achieve based on its present resources (refer to sub-section 1.16.2).
- **Appendices** will be included with spreadsheets to support the text.

The management will then amend the business plan and incorporate the business strategy (outlined in section 1.16.2) before its final adoption. Any potential weaknesses should have been removed at this stage and revised target projections for future trading agreed. The business plan will be a valuable document where it is also to be used to support an application for bank borrowing. The lending banker is familiar with mnemonics to shorten those parts of the business plan that should be carefully assessed. Taking probably the most widely one used, known as CAMPARI, a comparison can be made with the contents of the business plan outlined earlier as follows.

- ♦ **Commitment by the borrower:** the extent and content of the business plan will show whether the commitment has been well planned;
- ♦ **Ability of the borrower to manage the business:** the track record of management decisions will indicate their effect on business operations and how responsibilities are delegated to implement the operating plan. This will also assist to judge any individual personal abilities;
- ♦ **Management quality:** the organization chart will show the teamwork and individual management cv's will show their qualifications;
- ♦ **Purpose of the borrowing:** the business plan and talks with management will build up a full picture of why finance is required;
- ♦ **Amount of finance requested:** there should be sufficient information at hand to judge whether the sum requested is adequate or not;
- ♦ **Repayment capacity:** the cash flow forecasts will indicate how repayment is to be made – whether or not from operating surpluses;
- ♦ **Insurance offered in the form of available security:** the analysis of fixed assets and the balance sheet will generally indicate what security is held within the business and whether it is suitable.

1.16.2 Projecting future trading

Most businesses of reasonable size will compile ongoing monthly forecast of financial results for the first year ahead, with quarterly forecasts for the following year and annual forecasts thereafter, perhaps as long as up to five years in advance. The larger corporations will set out financial and business projections for even longer periods, either to match long-term sales contracts, long-term mining/exploration production or the payback period, when investing long-term in an individual project.

The lending bank should enquire how the forecasts have been compiled and test the system, rather than going into the detailed checking of complex calculations. Usually a 'bottom-up' approach is adopted, where forecasts are brought together for each group division or subsidiary company and amalgamated into a group picture. In the final analysis, any inter-group sales should be eliminated, together with any consequent duplication of trading profit. A final check should be made on the overall forecast to ensure that all operating assumptions correlate: that is, that subsidiary A is not assuming to sell 100% of its production to holding company B while company B is only willing to accept 50% of company A's production; company A may also assume that certain external factors will aid sales, while company B may be more cautious.

A different approach may have to be taken when forecasting financial results of smaller trading companies. Sophisticated projections may not be available beyond three months ahead and the answer to the question 'what are you forecasting for turnover next year?' may be 'a small increase if we are lucky'. Actual turnover results achieved monthly in the preceding year may be a good starting guide; these then have to be adjusted for seasonal and exceptional occurrences between last year and the next year and a view taken on the future trading outlook. The average gross profit margin for the past year will be known and this may be adopted for the coming year subject to variations in selling and raw material prices and to changes in direct wages costs. A broad percentage adjustment can be made to indirect costs to arrive at the net profit forecast.

1.16.3 Forecasting profit & loss accounts and balance sheets

Public companies will be able to provide a full breakdown of profit and loss accounts and balance sheet forecasts over the medium-term. Private companies may not provide formal projections beyond the gross profit figure, since it will mean having to estimate the future tax charge, to decide what expenditure will be capitalised in the balance sheet and to judge how current assets (debtors, stocks) and current liabilities (creditors) will change. It will be important, however, for the lending bank to get some idea how the future balance sheet will look in order to estimate the net worth of the business relative to its future borrowings.

As an approximate guide, the standard corporation tax rate can be applied to the forecast gross profit and, if dividends are usually declared, the same payout ratio can be adopted as for the previous year. Fixed asset expenditure may be adjusted for any significant costs known to arise in future. Depreciation at the company's standard percentage rate may be calculated on existing and future fixed assets (thereby writing down the balance sheet asset figure and reducing the net profit figure in the profit and loss account). In the absence of other information, stocks, debtors and trade creditors can be increased in proportion to the estimated annual increase in turnover. After including the tax charge and dividend payment in other creditors and adding retained earnings to shareholders funds, any balance sheet 'difference' can be added or deducted as the case may be from last year's cash in hand or overdraft figure.

1.16.4 Calculating a cash flow picture from the forecasts

Public companies will include in their published accounts a separate cash flow statement. The importance of this statement for the lending bank will be threefold: first, in separating the cash flow arising from continuing trading operations to that arising from non-recurring sources (eg sales of fixed assets or profit from discontinued operations); secondly, in showing the total actual expenditure on fixed assets in the year relative to the surplus funds available from trading (ie is the asset expenditure self-funding?); thirdly, for the trading year as a whole, identifying the overall accrual or shortfall of cash.

Private companies (depending on size) are unlikely to have compiled a cash flow statement and its inclusion in the accounts of small businesses is optional under present accounting regulations. If a broad estimate is requested by the lending bank, both the turnover and expenditure forecast figures will need to be grossed-up to allow for the inclusion of VAT (by multiplying each aggregate figure by 1.175 where the VAT rate is 17.5%). Non-VAT expenditure items have to be excluded: principally, wages and salaries, rent, rates and loan interest; gas utility overheads have a multiplying factor of 1.05. The difference between the two (income and expenditure) VAT totals will be the net figure that must be settled with Customs & Excise and this should be included as a net cost.

Expenditure on fixed assets generally is also subject to VAT and, where this is significant, the company may be able to recover VAT, so that the overall net figure as described in the preceding paragraph may be a receipt. For simplicity, the rules on zero rates and partial exemption from VAT have been ignored. Having adjusted the trading forecast(s) for VAT, the final adjustment will be adding non-trading receipts and costs to arrive at an overall cash flow projection. Non-trading items may be sales and purchases of assets, loan receipts/repayments and new capital invested in the business. The lending bank will then have a cash flow benchmark by which to determine the company's present cash requirement and to monitor its future cash needs.

1.16.5 Re-appraising the assumptions and comparing with targets

At this stage of assessing the company's financial strategy the bank will have built up a good understanding of the company's expected profitability and cash flow. Where these do not match the company's original targets or where the projections fail to support the company's desired level of borrowing, the bank should ask the company to review its planning and re-calculate its forecasts. The bank will also be appraising the risk factors it may be asked to accept in the light of this information, and be forming an opinion of the lending margin to charge the company.

1.16.6 A revision of the financial forecasts

The bank should enquire as to the grounds for revising any original forecasts made by the company. Alternatively, the bank may itself suggest changes as, for example, where interest rates generally are likely to be raised in the future and the company has been assuming too low a cost for its variable interest rate borrowings.

1.16.7 Reviewing future cash requirements to attain the forecasts

Arising from paragraph 1.16.4, the achievable cash flow calculated may be insufficient to support both future development costs of the company and the level of trading forecast. The shortfall may be a permanent feature of the cash flow or it may arise for just a few months ahead. In the former respect, the company will need long-term financing through borrowing or the injection of new capital. In the latter case, the use of derivative borrowing (such as a 'forward-forward' deal) may be suitable. This is mentioned further in paragraph 1.16.11 and section 7.

1.16.8 Deciding how the cash requirement is to be achieved

Apart from raising new money (referred to in paragraph 1.16.7), the company may decide it would be best to prune costs and/or reduce production capacity, thereby preventing overtrading (section 6.8) where there appears to be inadequate financial support to expand sales. Overtrading occurs where the business grows too quickly for its daily expenditure demands to be met out of the daily income received.

1.16.9 Providing a sensitivity analysis of the final financial model

Sensitivity analysis indicates how incorrect assumptions when estimating one or more variables that affect trading will change the conclusions to be drawn from those estimates. The analysis will calculate the extent of each change in value in relation to the other estimates. The variables may be internal or external to the company. Internal changes may be different production rates; higher operating costs; movements in sales and raw material prices and different staffing levels. External changes may occur to product demand by the market (resulting in higher or lower turnover); changing terms of trade (debtors taking longer to settle); variations in interest rates (as applying to variable rate debt) and exchange rates.

1.16.10 Incorporating a risk assessment to account for the unexpected

Contingency planning should be mandatory when raising a financial strategy. From the company's viewpoint this can be tackled in several ways:

- asking the bank to agree to a standby credit facility;
- taking a conservative stance when forecasting the cash need;
- using derivatives to offset the risk (refer to the next paragraph);
- changing trading policy now rather than later.

A standby facility will increase the bank's credit exposure and this may, or may not, be acceptable. More conservative forecasting will increase the amount of money to be borrowed; the cost will be more expensive than a standby facility and the additional sum may never be required. If the contingent risk is very likely to occur, or the company does not wish to endure a loss if the risk crystallizes, it may be better for the company to adopt a more conservative trading policy at once (eg by postponing a new project or reducing trading stocks) without waiting for the adverse event.

1.16.11 Considering reducing risk through using derivatives

The company may have a sophisticated treasury function in-house that uses, or could use, derivatives to lock in beneficial interest or exchange rates. The various methods are described in section 7. If the company does not have sufficient financial expertise in-house, the bank should outline what derivatives may be appropriate for consideration.

1.16.12 Finalise the cash amount to be raised and the timing

By this time, having worked through the prior steps to create a financial strategy, the sum to be borrowed by the company will be known, as will its timing. The company should regularly monitor its trading performance and cash flow to ensure that the financing requirement remains as forecast, so that no future amendment becomes necessary. The bank will also be monitoring the situation through the day-to-day conduct of the company's transaction accounts, to ensure that the business is operating within the credit limits imposed.

Corporate goals

1.17 Background

The corporate goals or objectives to attain may be regulatory or financially based. **Regulatory** goals have set dates to which to adhere and may be mandatory or voluntary, depending on the size of the company. Publicly quoted companies must report annually on an increasing number of corporate responsibilities separate from those relating to financial accounting and Generally Accepted Accounting Principles ('GAAP') that are discussed in section 3. These responsibilities are as follows.

- ♦ Corporate governance, as set out in the Combined Code of the Committee on Corporate Governance (June 1998 as amended by the 2003 Higgs Report: the role of non-executive directors) specified by the Financial Services Authority.

- Director's remuneration: the company's policy as reported to the Board of Directors.
- Statement of director's responsibilities: that the financial statements give a true and fair view of the state of affairs of the company.
- Independent auditors' report, as established by Statute (the Companies Acts) the Auditing Practices Board, the Listing Rules of the Financial Services Authority and general professional ethical guidance, to report on the financial statements and certain of the directors responsibilities (as shown above).

The Combined Code (the principles of good governance and code of best practice) covers: the working of the board of directors and the powers of the chief executive; the company's internal controls that are in place; investor/shareholder relations; the auditors' independence and fees; the directors' satisfaction that the company has adequate resources to act as a going concern. Where the company is quoted under the Alternative Investment Market ('AIM') rules, adherence to the Combined Code is only voluntary.

The requirement for companies to have an audit has changed recently. Companies with an accounting year ending on or after 30 March 2004 are exempt from an audit providing their annual turnover does not exceed £5.6 million. The previous threshold was £1 million. This relaxation in the regulations will put a greater onus on banks and other institutions to tighten their credit assessment of small and medium-sized enterprises.

Publicly quoted companies usually raise in their Annual Reports what strategic and financial goals have been set. The following examples have been taken from the 2002 results of two nightclub operators and the words have been paraphrased.

Company 1

'...a strategy focused on three key objectives: to continue to develop our successful large capacity lead brand situated in primary population centres in the UK; to launch a smaller capacity format in smaller UK markets; and to build on our London West End presence mainly through acquisition...'

Company 2

'...following four years of outstanding growth we have experienced difficult market conditions necessitating a degree of retrenchment and consolidation. We attribute the downturn to an unexpected decline in (participants) when trade did not expand to take up the substantial increase in capacity that has been coming on stream. (The company) has also been hampered by a lack of capital to finance the redevelopment of the acquisitions made during the year ...'

Not surprisingly, company 1 increased pre-tax profit by 10% whereas company 2 reported pre-tax profits lower by 31% compared with the previous year. Company 2 over-stretched itself financially for both internal and external reasons. It reported a small increase of 7% in borrowings at the end of 2002 and total gearing (borrowed debt to tangible net equity worth) was also reasonably modest at 130%. On the other hand, company 1 increased its borrowings during the year by 95% and had a gearing exceeding 400% at the end of the year.

The table below features some financial data taken from their published Annual Reports. It may be useful for readers to suggest at this point (before reading further) what other conclusions may be drawn from the results.

Year 2002 (continuing operations)	Company 1	Company 2
Turnover (£ million)	59.9	32.3
Pre-tax profit (£ million)	7.90	3.00
Change on previous year (%)	+ 10	- 31
Pre-tax profit return on turnover (%)	13.2	9.3
Cash flow (£ million)	9.25	4.24
Capital expenditure (£ million)	14.55	12.3
Total borrowings (£ million) (A)	32.38	36.85
Borrowings: margin cost (average % pa)	Libor + 0.75/1.25	Fixed 7.0
Tangible net worth (£ million) (B)	7.78	28.31
Gearing (%) (A)/(B)	416	130
Tangible fixed assets (£ million)	32.8	65.4
Sites capacity (per capita)	26,437	51,018
Turnover per sites capacity (£ pa)	2,265	633
Number of employees (average pa)	1,127	1,024
Cost per employee (average £ pa)	11,096	6,881

Note: Company 1 converted £20m into 2 yr fixed rate of 4.94% pa by the year end.

Company 2 had a forward up to 2 yr hedging cap & collar arrangement on £12m debt.

It is clear that both companies have identical basic goals, to grow by expanding the number of operational sites. The capital spending of each business was more than its annual cash flow. Both companies partially safeguarded themselves from higher future interest rates that would otherwise increase their borrowing costs.

Company 1 achieved a turnover double that of company 2, and subsequently could be less flexible financially and more susceptible to a trading downturn in profit terms greater than that of the smaller company. This was not so, however, and the key to its success may lie in the facts that Company 1 runs a greater proportion of sites in London, bringing in 3.5 times the turnover pa per capita capacity, than Company 2 which is more provincially located.

Each company's corporate goals should not interfere with its business strategy and action should have been taken earlier to have standby borrowings agreed, in case liquidity faltered, and to have measures drafted to counteract any drop in turnover. Neither company has matched its long-term assets with long-term debt (although Company 2 aborted an equity issue during the year) and is relying on future trading from a greater number of sites to repay its borrowings.

Company 2 may have benefited from utilizing SWOT analysis to spot any trading weaknesses before they occurred.

1.18 SWOT analysis

The aim of SWOT analysis is to highlight the Strengths, Weaknesses, Opportunities and Threats to a business. The first two are generally internal measurements of the company and the latter two are external factors. From the known facts (not all shown by the table above), an analysis of Company 2 would raise the following comments.

Strengths   An established company building up market share by acquisition
A substantial amount of property is held for development.
Many sites are leasehold (not tying up cash resources).
There is a diversity of sites being operated in the UK.
The company has built up a strong group trading cachet.
Operating leasehold sites offers easy closure if unprofitable.

Weaknesses   A reliance on quality and service rather than per capita growth.
Relatively low earnings led to no dividends being declared
Poor cash flow could not support capital expenditure plans.
Many sites are leasehold (affecting security of tenure).
Many venues are not sited in prime public locations.
Free/leaseholds included £15m surplus on revaluation in 2002.
The group's bank temporarily financed acquisitions in 2002.
The group is undercapitalised in terms of risk (equity) capital.

Opportunities   Leisure activities including nightclubs continue in popularity.
Good management strengths can beneficially affect turnover.
The market for selling/buying venues is buoyant.

Threats   The company does not chase discounting by lowering margins.
Local Authorities can revoke nightclub registrations.
Competition in the more popular 'growth' areas remains strong
The company is in danger of overtrading #

Definition: expansion of the business without adequate financial support

It should be noted that there are two factors common both to the company's strengths and weaknesses: the leasehold interests and the locations of the nightclubs. If most of the leaseholds are held on relatively short-term tenancies, they will be liable to frequent rent reviews affecting profits but, conversely, unprofitable sites can be closed with less liability than exiting from long leaseholds that may also be subject to frequent rent reviews. Secondly, a good spread of locations will safeguard against a drop in usage in some areas, but will not benefit from the potentially high throughput achieved by nightclubs well situated in London.

In the event, the trading of Company 2 sadly deteriorated in the first half of 2003 to a pre-tax loss of £0.6 million, compared with a profit of £1.4 million for the comparative period of the preceding year. This was before allowing for an exceptional loss of £1 million due to the effect of losing trading licences in one city. A forthcoming property valuation is expected to raise a significant and material impairment charge in 2003; a substantial number of properties awaiting disposal are incurring onerous carrying costs; a severe downturn in trade continues. The Chairman has retired in order to maintain the continuing support of the company's bank, with which discussions are under way to secure a long-term credit facility.

Competitive environment

The summary described earlier in this section (paragraph 1.5) of the work done by Porter in the 1970/80's outlined the five principal sources of external competitive pressure to affect the profitability of an industry relative to its cost of capital. This will be important to the monolithic corporations of industry who trade worldwide but less important to the smaller entities trading in their specific markets.

1.19 Perfect market equilibrium

Perfect market equilibrium exists when the quantity demanded of a product equals the quantity supplied. No trading company can improve their position once equilibrium has been reached. Equilibrium for the price of a product is always equal to its value. This will ensure profit maximization in a perfectly competitive market, when buyers and sellers have no incentive to change the status quo. The equality of demand and supply (the demand curve) will alter according to changes in customer preferences. Buyers will tend to pay more if there is excess demand and sellers will tend to lower their prices if there is a lack of demand.

But markets are very rarely perfect. The effect can nearly reach perfection if there is one overpowering market provider who can dictate the extent of production and the price of the product. The customers will be buying at identical prices and only their efficiency in selling on to the end-user will determine the relative profitability of one customer to another. In practice, this works less well if there is an overpowering customer buying from multiple sources. The buying price initially will be uniform to the providers but some providers will operate on a lower cost base than others and can accept a lower price for their product. The pricing equilibrium is consequently disrupted and will cause on-going changes in supply and demand.

1.20 Trading in an imperfect market

The key to successful trading where market demand fluctuates is a matter of timing and placement. In the first case it will be ideal to be 'ahead of the game' and dictate the take-up of one's product(s) to the optimum speed of production and optimum profitability. This is usually achieved with a new product offering a new technology or 'sales gimmick' that the market will love to purchase. After a period, the novelty wears off and competitive products may appear. Competitiveness can be retained, however, through reducing the selling price and the profit margin, hoping that sufficient goodwill has been earned to retain existing customers.

The second key, that of placement, is to offer the market what it requires rather than raising a product, then trying to create a demand, and thereby sell the product in the market. The two most prevalent reasons why start-up businesses fail is that they are undercapitalized at outset and they wish to develop a product (or idea) rather than satisfying existing demand for a known product line in an established market.

Additionally, the company may be placed in the right environment at a time when market demand appears. There is the example of a freeholder wishing to build a golf course: the land was flat and barren, features were needed. The owner hired out the land initially as a waste tip and in time this created the landscape features. The owner gained income from tipping at a time when there was little land available for this use. Thereafter the new pay-and-play golf course proved a boon, placed as it was in an area wanting this facility.

1.21 How to combat competition

A company has the choices of fighting competition on: pricing; product quality; niche services; marketing; rapidity of supply; after-sales service; strength of market share.

Pricing is easy to re-arrange and can be adopted for only a limited period, especially if the lower margin(s) will increasingly affect the ultimate profit. The company can publicize recognized 'sales periods', following on from when the product(s) were sold at the original, higher, prices. Different prices may also be chosen for different markets or locations.

Product quality has to be recognized for it to take effect; when it does, the selling price may be put at a premium to similar competitive products. Quality is often synonymous with low quantity sales markets: what the company loses in quantity of sales it makes up through higher profit margins. The danger is that quality may deteriorate and the market be lost, or that an insufficiently high selling price will not generate sufficient profits.

Niche services hold several favourable characteristics: they have few competitors by definition; their selling prices are little affected by changes in demand; the market for the product or service is not subject to geographical limitation. There may be a risk that technological developments may adversely affect the business.

Marketing is used extensively by large businesses as a tool to raise awareness in the market for the company's products and thereby gain market share. Some retail businesses use increased marketing to trade themselves out of a poor sales patch. Marketing should not be confused with advertising: the former has a formal budget and programmed expenditure guidelines and monitoring procedures, while the latter is aimed at a reactive market and is more informatory.

Rapidity of supply can be an important attribute and many services concentrate on this feature to gain sales. If the consumer has a demand for a service or product, it will be an immediate requirement and important for the business to ensure that production is maintained and machinery is operated efficiently. The service is not particularly sensitive to pricing but the market can be competitive.

After-sales service, and its quality, will be important if the product(s) sold require regular maintenance. Many manufacturers try to tie in the initial sale with a maintenance agreement or recurring parts replacement (often at very high profit margins, such as branded motor car spares) to increase turnover. Warranty or maintenance contract cost risks may arise in this instance.

If the **strength of market share** is significant, this in itself will add to a growth in turnover by enabling the undercutting of competitors' prices due to economies of scale, partially or wholly eliminating competitors' products from public display. Competitors may have to rely on brand loyalty to retain their demand intermixed with marketing campaigns.

Strategic alternatives

So far the business environment has been discussed and comments offered regarding what the company must consider in order to achieve its objectives. The lending banker wishes the company to be successful and it may be pertinent at this juncture to review historically what characteristics the banker may pursue to identify successful companies in the future.

The following extracts are paraphrased and derived from an article by Michael Goddard in the March 2004 edition of 'Professional Investor' in relation to large corporations, but it should be remembered that no account has been taken of the time needed to achieve success and that what has occurred in the past may be due to the interaction of exceptional external events that may not recur in the future.

> A successful company has been one where the share price has been less than two-thirds of its net quick assets.

> [Benjamin Graham, co-founder Graham-Newman Corporation, lecturer at Columbia Business School, co-author 'Security Analysis' (1934) and 'The Intelligent Investor' (1949)].

This theory works on the principle that quick assets (ie assets that can be realized within about one month without any diminution in value) less its total current liabilities (all current creditors due within the next year) will be able to generate earnings and therefore net value; if the share price is less than the net quick assets divided by the number of shares in issue, the company is undervalued. The two-thirds increment is to reduce the eligible field and allow for conservatism.

> Go to five significant companies in an industry and ask each about the strengths and weaknesses of the other four.

> [Philip Fisher, author 'Common Stocks and Uncommon Profits' (1958)]

This is a very practical test and the best analogy for bankers is to compare the performance and aspirations of similar borrowing businesses with the comments of their lending officers. The nub of the test is to ensure that each bank loans officer asks the question how that corporate borrower reads its competitors, records the answers and learns by them.

> The company must have an undervalued price:earnings ratio, have good operating margins, have a liquidation value, and earnings growth must be consistent.

> [Sir John Templeton, principal of Templeton Growth Fund]

The price:earnings ratio (P/E ratio) is calculated by dividing the price (in pence) by the earnings of the company for that year (shown in terms of pence per share). Note that the earnings are historic but can also be applied to the earnings estimate for the current year. The number of shares to apply as the divisor will be those qualifying to share the earnings; share options are taken into account only when realized. The definition of this is the number of years' earnings that are being paid for through buying of the company's shares. On this basis, if it is 20 years rather than 10 years, the assumption will be that the company on a 20-year ratio will show, in a perfect environment, double the rate of earnings growth than the company on 10 years. The other terms in the assessment are self-explanatory.

> *Growth companies have superior research of products and markets; a lack of severe competition; relative immunity from Government regulation; low total labour costs but well-paid employees; and sustained high profit margins.*

[T Rowe Price, principal of T Rowe Price Assoc Ltd]

The problems with these valuation criteria are identifying whether the company has superior product research. Perhaps the best benchmark is in the size of research budget (assuming it is not squandered on poor research) to the total turnover achieved. Low total labour costs can be shown by calculating the turnover generated per employee. Again, one is speaking of comparative company assessments.

> *A good business should have a high return on share capital; create its profits in cash; have a rapid turnover of stock; have a high rate of return on the total of plant plus stocks; have predictable earnings; be able to pass on cost increases to its customers; and be a (near-) monopoly.*

[Warren Buffett, founder of Buffett Partnership (1956-1969) and acquired Berkshire Hathaway (1956)]

There are some points to note with these criteria: if the share capital varies significantly between the beginning and end of the year, it would be appropriate to take the average of these readings. Stock turnover is the number of times the company sells its finished stocks during its accounting year. The calculation is to divide the annual turnover by the average value of finished stocks held (ie at the beginning and end of the year). Note that the definition is *finished* stocks, a figure for which may be available in the 'Notes to the Accounts'.

The rate of return on plant and stocks is the earnings generated as a percentage yield on the value of fixed production assets and unsold goods. It is the return on assets invested specifically to enable them to be resold, rather a unique test. The most interesting criterion is for the company to create its profits in cash. It is important to distinguish between earning profits that can, or cannot, be converted into cash. If profits are not converted into cash how will any borrowings be repaid? The only other way earned profits can be recognised will be in the underlying intrinsic value of the business. In turn, it assumes that this value will be realized at some time in the future, say, through a sale of the business. The value of leaving earned profits in the business will be to increase its net worth and, for a banker, this will add to the security value of lending to the company.

Two

Canons of lending

Bank lending to a customer marries two different outlooks: what the customer would like and what the bank is willing to grant. How the two match determines whether the transaction is successful or not. Their different viewpoints are exemplified in the following table.

Customers view	Lenders view
The amount should be met in full	Is it affordable?
Its purpose is sound	Is the purpose valid?
It must be relatively inexpensive	It is sufficiently profitable
It should be recurring or renewable	It must be repayable
It must be easy to access	Access must be controllable
It is without onerous conditions	Security may be required
It needs minimum supervision	It is easy to monitor
The request must be granted	Assessment is called for
The business is a good risk	Is the business viable?

As an introduction to commercial corporate lending, consider the lender's position to each view taken by the customer.

2.1 The amount should be met in full

The lender will first check that the calculation by the customer of the amount requested fits the facts of the case. Is the forecast of trading by the business sound and are the assumptions of the parameters to forecast turnover and profits valid and accurate? Has the customer provided a correct cash flow from the profit projections and does it match the maximum shortfall that the borrowing will meet as well as leaving a margin for error? Is the amount requested overstating the financing requirement? If the sum requested is borrowed, will the repayment terms be met easily out of profits and cash flow? Can the lender suggest a better alternative borrowing structure?

2.2 Is the borrowing purpose sound?

The lender does not wish to advance 'good' money after 'bad' that the customer cannot repay. If the company is in temporary liquidity difficulties, the bank will test this validity and consider lending the necessary sum with conditions to tie the advance into the reasons for the additional help. An example would be a factory strike preventing completion of near-finished products; the advance would be short term with repayment tied to the proceeds of sale of the finished goods.

If the liquidity difficulty was more structural, ie a lack of equity investment in the business, or due to a downturn in trading, the lender would examine the business in greater detail in order to be satisfied that future trading can be profitable given a reasonable time, and that the additional advance could be repaid out of future earnings (or in some cases the sale of fixed assets).

2.3 Is the cost of borrowing relatively inexpensive?

The customer will expect to pay for the privilege of the additional financial assistance and, depending on the size of the business and whether it has more than one bank to request a loan so that competitive quotations can be obtained, it is frequently the case that 'beggars cannot be choosers'. The additional risk taken on by the bank supports the view of a higher lending margin and it should also be the occasion when all the bank's facilities can beneficially be reviewed.

2.4 The bank advance should be recurring or renewable

Many smaller businesses are undercapitalised and have limited means to repay all debt that is borrowed. The bank should continually monitor the recurring nature of the lending in case future trading prospects turn adverse. Larger businesses, by reason of gearing up their profit return, count on renewable facilities as a permanent feature of trading and the lender(s) will have default conditions included in the borrowing terms as part of their security. At all times the lender should remember that the bank must not take the place of the business owner/shareholders and become the prime holder of risk. This is why borrowings ideally should never exceed the value of investment by the equity (risk) shareholders.

2.5 The borrowing(s) must be easy to access

The customer would like nothing better than to have access at all times to more finance without resorting to a formal request to the bank for more credit. The bank will accept the commercial need for an overdraft facility within a stated limit when cash demand fluctuates from day-to-day, but will control any abuse of this acceptance through making the overdraft subject to immediate recall. Otherwise, a regular renewal of facilities, usually annually, will be adopted by the bank to ensure that the business remains viable and worthy of bank support. If the business runs into difficulties greater controls will be necessary to keep the bank in touch with the problem account, including segregating the salaries from the main banking account and asking for weekly performance figures.

2.6 The bank facility must be without onerous conditions attached

As has been seen in 2.5, the raising and type of conditions levied on the conduct of the customer's bank account will be determined by the strength of difficulties the business has incurred and by the estimated time required to resolve the problem(s). The bank's 'security' in these cases may be one, or a mixture, of trading covenants and formal charges on assets. Examples of the former might be restrictions on the payment of dividends and subordinating other debt in favour of the bank advance; an example of the latter would be a fixed and floating charge on the business assets. The conditions are laid down to prevent future happenings damaging the bank's interests rather than to affect the daily trading of the business.

2.7 The bank facility requires minimum supervision

The business does not want to spend a lot of time checking to see if it is breaking any bank lending covenants, or to have the need to refer to the bank each time it has or might have a liquidity problem. The bank would much prefer the customer to conduct the account within the conditions already agreed, but to refer in advance to the bank any potential problem area if it is likely to affect the existing agreed lending terms. Monitoring accounts, particularly problem accounts, is a costly business.

2.8 The request for an advance must be granted

It must not be granted, however, until due assessment is made of all factors affecting the business and the borrowing. The bank should take the position that it would like to assist the company, notwithstanding that there is a financial problem, but that it needs to know the complete underlying situation in order to make a valued judgement on the merits of the request.

2.9 The business is deemed a good risk

Business entrepreneurs are born optimists and even the largest companies and banks can turn a blind eye at times to factors known to exist but perhaps not easily quantified. Asbestos claims were known to exist for many years but the companies that were affected were increasingly supported by bank syndicates, presumably on an accepted 'risk to reward' basis. Lending banks operate in a very competitive market and it can be hard at times to turn away profitable business.

The balance between what is a good risk and what is not is a constant, important, judgement that has to be made by a bank. There are ways the bank can partially mitigate the effects of risk internally: accessing forecasts of the economy preceding a change of lending strategy; emphasising certain industry sectors to lend to over others; offering programmed lending based on the probability of failure; raising lending margins to dampen demand and/or improve the bank's reward margin; and taking additional formal security.

2.10 What determines good lending?

The first determinant is a well-structured preparation of the application by the borrower that gives the lender all the essential facts on which to base a risk assessment. The smaller business may have only a rudimentary idea of how to put together a proposition and it may be helpful up to a certain size of credit application for a questionnaire to be issued to the prospective lender for completion and return to the bank, preferably in advance of the initial interview, if it does not put the applicant off applying. The larger business will already have done its sums and perhaps even assumed some of the answers, eg the type of advance.

The lender will expect the borrower to explain the strategy behind the borrowing request. Many commercial propositions fail to gain credit because the strategy is flawed or has not been well planned. A request for additional working capital to promote a new product without having first test marketed the product would be flawed. A projection of future trading turnover without first checking that the required numbers of product can be produced to meet the sales forecast would not be a well planned application.

The borrower must have distinguished properly between 'turnover', 'profit', 'cash flow' and 'timing'. Turnover only becomes unrealized profit when the sales invoices are accepted, and profit is only realized as cash when the sales invoices are paid. Good management of the debtors' ledger is required. The timing gap between a sale and receiving the cash requires (working) capital to pay for production, wages and other costs.

The borrower must also distinguish between 'sales', 'profitability' and 'mix of products'. Increasing sales does not necessarily equate to a higher profit, or even a profit at all, if the pricing of the product(s) or service(s) is too low to recover the costs of production. The business will be inefficient if it concentrates on selling low margin products when it could just as easily and more profitably sell higher margin goods.

Thus far we have concluded that the prospective borrower must understand the key variables behind successful trading, have raised a well-prepared application, have managed the business well to date and have recognized, and accurately incorporated in trading projections, the earlier points raised. It is now time for the lending banker to exercise his/her skill and judgement on the lending proposition.

2.11 Safety

Will the advance be repaid on time? What risk attaches to the advance? What risks attach to the business? What formal security is required?

The business cash flow will indicate whether the advance can be repaid and over what period of time. A sensitivity analysis on the trading projections will indicate the margin of error to be allowed in the calculations before repayment is jeopardised. The type of business and the characteristics of the trading market will suggest what business risks to assess. The extent of free (equity) capital held in the business will determine the unsecured element of security and the assets that are unpledged to date will denote the scope for taking a legal charge.

A typical sensitivity analysis will change the borrowers turnover, profit margin and costs forecasts to see their effect on net earnings and how the revised projection(s) will affect the servicing and repayment of the proposed loan. For example, turnover may be reduced by 10% and 20%, and profit margins (or selling prices) may be similarly reduced. Materials and labour costs are likely to be reduced by smaller figures and the least likely change may occur for indirect costs. Care should be taken to make the changes interactively compatible: for instance, if selling prices are lowered, this may stimulate sales demand and raise turnover.

2.12 Liquidity

The lending banker will wish to turn over the bank's cash resources as quickly as is practical. A loan having an early repayment date will, in most cases, generate more fees quicker than a longer maturity loan with annual refresher fees. It will also have the benefit of being susceptible to the company's trading risks over a shorter period. Larger, medium-term loans tend to have a fee structure lower at commencement and higher after the early years. This reflects the greater exposure risk over time. Conversely, companies that can draw funds from several sources may well repay the loan early before the higher margin kicks in. The banker will also be aware that funds set aside but not drawn are unproductive.

2.13 Profitability

The bank has an armoury of loan charges to levy on the borrowing customer to cover certain lending costs and to earn income, in addition to the 'turn' on the cost of funds itself, when the interest margin is added to the money lent. In the London market, the interest margin will in most cases be based on Bank of England base rate, the London Inter-bank rate (LIBOR) or the European Inter-bank rate (EURIBOR). There will also be added a fee to cover the Mandatory Costs of borrowing, ie the cost to the lender of complying with the Bank of England's deposit rules and fees payable to the Financial Services Authority.

There is usually a standard front-end fee paid on the whole facility, either on signing the loan agreement or when it is initially drawn. There may be added a utilization fee payable on the average size of loan drawn and outstanding over set periods. The aim of this will be to act as an incentive for the borrower to use the facility more. There may also be a commitment fee payable on the undrawn part of the facility over set periods, acting as an incentive for the borrower to use the facility. Both of these fees will be smaller than the basic lending margin, typically up to 1/8% pa (ie 12.5 basis points, where 100 basis points equate to 1%).

Large loans syndicated between banks will have one-off lead arranger and manager fees, participation fees and underwriting fees. The lead arranger(s) will pilot the syndication and be paid for the work involved. Manager banks will be taking a larger share of the loan on to their lending book and will receive an additional fee for this exposure. If the loan is underwritten, as a guarantee that the whole amount of the facility will be taken up by banks making up the syndicate, then there will be a fee due to the underwriting banks for their potential risk in taking up a greater share of the loan should the syndicate not subscribe to the whole amount of the loan.

2.14 Pricing

Each bank will have its own pricing policy guidelines. For smaller credit facilities the fixed or variable interest rate pricing will be agreed privately between the bank and the borrower at the time of signing the facility agreement. Some banks make their general lending rates available to the public by publishing their standard rates in set bands and revising these bands each time there is a change in interest rates set by the Bank of England. Major companies, however, may wish to negotiate fees privately with their bank(s).

Large credit facilities will be priced at a fixed or floating interest rate margin over either Bank rate or Inter-bank as described in the preceding section. The lending agreement may have options for the borrower to change between a fixed and a floating rate at each renewal date of the facility. Where loans are based on money market inter-bank rates, the most frequent period taken for drawings is three months, with interest being paid at the end of each period. Conversely, if the facility is drawn by way of acceptance credits (bills of exchange), the interest cost is fixed at the start of the borrowing period. The interest rate margin is mutually agreed between the bank and the company and is determined by the credit standing of the company, the bank competition for the company's business, and the bank's propensity to gain the lending business.

The bank will be weighing up the loan application and its pricing in a number of ways: how will the loan fit in with the bank's existing perspective of country and industry exposure; what is the risk of a company default; what perception is held of retaining the company's business; what is, or will be, the total potential earnings from the company as a bank customer? It is worth remembering that it is easier to retain a customer than to gain one, and often a fine profit margin is accepted by the bank if it is judged that the fees being, or to be, earned on peripheral business will outweigh any shortfall in the loan margin.

2.15 Bank regulations affecting lending

The European Commission's original Basel Capital Accord laid down a capital adequacy framework for the regulated banks by way of a non-binding agreement, having the twin aims of strengthening the soundness and stability of the international banking system and of applying a high degree of consistency and fairness in the regulatory treatment of banks across countries.

Its first concept was to adopt an agreed categorization of bank capital between core capital (tier 1) and supplementary capital (tier 2). In essence, Tier 1 consisted of equity capital plus retained earnings; Tier 2 included reserves, hybrid debt/equity capital instruments and subordinated debt. Secondly, risk weightings were added to reflect the relative risks carried by different classes of counterparties. The aim was to assess capital in relation to the credit risk that the borrower would not repay its loan. Minimum target ratios of capital to risk were laid down, ranging from 0% to 100%, effective by 1992. A later amendment in 1996 added additional capital requirements relating to market risks of losses in outstanding trading positions arising from changes in market prices.

The standardized and foundation levels of Basel 2 are scheduled to come into effect from January 2007 and the advanced system, one year later, even though precise terms have still to be agreed by all participants. It intends to improve the treatment of sovereign debt (previously members of the OECD – the Organization for Economic Co-operation and Development – were effectively classed as risk-free but non-members had a 100% weighting) and to amend different Private Sector lending exposures that had been treated identically from a risk view.

Basel 2, in its present format, adopts a credit rating approach by introducing new methods of measuring and rewarding economic profitability and accurately allocating capital. There is more emphasis on operational risk and a revised assessment of credit risk. Banks adopting their own Advanced Internal Ratings Based (AIRB) approach for measuring credit risk or the Advanced Measurement Approach (AMA) for operational risk will have a minimum capital base to meet. There is a more basic (Foundation) Revised Standard Approach (RSA) for credit risk and a Basic Indicator Approach (BIA) for operational risk as an alternative choice. Market risk will be internally monitored in the advanced case but a standardized approach applies in the foundation case.

The effect will mean a re-pricing of products (by the banks and all other credit institutions and investment firms, as defined) to reflect the capital charge involved. The current market risk assessment is expected to remain unchanged. The aim will be to create a level playing field for participants. Its effect will mean that banks will have to improve their management controls to assess risk, have much greater data on which to judge risks (given the implementation of suitable IT programmes) and has to encourage the use of what may be termed economic profitability models.

Each bank will start with its own risk portfolio profile. It is believed that a lower regulatory capital requirement through a reduction in risk weights will apply to uncommitted and unsecured (retail) loans such as: overdrafts and credit cards; mortgages; investment grade (safe) corporate loans; loans to small- and medium-size businesses. Fee/service-based operations (asset management and specialized private banking) and un-rated (Sovereign) or non-investment grade loans will require increased capital.

Implementation of Basel 2 will be through three so-called 'pillars'. The first has been broadly explained and concerns minimum capital requirements. The second covers the supervisory review process to ensure that banks have good monitoring and risk management methods. The third involves market discipline and disclosure requirements to allow each bank's capital adequacy to be compared one with another.

The new regime is hoped to lead to a reduced risk of (a world) financial crisis and its effect on overall capital requirements to be broadly neutral. Because lending to the retail sector and high quality corporate borrowers will demand less regulatory capital requirements the theory is that their cost of borrowing will fall. It may be more likely that borrowing to these sectors will be stimulated. If this increases competition to provide loans to a market showing static demand to borrow then this might be so, particularly at a time of sluggish economic growth generally. Otherwise, during a period of a booming economy, it may overheat these sectors and lead to bad debt troubles further ahead.

2.16 Matching the lending to the corporate structure of the borrower

The smaller company will be looking to borrow broadly at the cheapest rate that can be satisfied by the cash flow of the business. In most cases this will put the onus of structuring the proposed borrowing on the bank. The bank lending officer will have the opportunity to satisfy both parties: the borrower as to the terms of the proposed deal, and internal bank policy as to the type of advance made (or to be 'promoted' by the bank) and at what lending rate. This is where the experience, knowledge and skill of the lending officer will be paramount.

The large company will have its own views on the structure of its borrowings, aided by a 'house' investment bank or specialist lending unit of the transaction (clearing) bank. Let us assume the lending officer is the sole 'specialist'. What steps should be invoked in order to advise the company? The factors to consider will be:

- the overall future annual cash flow estimated for the business for several years ahead;
- for those years, whether there will be any significant monthly fluctuations to the expected cash flow;
- confirmation that all new projects have been incorporated in the projections in respect of capital investment and operating revenue expenditure and trading income;
- a forecast of the profit and loss account and balance sheet at the end of each trading year;

- ♦ separate forecasts relating to any subsidiary undertakings;
- ♦ analysis of all existing group borrowings and repayment profiles;
- ♦ an assessment of the tax implications of trading and borrowing;
- ♦ an understanding of company policy in respect of the use of derivatives for hedging purposes and policy on cash management and dividend payments.

The company should have already provided the lending officer with its updated business plan wherein most of the above points would have been set out. Possibly not in evidence will be cash forecasts of each subsidiary. This will be required if the subsidiaries are autonomous financially and have to borrow locally rather than from the holding company. The tax implications will be important if public debt is raised in a country with a lower tax charge than the parent company's domicile, or where cross-border trading is made intra-group. In this latter respect, the company will not be able to shield profits arising outside normal commercial considerations to a low tax-bearing country. It will a wasted effort if the lending officer puts up suggestions that are contrary to the policy of the borrower.

Some of the more common lending structures that may be suitable for the bank to consider offering, subject to the particular borrowing circumstances of each company, are given in the next table.

Borrowing type	Borrowing structure to cover
Overdraft	Daily/periodic/seasonal cash flow swings.
Debtor and stock finance (factoring/invoice discounting)	Expanding businesses with low net worth/equity capitalization/property assets.
Produce finance (L/C's; bills)	Imports/exports. Seasonal crop financing.
Asset finance (HP; leasing)	Plant/machinery/vehicle financing.
Medium-term loan	Term to match the life of the asset.
Medium-term rollover (multiple option facility)	Expanding businesses but undercapitalized and wishing to gear up by borrowing.
Long-term loan	Property assets and trade investments.
Syndicated, sizeable, loans	Quoted companies. To spread banks' risk.

2.17 Lending to different types of businesses

Each business will have its own characteristics that will affect the type of loan advanced and the lending risks involved. All types of business will require working capital at some stage. A simplified table of the most common types of business with their specialist borrowing needs and particular credit risks below, followed by a more detailed description of each category.

Types of business	Typical borrowing need	Typical credit risk
Agricultural	Seasonal working capital	Market prices
Chemicals	Research and development	Market demand/competition
Conglomerates	Expansion	Multiple cash flows
Computers	Research and development	Technical developments
Construction	Working capital	Fixed price long-term contracts
Defence	Contract financing	Fixed prices/ technical developments
Electronics	Research and development	Technical developments
Engineering	Contract financing	Contract pricing/demand
Entertainment	Promotion/asset replacing	Lack of profitability/demand
Exploration	Long-term investment	Cash flow
Financial institutions	Working capital	Bad debts/investments
Food	Expansion	Competition/pricing
Fuels	Asset exploitation	External environment
Investment companies	Long-term investment	Investment losses
Leisure	Asset investment	Changing fashions
Non profit-making	Working capital	Financial management
Partnerships	Working capital	Capital withdrawal
Pharmaceuticals	Research and development	Non-productive R & D
Property	Long-term investment	Market demand/rent yield
Retailers	Working capital	Competition/sales demand
Telecommunications	System development	Long lead-in time/competition
Transport	Working capital	Demand/operating costs
Utilities	Supply financing	Regulatory environment
AIM-listed companies	Expansion	Lack of profitability

Agricultural businesses will be dependent on crop yields, the vagaries of the weather affecting the growing season, and market prices when selling the harvested produce. There is a constant seasonality to income and financial resources of the farm will have to meet the prior expenditure of tending the ground, planting, fertilising and harvesting. Milk quotas offer a regular income and, as such, are a valuable asset to hold, but sales are subject to market prices. There are many different forms of Government/EC grant that can be claimed to boost farm turnover and aid diversification.

Chemical companies need to maintain a research capability to remain competitive and provide the products the market demands. New products marketed by competitors may wreck sales forecasts and lead to problems in completing planned capital expenditure programmes. The lending bank should be aware of the principal products of the company that generate the greatest share of profits and relate this to the risk of these products incurring a reduced demand in the future, particularly when the patent period expires.

Conglomerate companies will comprise a number of major businesses operating in different markets subject to different trading factors and unrelated cash flows. Each separate business should be independently assessed for its own borrowing requirement and risk factors, and then assessed regarding whether all the requirements can be met through raising one universal borrowing facility or whether an amalgam of several separate facilities should each be considered on their individual merits.

Computer companies may be involved in hardware or software development. The speed of technological change has been evident for several years and what might be a strong development marketed in one year may easily be overtaken by a more sophisticated product the next year. The business may have a long-term contract production run, however, and this may give the company time to stay at the forefront of market demand and to continue to expand and be increasingly profitable.

Construction and building businesses need to have sufficient capital to finance the work before completion, notwithstanding the receipt of regular progress payments. There should be an accurate tendering system in place to ensure profitable trading. In cash flow terms, the profit is not received until near the end of the construction cycle, with the final sales of individual properties, the latter being an important factor to consider where residential housing is concerned.

Defence suppliers also have to tender, usually at fixed prices subject to some price escalation. Much of the specialized work can be sub-contracted and the financial standing of the contract is only as strong as the weakest link, whether meeting performance criteria or accurately forecasting profits when tendering. Cost overruns due to work delays or technical problems can be very expensive due to the size of contracts in this field. The lending bank should enquire about the present status of all major contracts. There is also the risk of suffering from the lack of a continuous order train.

Electronics companies have characteristics similar to those mentioned for computers. They may be trading at the 'heavy' end of the market and be subject to the same risks as large contractors/suppliers of equipment, or they may be more specialized at the 'light' end of the market situated in a niche product area. If the latter, it is more likely that the company will be relying on just one or two main products, so an assessment of their continuing viability to sustain business turnover should be carried out.

Engineering is a wide field and can also be divided between heavy and light engineering work. The work can be very competitive and relatively unskilled, as with the small 'metal-bashing' business, or be highly skilled, involving large contracts taking a long period of time to complete and where there are few competitors. The market(s) in which the company is trading should be examined for movement in demand (ie seasonality; cyclical trends) and how this might affect the business. It would also be pertinent to benchmark the company's profitability to its peers. Significant contracts may be suited for their own financing, particularly if the work is situated overseas, otherwise general lending products may suffice.

Entertainment is also a wide field and can encompass music, shows, radio and TV media, to bookmakers. Each depends on participation of the public for revenue and requires capital spending to upkeep their assets to provide this service. The advertising income generated has to be adequate to provide a satisfactory cash flow. The difficulty arises in that money has to be spent before the profit return can be realized. If this is overdone, a loss will ensue. Competition can be fierce but pricing limitation is muted since the public would prefer to pay to see or hear its choice rather than not at all. Capital investment is generally through equity capital backing.

Exploration requires capital funding that may extend over many years before a 'find' is discovered and exploited. Meanwhile, the company will need working capital to support its activities. The income from past discoveries will assist to a degree in meeting ongoing expenditure. Any long-term borrowing should be on a speculative 'equity risk' basis, perhaps topped up through a minority of long-term debt. The security offered by a mine should be considered as there is income flowing from the sale of the minerals extracted and the estimate of the known reserves.

Financial institutions depend on several income streams for their profit: there will be a 'turn' on lending; fee income raised; account management charges; and revenue from specialized services such as export/import business. The niche financial institutions will be looking to set up credit (working capital) lines with larger banks. Their risk to a lender will be in the type of business being conducted and the degree of security they will hold from their borrowers. This can range from an unsecured consumer loan to a term advance secured by a first charge on the borrower's property.

Food and drink companies are trading in a relatively stable market and particular brands can have a regular public following for many years, especially if they are well marketed. When a brand gets 'stale' and loses its turnover momentum, it is often re-marketed under a revised or new label. Finance may be requested to help support a new product launch. This can be risky if the public does not respond well.

49

Unexpected raw material price increases may be difficult to pass on to the public and existing competition will limit the scope to improve selling prices and margins. Having said that, there will always be the need to purchase food and drink. Lending to these companies should take such factors into account.

Fuels such as oil and gas, like exploration companies, rely on sufficient reserves to act a security for current research and exploration work. In these cases, however, the oil and gas is already being piped out and the long-term sales contracts are security in their own right, after allowing for variations in future fuel prices, and will generate the cash flow to support new developments. The main risk will be in fuel recovery if the wells are situated in territories with an unstable political background. The size of funding required will mean that most corporate borrowing will be through the international money markets.

Investment companies will also rely significantly on the money and equity markets to raise new capital. Banks are not in the business lending money on a long-term investment basis unless it is through their specialized venture capital vehicles. There may, however, be short-term requirements that can be satisfied in the normal course of business, with formal security being taken on the underlying investments. There may also be a bridging finance demand where a change of investments within the portfolio is to occur. The investment company in this instance may take advantage of derivatives to safeguard the immediate value of its portfolio.

Leisure activities can embrace hotels and football clubs. Capital expenditure on hotel rooms requires a certain average percentage occupation to be profitable. Tourism is a fickle business and demand can vary widely from year to year. There is an inherent risk when lending to a hotel chain with ample asset value but poor cash flow. A forced sale of assets may, or may not, be easy. Football clubs, on the other hand, are rarely asset rich but do have the nebulous benefit of selling players potentially profitably. Many have succumbed recently to a heart-over-head attitude in paying out exorbitant wages to players (and incurring heavy financial losses) rather than tying a large element of pay to a bonus scheme based on financial results. The risk was there for all to see. Diversification of income will mitigate any turnstile operating losses.

Non profit-making entities, depending on their size, may have little or no professional financial management. The lending risk to them is that they overstretch their expenditure budget and have no clear means to raise further financial resources. Where their rules permit borrowing the lending bank should check how commercialised is the business: what are its objectives; can income be increased rapidly if it is needed; is it an association (possibly a company limited by guarantee) where the membership may fluctuate from year to year, or a more established large company having underlying legacies providing a high annual income? It should be noted that a registered charity has no powers to borrow funds.

Partnerships may be limited, or unlimited, or have limited partners within an unlimited partnership. The more limited partners there are, the less availability of partners' assets there will be to support borrowings. The partnership may be a professional business (accountants, solicitors), or a commercial business that has not decided to convert into a limited company. Professional partners will be looking to the annual profits of the partnership to earn a living; nevertheless, this should not prevent the partnership agreement from having a clause therein about maintaining a certain level of capital investment in the business. Professional partnerships will have a clients' account to hold money on deposit pending payment, say, for investment or a house purchase that will be additional deposit business for the bank. The risk inherent to a commercial partnership should be viewed as similar to that of a commercial company.

Pharmaceutical companies will have large research and development units and their products can take many years before they are commercially viable. Their research should be safeguarded with patents. The risk is that too much expenditure over many years may lead to abandonment of the project. There is also the risk of supplying drugs to the public that are subsequently proved dangerous and so raise litigation. Depending on the size of the company, access will be needed to the money market(s) for raising ongoing long-term capital.

Property companies will be retaining a portfolio of assets for the long term to generate rental income and eventual capital gain. They will also be developing existing buildings or new sites. Where a bank provides a long-term loan this may be tied to a particular development or property; the quality of the tenant(s) should be assessed for risk and the overall rental yield compared with the cost of the money lent. A development that has, as yet, no firm tenants should be supported by additional security. Market demand for office accommodation at the time determines the rental that can be obtained on the property. Residential property will frequently be acquired for resale and, again, current market forces will influence the selling prices that can be realized.

Retailers will be selling to the public who will, in most cases, be price-conscious unless ease of location of the shop(s) determines custom. Profit will depend on rapidity of turnover and the volume of stock of good selling lines on display. Higher stock levels will require more working capital for their purchase. The bank should check that stock turnover and the overall profit margin, after allowing for any change in the mix of sales, are maintained and that losses from unsold lines, wastage and theft are kept to a minimum.

Telecommunications, now unregulated and open to competition, will be relying for growth on the public paying for new services and products. This will demand a high investment followed by active marketing in order that businesses achieve 'critical mass' in a competitive environment. It will be important for the bank to check with some accuracy the cash flow expected by the business on which to base a lending decision. Preferably, new developments should be largely financed on a regular basis from existing business turnover.

Transport businesses require capital for fleet acquisitions, regular replacement and overheads such as duties levied by the government and tolls that are beyond control. Delivery times for perishables must be strictly adhered to and a truck's use may be limited to the same type of load previously carried. The lending risk may be lessened where long-term hire contracts are employed, especially if the contract is on a cost-plus basis. Asset security is a problem since vehicles are always on the move, frequently overseas, and depots are often rented rather than owned freehold.

Utilities are also now unregulated and subject to competition. This is particularly evident where a competitor from another geographic area is allowed to sell electricity and/or gas at a unit price lower than the incumbent supplier. There may be liability in having to upgrade the infrastructure and/or create new supplies to meet an expected higher demand from the public. These operating risks are mitigated by the fact that there is a captive market that cannot do without the services provided. A loan proposition should incorporate an assessment of long-term expenditure needs and compare this with the potential rewards for the company.

AIM-quoted companies, rather than companies having a full Stock Exchange quotation, will incur the benefits of less official regulation and lower costs towards the advantage of access to public financing. The majority of companies will be fledgling businesses, neither yet achieving profits nor having established a mature market for the product(s) or service(s) being developed. To this extent, equity financing coupled with some venture (risk) capital from specialized financial organizations will comprise the bulk of the initial funding package. There can be the modest addition of an overdraft from a traditional banking source or, by choice, a secured short-term loan. The skills and qualities of management will be of prime importance when deciding whether to advance commercial funds.

2.18 Lending to company groups

When considering offering a loan facility to a group of companies the bank should examine a number of special points of risk:

- what subsidiaries have been consolidated?
- what subsidiaries have not been consolidated?
- what is the choice of lending vehicle?
- what are the principal trading companies?
- what intra-group policy is laid down?
- are any subsidiaries and/or assets ring-fenced for security?
- are any lenders to the group ring-fenced?
- will the domicile of any subsidiaries affect lending?

What subsidiaries have been consolidated?

The Companies Act section 228 exempts a company (unquoted) from preparing group accounts if it is itself a subsidiary of a larger group; the parent company must be named in the subsidiary's report. A subsidiary is one where more than 50% of its issued shares are held by the parent company. Minority shareholders in a subsidiary can apply to overrule this exemption if they hold a majority of the minority shares in issue or hold at least 5% of the subsidiary's total issued shares. Exemption also applies to private companies (if eligible, as defined) and to small and medium-sized companies (as defined by maximum aggregate turnover, balance sheet total and number of employees) when taking all group companies into account.

The bank should determine whether consolidation (or otherwise) would affect a lending proposition in any way – either through a subsidiary not coming under the umbrella of the facility terms for loan covenants or security purposes, or through missing the availability of an eligible subsidiary to join in the facility – and if so, whether the reasons for ring-fencing that company are sound.

What subsidiaries have not been consolidated?

Under the Companies Act 1985 section 229 a subsidiary may be excluded from consolidation inter alia if:

- it is not material for the purpose of giving a true and fair view in the financial statements;
- severe long-term restrictions substantially hinder the exercise of rights over its assets or management;
- the necessary reporting information cannot be obtained without disproportionate expense or undue delay;
- the subsidiary is held exclusively preparatory to a sale;
- the activities of the subsidiary are so different that to consolidate them would be incompatible to show a true and fair view.

This last reason is probably the most frequent met in practice. The notes to the financial statements must show the reasons for excluding the subsidiary(s). Consolidated or not, the lending bank should still examine the effect on operations of the subsidiary with other group companies in terms of earnings, borrowings, potential transfer of assets and security for any credit.

What is the choice of lending vehicle?

Many companies choose for tax and debt issue reasons to have a 'shell' group holding company domiciled overseas as the parent company, with its assets solely being investments in other group operating companies. Such offshore holding companies, for the borrowing group, will ideally be situated in a location with no (or minimal) capital gains tax, beneficial withholding tax treaties, minimal intra-group interest and dividend transfers, and advantageous corporate laws.

The danger for a lender is that there is no direct access to the assets of the operating companies and the value of shares in the operating subsidiaries in a forced liquidation may either be negligible or their value difficult to realize. Cross-guarantees between all group companies will partly safeguard the lender but there should also be strict supporting covenants against transfers of assets, distribution of earnings, limitation of local borrowings and priority of security.

What are the principal trading companies?

The lender should know what subsidiaries constitute the main operating entities of the group. If these companies are not to be the borrowing vehicles, there must be valid reasons for this set-up. It may be that the group operates a central treasury function, netting out balances daily and lending money within the group, as required. Particular care is needed where an important subsidiary is a jointly owned venture with an outside group. In this case, what are the terms of the joint venture as to management, apportionment of profits, borrowing rights, ownership of assets and the rights of each party on a cessation of the venture, voluntarily or involuntarily?

What intra-group policy is laid down?

The companies of a group may be structured in the form of a manufacturing subsidiary and a sales subsidiary. The manufacturing company may sell finished goods to the sales subsidiary at a small percentage mark-up and the bulk of profits are to arise in the sales company. These companies may be domiciled in different countries. If the bank is lending only to the manufacturing company, there will be restrictions on the earnings to arise in that company and the turnover will depend on the amount of goods that the sales company will take up to resell. It will be important for the lending bank to have knowledge of the corporate policy of the borrower in matters affecting its subsidiaries.

Are any company assets ring-fenced for security purposes?

If the group is pledging its book debts for the purposes of running an invoice discounting or factoring facility, these debts will be charged to the lender of that facility and ring-fenced from their use as security for other loans (but only to the extent of the amount outstanding at any time under the invoice discounting or factoring agreement). A subsidiary situated overseas will often find it easier to borrow locally in that currency and this borrowing may need to be supported by local assets. The prime lender should take into account the amounts of these additional facilities when setting an overall lending limit, as well as allowing for the loss of security that will be suffered.

Rather than losing the freedom of putting an overall first charge security package in place, a local lender may accept a bank guarantee instead. If the corporate group is deemed a very good credit risk, a **letter of comfort** may suffice. This is issued by the parent company, in respect of a subsidiary that the bank will finance, in place of any formal security for the lender. It is not a guarantee of support. An example is as follows.

> 'This letter of comfort is provided by us [x] in respect of [y] which is a wholly owned subsidiary of this company. We hereby confirm that it is our policy to ensure that [y] conducts its affairs with a view to maintaining a sufficient financial standing to meet all its obligations. We confirm our willingness to safeguard the operations and financial stability of [y]. We warrant that the ordinary shares of [y] are wholly owned by us and we will not reduce our ownership without your written consent. We also warrant not to permit the borrowings of [y] to exceed a maximum level [z] as defined and agreed from time to time between you and [y]'.

In its widest sense, a syndicate of lenders may accept 'security' as through negative pledge and pari passu clausing (refer section 6.12).

Are any lenders to the group ring-fenced?

Where there are several lenders to a group (so inferring a sizeable borrowing requirement) it is usual to have a syndicate of banks offering credit on a pari passu basis. Where there are just two or three banks, there may be a demarcation of security between them, for example as between a bank supplying an overdraft facility and another supplying a term loan. The security may be shared or split between them or the prime bank may take a first charge, leaving a second charge to the other bank. A problem may arise if the bank holding the second charge suffers a default and pursues repayment, leaving the first bank either to follow suit or to pay off the second chargee in order that the company might continue trading.

Will the domicile of the borrower affect lending?

The loan agreement will have a clause stating what country's laws apply to the agreement. There may be difficulty, however, if any rights of the lender have to be upheld in a court overseas and/or where the recovery of assets is involved. The lender should be aware of any contingent liabilities that may arise through a transfer of ownership. For example, a change of owner where a bank exercises its security rights may crystallize local pension commitments for the existing workforce.

Three

Financial statements

3.1 Background

An important part of assessing the success of a business in achieving its financial goals is to interpret correctly and fully its historical trading record. The figures themselves may be historic but they will provide the means to assess past actual results with the benchmark of what was forecast, as well as by which to judge the financial acumen of management. To do this, knowledge is required of what is shown in the financial accounts.

Historical accounts

A general definition of a company (or corporation, the words are synonymous) is 'an association of persons formed as a separate legal entity to carry out a business enterprise and with the authority to act as an individual'. Where a UK commercial business is concerned this 'individual' usually takes the form of a private or public limited company, incorporated and registered under the Companies Acts (1985 or earlier). The business may otherwise be unincorporated as a partnership, with or without limited liability partners. Companies so regulated have to issue financial statements in a certain format showing the result of their past trading annually (for other periods exceptionally at either commencement or cessation of business or at a change of accounting date). In order properly to interpret these trading results, bankers should have an understanding of the Disclosure Regulations, what to look for when examining the accounts and where relevant information is displayed.

Apart from showing the necessary regulatory information, the accounts must either conform to general guidelines issued by the accounting authorities or provide a statement of why there has been a divergence and what its effect has been on the operating figures being reported. The Accounting Standards Board ('ASB') has set UK accounting standards in the past and various additions and amendments have been published over the years. These standards are now being superceded by International Financial Reporting Standards ('IFRS') for the consolidated accounts of quoted companies to apply from 2005. The expectation is that global companies will report under IFRS, but the option to remain under UK ASB standards will still be available for smaller companies. There will be two different standards, but rather the UK rules will be less onerous in terms of providing the quantity of information. In some respects, the IFRS requirements are less stringent than current ASB standards.

3.2 Proposals for accounting standards from 2005/6

The IFRS disclosure standards at present recommended for companies to implement shortly, as far as they may affect bank loan assessments, are as follows.

Aspect	Content
Business combinations	Assets acquired at their purchase cost
	Goodwill capitalized but not amortised
	Intangible assets to be capitalized
Discontinued operations/assets for sale	Show separately, not depreciated
Derivative hedge accounting	Fair value definitions allowed
Financial instruments	Presentation & measurement
Retirement benefits gains or losses	Fully recognized as they arise
Post balance sheet events	Disclosure requirements
Earnings per share (listed companies)	Calculation thereof
Related party disclosures	Definition and disclosure

There are similarities between the disclosure requirements of financial information required by private and public companies. In broad terms, public companies have a greater degree of disclosure as befits their public ownership standing.

Financial information to be published in the accounts:

Content of the company report	Full disclosure	Abbreviated medium-sized company	Abbreviated small-sized company
Chair and/or Chief Executive's operating review of the year	Shown	Usually not shown	Not required
Company information: including directors and advisers	Mandatory	Mandatory	Show company number
Report of the directors	Mandatory	Mandatory	Not required
Corporate governance with directors' responsibilities	Mandatory Mandatory	Optional Mandatory	Not required Not required
Independent auditors' report	Mandatory	Mandatory	Mandatory if not exempt
(Consolidated) profit & loss account	Mandatory	Mandatory	Not required
(Consolidated) balance sheet	Mandatory	Mandatory	Mandatory
(Consolidated) cash flow statement	Mandatory	Not required	Not required
Note of historical cost profits & losses	Mandatory	Not required	Not required
Reconciliation of movements in shareholders' funds	Mandatory	Not required	Not required
Notes (forming part of the accounts)	Mandatory	Mandatory	Mandatory
Other financial information & notices	Optional	Usually not	Not required

Reference has been made to medium and small companies. These definitions are laid down as follows.

Defining conditions satisfying at least two criteria in the current and the preceding year	Medium company	Small company
Turnover not more than	£ 22.8 million	£ 5.6 million
Balance sheet total not more than	£ 11.4 million	£ 2.8 million
Employees average number not more than	250	50

In the following sections, we will imagine that the banker will shortly be interviewing the managing director of a substantive company that is a prospective new client and that the only information at hand is a copy of the most recent, but nevertheless historic, accounts of the business.

3.3 Companies requiring full accounting disclosure

The **operating report** will summarize the trading highlights of the year and the board of directors' strategy for the future. This will be useful in preparing questions for the interview. A comparison with financial results for earlier years may be shown here or otherwise given in the information at the back of the report. Particular note should be made of any drop in returns compared with the previous year and the reasons given for the fall. Is it likely to recur? Was it due to internal or external factors? Why was the company not better prepared to counteract the fall?

The next important search will be to read the future plans proposed for the company. Additional information may be given in the report of the directors' and further clues shown in the notes to the accounts under the headings for capital commitments and post-balance sheet events. It may be possible to access additional information from public sources about the company. If it is appropriate, a breakdown of turnover, profit before tax and possibly capital employed (net assets) both geographically and for the different divisions of the company will be set out, together with a summary of continuing and discontinued operations resulting from acquisitions and disposals made during the year.

The **company information** pages will state the principal bankers to the company and list the directors, including non-executives. Their shareholdings and share options in the company and holdings of other investors owning more than 3% of the issued share capital will be revealed in the **report of the directors'**, which is otherwise a summary of the important events that have occurred during the year.

Corporate governance has had some prominence of late and a new code (of best practice) became applicable to listed (quoted) companies with reporting years beginning on or after 1 November 2003. A prospective banker to the company should note that the directors must report that the business is a going concern with supporting assumptions or qualifications as necessary. The principle is that the board of directors should present a balanced and understandable assessment of the company's position and prospects and, for this objective to be met, there should be supplied, in a timely manner, information in a form and of quality appropriate to enable a proper discharge of these duties.

The **independent auditors' report** should be read for any possible stated qualification. Apart from reassuring the lending banker that proper accounting records have been kept, the audit report also gives a true and fair view, after a test basis on the evidence provided, and reasonable assurance that the amounts and disclosures in the financial statements are free from material misstatement. There is now an audit exemption threshold affecting companies having a year-end on or after 30 March 2004, which may now opt out of a statutory audit if their turnover does not exceed £5.6 million (previously £1 million) or where their balance sheet total does not exceed £2.8 million (previously £1.4 million)

The **profit and loss account** can be set out in one of two formats to comply with the Companies Acts. The essential difference is in disclosing operating costs, which may be stated either in a summarized or an analysed form.

Summarized form	Analysed form
Turnover	Turnover
Less Cost of sales *	Change in stock of finished goods & work-in-progress
= Gross profit or loss	Own work capitalized
Less Distribution costs *	Add Other operating income
Administrative expenses *	Less Raw materials & consumables
Add Other operating income	Other external charges
	Staff costs *separating social security/pension costs*
* *including Depreciation that is shown separately in the Notes to the Accounts*	Depreciation & other amounts written off assets
	Exceptional amounts written off current assets
	Other operating charges
Add other income and interest received less paid	As opposite
Less taxation	
Less extraordinary charges	
= Profit or loss for the year	

The **balance sheet** disclosure requirements have been standardized in successive Companies Acts. Generally speaking, the reporting figures to be shown are identical for all types of company but publicly quoted companies must disclose more information in their attached **notes to the financial statements** than private companies.

3.4 Companies not requiring full accounting disclosure

Abbreviated accounts may be filed by choice by medium and small companies. For medium companies the format is identical to the full accounts shown above except that no separate turnover, cost of sales and other operating income has to be disclosed. For small companies no profit and loss account is required and the notes to the accounts are more limited in disclosure. Small companies may also opt for **minimum disclosure** requirements (with less extensive balance sheet notes and without the need for a cash flow statement) or, as a further choice, disclosure under the Financial Reporting Standard for Smaller Entities (**FRSSE**). There are greater non-disclosure benefits through adopting FRSSE rather than minimum disclosure. The details of these regulations are outside of the scope of this text.

3.5 Specimen layout of financial statements

Profit and loss account

Statutory layout	Values	Comments on the disclosure requirements
Turnover	x	split between continuing and discontinued operations
Cost of sales	x	or show separately change in stocks; raw materials; staff costs; depreciation of fixed assets; other operating charges.
Gross profit	x	
Distribution costs	(x)	shown as negative (in brackets)
Administration costs	(x)	shown as negative (in brackets)
Operating profit	x	split between continuing and discontinued operations
Fixed asset changes	x	book profits and losses realized
Investment income	x	
Interest receivable	x	
Interest payable	(x)	shown as negative (in brackets)
Profit before taxation	x	on ordinary activities
Taxation	(x)	on ordinary activities profit
Profit for the financial year	x	
Equity dividends	(x)	declared and proposed
Retained profit	x	for the financial year

Balance sheet

Statutory layout		Values	Comments on the disclosure requirements
Fixed assets			
Intangible assets		x	goodwill, patents, development costs
Tangible assets		x	land, buildings, plant, assets in construction
Investments		<u>x</u>	group and other shares & loans
		x	
Current assets			
Stocks	x		includes work-in-progress, payments on account
Debtors	x		separating trade other debts and accruals
Cash	<u>x</u>		
	x		
Creditors amounts due within one year	<u>(x)</u>		separating trade & other creditors, loans,
			payments on account and accruals
Net current assets/(liabilities)		<u>x</u>	
Total assets less current liabilities		x	
Creditors due after one year		(x)	items as for creditors due within one year
Provisions for liabilities & charges		<u>(x)</u>	taxation, pensions, other provisions
Net assets		<u>**xx**</u>	figure equals shareholders funds
Capital & reserves			
Called up share capital		x	
Share premium account		x	
Revaluation/other reserve		x	
Profit and loss account		<u>x</u>	
Shareholders funds		<u>**xx**</u>	

Cash flow statement (where required)

Reconciliation of operating profit to net cash inflow from operating activities

(This reconciliation may alternatively be found in the notes to the accounts)

Operating profit	x	
Depreciation charges	x	
Profit or loss on sale of fixed assets	x	a profit will be negative
Increase in stocks	(x)	a decrease will be positive
Increase in debtors	(x)	a decrease will be positive
Increase in creditors	x	a decrease will be negative
Grants released to income	(x)	
Net cash inflow from operating activities	x	carried down to next statement

Cash flow statement

(A detailed analysis of these items may alternatively be shown in the notes to the accounts)

Net cash inflow from operating activities	x	
Returns on investments & servicing of finance	(x)	interest, dividends, rents
Capital expenditure	(x)	sales, grants less acquisitions
Equity dividends	(x)	
	x	
Financing	x	borrowings less repayments
Increase in cash	x	carried down to next statement

Reconciliation of net cash movement to the movement in net debt

(This reconciliation may alternatively be found in the notes to the accounts)

Increase in cash	x	
Cash inflow from financing	(x)	new loans less repayments
Cash spent on finance leases	(x)	capital element only
Change in net debt resulting from cash flows	x	may be positive or negative
Exchange differences	(x)	may be positive or negative
Movement in net debt	(x)	may be positive or negative
Opening net debt in the period/year	(x)	
Closing net debt in the period/year	**(x)**	

Notes to the financial statements

(The following comments relate to a company with full disclosure)

The following text offers guidance on the more important aspects of the declared information as it relates to a corporate lender. In all cases, a comparison with existing benchmarks set down by the lending bank should be made, as well as a comparison with the policies adopted by peer corporate borrowers operating in similar markets. Where these values or policies differ, a judgement should be made of their materiality to the lending risk. The comments supplied offer a broad outline to understand what can lie behind a company's published information and are not intended to be a substitute for appropriate legal definitions or accounting recommendations or for exceptions only rarely met in practice.

3.6 Accounting policies

Certain subsidiary and/or related or associated companies may not be **consolidated** in order for the group accounts to reflect a 'true and fair view' and this can override company law requirements. Care is needed to trace back through any cross-guarantees or contractual liabilities, whether the lack of consolidation is material and how it may affect the borrowing company. An important example would be where the borrowing company is a 'shell', with its assets being shares in other group companies who trade and have asset substance. Lending to the shell company could be very risky without the security of cross-guarantees. A comparison of the consolidated balance sheet with the parent balance sheet will show how the assets and liabilities are distributed.

A **subsidiary company** is one where the parent or holding company owns more than half its issued share capital or can effectively control the subsidiary company through the exercise of voting powers. These voting powers may be direct or indirect through other group companies, and either share-driven or through majority control of the board of directors.

A **related or associated company** is one not wholly owned by the parent company. Disclosure of financial information of a related or associated company is governed by the Companies Acts and recommended accounting principles. Disclosure of shares owned, loans and amounts owed, and income attributable to the related or associated company will be shown in a separate note to the accounts.

The company's policy on **research and development** will be described. The carrying forward of expenditure in the balance sheet, rather than charging it to the profit and loss account as it occurs, can materially affect the company's profit (or loss). The lending bank should be aware how the company expects to amortise this amount, by how much is it likely to increase in future years and whether the full amount is expected to be recovered through future sales relating to this expenditure. The standard practice is to write off this expenditure against earnings arising from the project.

Goodwill is the excess of the cost of an acquired entity over the total of the fair values of its identifiable assets less liabilities. It is currently written off (against profits) over its estimated useful economic life and there can be an additional 'impairment' charge arising at any time if the value of the net assets falls below book value. Where a company is requesting finance to acquire another entity, the extent of the goodwill to be created arising from the purchase price should be weighed against the earnings prospects of the entity being purchased and the period required before these earnings show a positive return net of acquisition costs.

A valuation shortfall of the company's in-house **pension fund** may give rise to a significant current liability where the annual contributions charged against profits are insufficient to match the long-term actuarial pension liabilities. The bank should allow for the revenue shortfall in any earnings forecasts but be aware that, where it is a defined (retirement) benefit scheme, the underlying assets value (and the company's contribution liability) will fluctuate from year to year.

Foreign currency dealings have previously been translated at the rate of exchange ruling at the balance sheet date. The proposed new standard IAS 39 due for implementation from 2005 is still being amended: it will require companies to measure financial instruments (derivatives) at fair (or market) value and the trade result taken to profit and loss account, rather than being valued at their original cost as at present, with any amortisation in value spread over their effective life. In practice, it will make company profits far more volatile and will be particularly important for banks' accounting and evaluation of company earnings. The main proposals currently are:

♦ only items that are assets and liabilities are to be recognized as such in the balance sheet. Hedged items are therefore excluded and their interim changes in value do not have to be calculated and accounted for;

♦ gains and losses from hedging do not have to be allocated across all the individual items being hedged;

♦ any prepayment risks are to be priced based on expected rather than contractual time periods;

♦ fair values are limited to the first date when the counter party can demand payment.

3.7 Turnover

Depending on the size of the company, turnover will be analysed by activity and by geographical market. Any significant changes to the mix reported should be enquired after. Not necessarily shown, but nevertheless very relevant, will be the profit earned from each activity. Going a stage further, the estimated market share the company enjoys and the proportion of turnover arising from the largest two or three customers will also be important information by which to judge the future value of the business. if this information can be obtained.

3.8 Changes in operations

The profit and loss account or notes to the financial statements must show separately turnover, cost of sales, selling and distribution costs and operating profit/loss for continuing operations, acquisitions made and discontinued operations. When a bank assesses the company's earnings forecasts it should rely on projections of continuing operations together with an estimate of the full year's contribution attributable to any acquisitions, ensuring that the latter also includes the cost of the acquisition on a full year basis. This may then be compared with the return from continuing operations for the previous year and a judgement made on the acquisition strategy and whether the lending risk has been increased.

3.9 Staff numbers and costs

Production and sales numbers divided into the sales achieved will be a guide to the efficiency of operations as will changes in overall wage costs. The figures will be the averages for the year and it is advantageous to compare the analysis with year-end figures, if they can be obtained from the company, to reveal the recruitment trend.

3.10 Taxation

Corporation tax will be deferred if the total capital allowances claimed on assets exceed the current tax charge on profits. The reconciliation of current tax will show the extent of this deferral and also whether there are any group losses set against profits. This will be helpful if the bank is not aware that a part of the group is loss making.

3.11 Tangible and intangible assets

The specimen financial statements provided earlier mentioned the analysis of items grouped under these headings. The cost of additions will be necessary to include in the calculation of the company's cash flow. There may have been a revaluation of land and buildings or other assets in the past and any surplus arising will also be shown under shareholders' funds as a revaluation reserve. The date and type (eg open market current use basis) of revaluation will be shown. If property values have since fallen there should be a note to this effect but it will not necessarily indicate a firm revised value, rather than a directors' opinion.

3.12 Acquisitions

Subject to the size of the company and whether it is publicly quoted, a summary of the financial effects of acquisitions made during the year may be included. Any deferred consideration for these purchases may still be outstanding and will affect future cash flow. There may be conditions attaching to the deferral (ie the purchase price being subject to future trading returns of that business) that will be of note to the bank. Full financial information about the acquisition may not be evident, particularly where the vendor has sold a division of its company that does not compile separate financial statements other than management figures.

3.13 Borrowings

It will be of interest to the bank if the company discloses information greater than the statutory requirement of disclosing total borrowings repayable within one year, between one and two years, between two and five years and after five years. Some analysis by type of borrowing will be given: between overdraft, bank loans, hire purchase and finance leases and loan stock. Public companies will additionally report on the amounts and cost margins of fixed and variable rate debt, the effect of derivative dealings, the security taken for the borrowings, the extent of undrawn facilities and a statement of risk management.

3.14 Post balance sheet events

The lending bank should not forget to read this section of the notes for up-to-date information valid at the date of issuing the annual report.

3.15 Monitoring actual performance against budget

Annual monitoring of a company's performance is not conducive to the bank's rapid influence of its trading and cash flow. This is more a case of going through the motions in the absence of any known problem. The bank relationship, however, should instead be a two-way procedure and, in practice, it is surprising how much new business can be gained through occasional but regular contact with the customer. Contact of this type does need familiarity with the financial background that, in turn, suggests reading the most recent accounts supplied by the company, either at the time they are received or just prior to contact being made with the company.

On the occasion of a monitoring visit, the banker should prepare a checklist of items to be updated, together with a history of the account, its past needs, and points of particular interest in the company that should be regularly raised. The checklist will be individual to each bank but a suggested example is given as follows:

- ◆ company details/address/management/personnel contacts;
- ◆ customer relationships/record of business contacts;
- ◆ past and current business record with the bank (margins/profitability);
- ◆ follow-up requests and results;
- ◆ regional or central office data/credit limits;
- ◆ salient most recent financial results (turnover, net profit, outlook);
- ◆ information or news arising since the last contact;
- ◆ points to raise at the next contact.

Where the monitoring is to check on the ongoing financial well-being of the company, the information requested from management on a regular basis will be specific to the case. The usual monthly figures requested will be selected from the following: firm orders received; sales achieved; lists of debtors and creditors outstanding; list of deferred payment accounts; ages of trade balances; totals of cash and bank etc borrowings outstanding (where more than one bank is involved); intra-group balances (if any). The aim is to be aware of the key components of trading and cash flow.

A further type of monitoring will compare trading results against the budget set by the company. It is not assumed that the business is about to incur financial difficulties or may require assistance to trade out of an adverse financial condition. There are presumed indications, however, that the bank is not prepared to allow the company to monitor itself: perhaps the account is seen regularly near to its agreed credit limit, or should be improving its cash flow, but this is not apparent. For prudence, a monthly comparison of trading against budget projections is requested. In this case it will be important to query, as soon as possible, with the company why any significant divergence of any figure has occurred, so that remedial measures may be undertaken.

As an example, orders received and/or sales may be lower than budget. This may be due to one or more reasons such as: uncompetitive pricing; greater competition; poor quality control; late deliveries; a reduced level of production; generally lower demand for the product(s). There is a choice of remedial action that the company can take: sales prices can be lowered for a period to stimulate demand; internal measures may be taken to improve quality, deliveries and production. Alternatively, the company may choose to live with lower sales and reduce operating overheads on the assumption that trading will soon recover. Either way, the bank will need to be satisfied that the remedial action adopted is appropriate.

3.16 Cash flow forecasts

The cash flow statement shown in a company's accounts at the end of the year will:
- take the operating profit figure for that year;
- add back depreciation charges (as these are not payments in cash but a provision against future diminution in asset values);
- account for the increase or decrease in net current assets (excluding cash-in-hand and borrowings);
- deduct taxation, capital expenditure and any dividends declared;
- before adding any money received from new financing to arrive at the increase (or decrease) in cash borne during the year.

There is no set format to interim management accounts but they should incorporate cash flow forecasts based on future trading projections. Different types of company will each adopt their own preferences to suit their circumstances. Cash flow, of course, must account for income and expenditure inclusive of value added tax; although the overall effect of VAT will be neutral over time, there will be monthly or quarterly timing differences in money spent and received before it is settled with Customs and Excise.

A general pro forma of a cash flow forecast sheet follows. The assumption is that the lending banker has been provided with a year's management forecasts and wishes to verify his base assumptions. The important task will be to verify that the monthly closing cash balances forecast earlier reflect reasonably accurately the actual balances attained and, if there are significant discrepancies, to discover the cause.

Trading forecasts	Month 1	Month 2	Month 3 etc
Invoiced sales	note 1		
Less materials	note 2		
direct labour	note 3		
other direct costs			
Gross cash flow			
Less indirect labour			
other indirect costs			
+/- VAT settlement	note 4		
Net cash flow before tax			
Less tax payable	note 5		
Less distributed dividends			
Net operating cash flow			
Asset sale receipts			
Less asset purchases			
+/- exceptional items			
Add capital/loans introduced			
Less capital/loans repaid			
Net non-operating cash flow			
Overall net cash flow	note 6		
Add opening cash resources			
= closing cash resources			

Notes to the pro forma

1   Comparative monthly returns for the previous year should provide an initial basis for forecasting future months, adjusted for any exceptional returns and allowing for seasonal demand. Future months can then be adjusted for known occurrences (eg estimates of new product income, forthcoming price increases, changed sales mix). If greater accuracy is required, the number of working days in each month can be set out and turnover calculated accordingly.

2   Materials costs as a proportion of sales should not differ materially if the use of future production materials to manufacture goods for resale in the coming year will be similar to that in the previous year.

3   A check should be made of the average number of operatives employed in the past year and their overall annual cost as a guide to their total cost in the coming year. Wage increases should be accounted for as well as overtime working, if this is material in amount.

4   The VAT settlement is most likely to be a payment rather than a receipt unless sizeable capital expenditure is incurred on which VAT can be reclaimed. There can be an annual reconciliation of the liability as well as the regular monthly or quarterly settlement dates.

5   The tax liability for companies will be self-assessed: small and medium companies will pay corporation tax (at rates varying according to their profits) due nine months following the end of their accounting period; large companies (having a corporation tax rate currently of 30% and reporting a profit exceeding £1.5 million) may pay in four instalments, due in months 7, 10, 13 and 16 of the accounting period.

6   Overall net cash flow will be calculated as the sum of net operating and non-operating cash flows.

3.17 Profit and loss account forecasts

Management accounts are typically compiled from monthly accounts postings. These will not mirror the actual profit or loss for each month unless the company has an accounting system that includes the provision of monthly stock figures, detailed creditors accruals and apportioned depreciation on fixed assets. The major deficiency to an accurate profit (or loss) estimate will be the lack of a stock figure. The lending banker can mitigate this shortfall by working the following sum:

Stock held at the last stock count	£x
Add materials purchases delivered during the succeeding month	£x
	£x
Less materials used in sales for the succeeding month	£x
Revised stock figure at the end of the succeeding month	£x

The management accounts will show the purchased materials paid for during the succeeding month rather than the value of materials delivered. This value may be obtained from the record of deliveries inwards kept by the company to check what deliveries have been made and whether they are as the company has ordered. The company's order book will be a further partial check on deliveries received. Materials used in production and sold in the month may be obtained by analysing the sales invoices and deducting the average profit margin earned on materials invoiced.

Where the company cannot easily extract the above materials information, an approximation for stock can be made by taking the percentage historic usage value of materials purchased relative to sales made in each period. This figure is then compared with the cost of materials purchased (over two months if the usual credit period allowed by suppliers is 60 days).

Example

Sales made in the previous year	£2,420,000
Materials purchased in year	£1,370,000
Materials purchased two months ago	£130,000
Percentage of materials to sales	57%
Management forecast: month 1	
Sales expected	£200,000
Materials calculated @ 57%	£114,000
Month 1: opening stock (actual) value	£440,000
Add estimated purchases (as given above)	£130,000
	£570,000
Less estimated sales (as given above)	£114,000
Revised stock value, end of month 1	£456,000

3.18 Sensitivity analysis

Consider the following hypothetical profit and loss forecast by management (for brevity the figures are shown quarterly); management has projected a gradual increase in sales and a steady gross profit percentage; additional direct labour has been recruited in the third quarter; other costs have been assumed pegged at their current levels.

£'000	Quarter 1	Quarter 2	Quarter 3	Quarter 4	Full year
Turnover	440	480	520	560	2,000
quarterly increase		+9.0%	+8.3%	+7.7%	
Materials	179	205	212	238	834
Labour	120	121	142	143	526
Cost of sales	299	326	354	381	1,360
Gross profit	141	154	166	179	640
Gross profit %	32%	32%	32%	32%	32%
Indirect costs	90	90	90	90	360
Finance	20	20	20	20	80
Net profit pre-tax	31	44	56	69	200

The bank believes that certain forecasts are flawed and a sensitivity analysis is required. Turnover is not expected to rise by more than 5% in the second and third quarters and to fall by 5% in the fourth quarter as industrial confidence wanes. In addition, the bank economist believes that raw material prices will rise by 10% for the third quarter and a factory floor general wage award of 5% will occur within the fourth quarter. Rates, amounting to one-tenth of indirect costs, are also expected to increase from the second quarter by 8%, an increase that the company has not taken into account since its estimates were raised. The dealing room reads the market as expecting a small gradual increase in the cost of borrowing over the year. How will these changes affect the profit forecast?

Revised £'000	Quarter 1	Quarter 2	Quarter 3	Quarter 4	Full year
Turnover	440	462	485	460	1,847
quarterly increase		*+5.0%*	*+5.0%*	*−5.0%*	
Materials *	179	191	218	215	803
Labour	120	121	142	150	533
Cost of sales	299	312	360	365	1,336
Gross profit	141	150	125	95	511
Gross profit %	*32%*	*32.5%*	*25.8%*	*20.7%*	*27.7%*
Indirect costs	90	91	91	91	363
Finance	20	21	21	21	83
Net profit pre-tax	31	38	13	−17	65

* **Note:** materials costs have been adjusted for the proportionate change in turnover projected and for the increase in prices.

The bank will discuss with the company whether the new assumptions and outlook are valid and, if changes are necessary, a compromise must be found. The bank will want two decisions to be resolved: what the company will do to avert the sensitivity forecast fall in profits and how this will affect both cash flow and the credit advanced to the company.

3.19 Ratio and returns analysis

Calculating a ratio or a percentage trading return (by itself described commonly as a ratio), conveys little explanation as to the strength of the business or why it may have sustained a change in fortune. A comparison must be made with earlier ratios and returns to find out whether there has been a variance, followed by an assessment of why this has occurred. A benchmarking exercise with peer (groups of) companies will be helpful if it is available, as will an enquiry regarding management of the return that was budgeted for that trading period with an explanation of why this was not achieved.

Benchmark ratios taken from public sources, unfortunately, do not necessarily include important information that adds significantly when assessing a company's trading returns. An example of this would be a business having two principal sales lines, one being labour intensive requiring little raw material and offering a relatively low profit return, and the other selling on goods made elsewhere at a high profit return. Calculating an average gross profit return on total sales will not indicate how each part of the business has been trading unless figures for each division are available and a comparative ratio analysis is done separately.

There is what may be termed 'primary ratios' and 'secondary ratios'. The former provides the analyst with the most pertinent information to conduct a more intensive assessment to judge the health of the company. The latter may be useful supporting data but their worth will depend on the type of business undertaken and other factors specific to the company.

Primary ratios – profit and loss account

Gross profit percentage return on turnover will show whether average sales margins on trading have dropped, been maintained or improved. For greater accuracy, where the company analyses its turnover and gross profit, the return for each division should be calculated separately. There may be several reasons for a variance, such as:

- ♦ not passing on higher production costs in higher selling prices;
- ♦ selling goods at reduced margins (old stock, sales reductions);
- ♦ more or less employment of direct labour leading to changed costs;
- ♦ inaccurate tendering for work leading to changed turnover margin;
- ♦ stock loss, for whatever reason;
- ♦ changes in the mix of goods being sold;
- ♦ changes in internal production efficiency (machinery breakdown);
- ♦ changes in delivery charges (own delivery or outsourced);
- ♦ changes in stock valuation.

Changes may occur in the valuation of stocks even though audit requirements insist that the basis of the valuation must be consistent. For example, raw material replacement costs may increase significantly so that where the company is adopting a first-in-first-out valuation basis, the value of stock at the end of the period will be much higher while the quantity of stock held may be unchanged. This will lead to a higher average production cost figure for the year until the new stock is used in production or selling prices are changed to recoup the loss of profit.

The **stock turnover** figure will measure the speed of the business in selling its stock of goods for sale during the period of assessment. This may be calculated in one of two ways:

- the number of times the average value of goods held during the year will divide into the turnover;
- dividing the cost of goods sold during the year by the average value of stock of goods held converted into a number of days.

Example

(Note: stock is defined as raw materials, work-in-progress and finished goods)

Turnover for the year	£28,477,000
Beginning of year stock value	£ 1,125,000
End of year stock value	£ 1,967,000
Hence average stock value	*£ 1,546,000*
(Production) Cost of sales (goods sold)	£16,770,000
Calculation 1: 28,477,000/1,546,000 = 18.4 times	
Calculation 2: (1,546,000/16,770,000) × 365 = 33.6 days	

Calculation 2 is not directly dependent on the level of turnover and measures how fast stock is shifted into production. It is a direct measurement of the value of stock as a proportion of all production costs. Calculation 1 measures the stock requirement to generate a certain level of turnover. Calculation 1 is used more frequently in practice and it does provide a more direct comparative measure as to how much stock is necessary to support the turnover achieved.

Capacity of production and its use will measure the realized value to the maximum value of production that can be achieved with existing (human and machine) resources of the business. It will be the actual percentage production efficiency of the business measured against full production, after allowing for unproductive labour hours and idle machine time. The ratio is calculated as the average value of production (or perhaps the number of widgets produced) achieved in the year divided by the maximum production possible and it is shown as a percentage. This information is not usually available directly from the financial statements although the lending banker may be able to request it from management. By calculating this ratio companies will be able to assess whether they should:

- ♦ employ more staff or use existing staff more efficiently to raise production;
- ♦ consider replacing some production machinery to reduce breakdowns;
- ♦ estimate by how much turnover can be increased before additional production resources are needed to be implemented;
- ♦ evaluate where best economies of production can be made to reduce costs.

The ratio of the value of **trade debtors to trade creditors** will show the efficiency of the company in collecting debtor balances to improve cash flow, and in using deferred-payment credit made available by trade creditors to expand the working capital employed in the business: it is usually shown as the value of trade debtors divided by trade creditors. Taking this ratio a stage further, by subtracting the end of year trade creditors from the trade debtors and comparing the figure to the calculation one year earlier will show the change in cash flow resources. If this is subsequently divided into the turnover achieved during the year, it will show whether or not the higher level of sales is reflected in an improving trade cash position (as is calculated in the following example).

Example

end of	Year 1	Year 2	Year 3
Turnover (£ millions)	180	200	240
Trade debtors	35	40	50
Trade creditors	17	20	20
Debtors less creditors (net trade balance)	18	20	30
Improvement in cash flow		+ 2	+ 10
Net trade balance/turnover	10%	12.5%	

Primary ratios – balance sheet

Gearing is the measurement of third party debt against the net worth of the business. Different businesses, by their nature, operate with different levels of debt and there is no single ratio by which to judge them all. Bankers most frequently look to a one-to-one basis of debt to net worth as being the benchmark by which to formulate an opinion on whether the business is over-geared or not; this means working on the principle that if the ratio is higher, the bank is putting more working capital at risk than the owner's equity. The reasons why a company will request debt may be because the business is under-capitalized and further share (risk) capital cannot be easily raised; it may alternatively be because the business is expanding rapidly and/or the profit return being enjoyed is more than the cost of raising debt (ie the company is 'gearing up' its return).

Example

	(£'000)
Annual earnings available for distribution	375
Share capital (2,000) and reserves (500)	2,500
Total borrowings	2,000
Gearing	80%
Return on share capital and reserves	15%
Cost of dividend @ 10% pa	200
Retained earnings after dividend	175
Further borrowing requested	400
Revised gearing	96%
Cost of borrowing @ 6% pa	24
Additional earnings on new money	60
Dividend cost of new equity	40
Net return if debt was raised	36
Net return if equity was raised	20
Benefit of gearing up	16

Note: It is assumed that the new money will earn an identical earnings return to that of the existing capital and reserves.

It is usual to include all borrowings in the gearing ratio (overdraft, bank loans, other loans, hire and lease purchase debt) and not to net out any cash in hand, on the principle that all debt will have prior repayment rights over equity holders. If priority of debt repayment is to be accounted for specifically, the borrowings figure will only incorporate debt that has a prior charge over the bank indebtedness. In both cases, the definition of share capital and reserves will be net of any goodwill but not of other intangibles with an unascertainable market value, eg patents.

Similar to the gearing ratio is **debt interest cover**: this is defined as the ratio of earnings (ie profit) before debt interest and tax to the interest payable in the same accounting period and is quoted as the number of times covered. In the earlier example given, the profit before tax (at 30%) would have been 536 and before interest (at 6% pa) would have been 656 before allowing for any additional borrowing. The interest cover, therefore, would be 656/120 = 5.5 times. When the interest cover approaches unity, the bank will be asking itself whether the business will be able to continue to pay interest on its loans as they fall due.

A supplementary ratio not frequently met is to redefine the interest to include repayments of borrowing principal over the same operating period, on the principle that a failure to pay either sum will constitute an event of default. Where a company raises new debt during the year, the interest should be taken as a full year's charge, on the principle that this will be the amount to be charged against future profits.

The **return** (percentage) on **capital employed** is used to measure the value of success the business has achieved in investing its capital. It is the ratio of profit to capital employed over the same period of time. As with some other ratios, there is more than one definition of the terms used: 'profit' can be taken to mean 'profit before long-term debt interest and tax' to be divided by the total of 'share capital and reserves and long-term debt', recognizing that long-term debt is as much operating capital as shareholders' funds. It seems illogical to include only long-term debt and to ignore all borrowings, since borrowings are used to generate earnings and some companies exist through the constant use of overdraft finance.

Alternatively, profit may be defined as 'profit after interest and tax that is available for distribution as dividends' divided by 'share capital and reserves', reflecting the purist return available only to shareholders of the business. This ratio would appear to be more appropriate, since shareholders may wish to compare an investment return from the business (whether or not all available earnings are withdrawn as dividends) with the return offered by other forms of investment. Comparative use of the ratio will be effective as long as the lending bank accepts one consistent method of calculation on a regular basis.

Liquidity of a business generally is discussed in section 3.21 and its most common balance sheet measurement is by the 'current ratio': current assets divided by current liabilities, on the principle that these assets and liabilities are quickly converted into cash. Sometimes this is modified and the 'acid test' or 'quick' ratio is used, by deducting the value of stocks from current assets before calculating the ratio. This seems rather incongruous since stocks are turned over several times a year and debtors and creditors can be outstanding for up to 60 days or more: why should stocks be treated differently to trade balances? As ever, there can be exceptions: manufacturing companies may carry work-in-progress and finished goods in their 'stocks' figure for long periods that are not rapidly converted into cash.

Secondary ratios

When analysing balance sheets it is sometimes advantageous to measure the turnover of a company in relation to its use of **business resources**, both human and assets. The former is calculated through dividing turnover by the average number of staff employed in the business and the latter by the average total book value of fixed assets shown by the balance sheet. A comparison with previous years will indicate the trend: whether the company is achieving more or less sales from its workforce and investment in assets.

The definition of assets requires care: probably the best indicator is to take only plant and machinery, equipment and vehicles necessary for production and sales, since to include land and buildings (likely to remain a static figure without addition) will disguise the operating trend. Assets should be taken before deducting depreciation, since this is a provision to build up book funds for their replacement, while the trend being measured is the return earned on the original cost of the fixed assets.

The trends of various **expenditure ratios** (of their individual costs to turnover) may need to be monitored: marketing costs are one example and labour costs are another. They are most beneficial when the company is going through a period of change or is examining the potential result of a new project and whether its implementation will affect the historical trend. Companies can let labour costs balloon as much as expenditure on equipment and keeping an eye on the relationship between fixed assets and the business' net worth (share capital and reserves less goodwill) may also be relevant.

The calculation of **earnings per share** (the distributable earnings in pence divided by the number of shares in issue) is more an investment tool than a banking guide, since it informs shareholders and investors of the profit earned by the business as relating to the share capital employed. The **earnings yield** (the distributable earnings in pence per share as a percentage of its market price) is the return the company has made on the full value of the company and, where the earnings are partly distributed as dividend, the **dividend yield** (the annual total dividend in pence per share as a percentage of its market price) will show the income return attributable to investment in the company's shares at that time. The inverse of the earnings yield is the **price/earnings ratio** (the price of a share divided by the annual earnings, both in pence per share), which shows the number of years earnings that are required to purchase a share as represented by its share price.

These investment valuation instruments can be useful to a bank in judging, for example, whether a company is distributing too much of its earnings by way of dividends, is about to pay too much money to acquire another company for which loan support is requested or, in the perception of the stock market through the share's price/earnings ratio, is too highly valued in respect of its future earnings capacity. There are two valuation concepts, however, that are helpful to a bank, as follows.

First, the trend of **earnings before interest, tax, depreciation and amortization** (of fixed assets), otherwise known as **EBITDA**, will show the value of future earnings in cash terms. If several future years' projections of this figure are discounted back to a present day value, this can be compared against the present day total of share capital and reserves plus debt. The greater the differential by which EBITDA exceeds share capital and reserves plus debt then the greater the value of the business and the less risk when lending to the company (subject to other issues).

Secondly, banks will also be interested in viewing the enterprise value of a quoted business. This is similar to EBITDA but only accounts for long-term debt and the figure for share capital and reserves is substituted by the market share value of the company. The net enhancement of the company arises through the retention of earnings, a factor that banks wish to see as companies grow.

3.20 A comparison of financial trends

The trend is the direction that the company is reporting: it may show an improvement or a decline in financial performance. Sadly for both income and expenditure forecasting, it is rare for all variables to perform at the same time in an expected manner. Income may reduce due to changes in the weather pattern and stocks of winter clothing will be left on the shelves during an unexpected heat wave. The clothes may be mothballed until the following winter season, at risk of being 'out-of-fashion', or the more likely result is to initiate a sale at reduced prices, so lowering the overall trading margin and eventual profit to be earned. While profits may be maintained, unexpected expenditure on infrastructure, perhaps roof repairs due to a leak, will reduce cash flow and create another drain on resources against forecasts.

One benefit of comparing trends is to gauge past results as an indication of possible future performance. An established product that has been on the market for many years is likely to retain its public following unless a dramatic event materializes, such as contamination of food being sold, causing a product recall and adverse publicity leading to lower sales in future for an unknown period. With the former, the sales trend will be a good barometer of future sales; with the latter, the historic sales trend should indicate to what level future sales might pick up once the contamination scare is lifted.

There are sophisticated mathematical models to measure and value empirical trends, namely probability choice matrices and 'least squares linear regression' modelling. The latter consists of taking an average relationship between two variables (say turnover with net profit) and measuring these historic observations based on the assumption that they will revert to their average values over time, so that they can form a trend line for the future ie the line of best fit.

3.21 Financial statements and lending propositions

Lending to a company is based on the same principle of lending to an individual; the size of credit may be different and the rules of engagement will not be the same, but the risk to each proposition is as good as the individual(s) that invest the funds for a profit. A company, like an individual, will be measured by the results it achieves: profits earned; return to its shareholders; its success in repaying all of its debts on time. Measurement of the company is made through assessing the performance of its management and analysing its financial statements; the second part being itself a measure of the first.

When looking at a company borrowing proposition a bank should be aware that its prime consideration will be **security of repayment** of the loan. The company and management may be top class and the reason for the advance may be fully acceptable, but this will not count for much if the loan is not repaid. Financial statements may be the only firm evidence (ie independently audited) of the security of the company as a creditor to the bank. As these statements must disclose certain minimum facts about the business they are important for the bank in evaluating its credit assessment. Ancillary information in the form of business plans and forecasts are unlikely to be audited unless they relate to the company obtaining a public quotation.

Small and medium companies have now gained exemption, if they wish, from a formal audit. This will put even more emphasis on the bank to conduct a thorough risk assessment of these companies. This trend can only increase the likelihood that banks will be more cautious in future when granting credit facilities and will increase their commitment to take formal security for any advance.

Credit repayment risk and **liquidity** are virtually interchangeable: if the company has constant good liquidity, then there are hopefully sufficient funds available to repay the bank facility over time. The measurement of liquidity is shown by the company's balance sheet at the date it is drawn up. Future liabilities and their time of crystallization into immediately repayable debt will be shown either by the balance sheet or by the notes to the accounts. Examples of the former are 'current trade and other creditors' and 'creditors falling due after more than one year'. Examples of the latter are liabilities analysed under time bands when loans, leasing payments and the amount of future capital commitments authorized become due for repayment.

A useful (and conservative) exercise when considering future liquidity is to extract from the balance sheet those assets and liabilities that have to be settled within the next year. In the example following, it is assumed that the value of stock held will be unchanged. The company has not provided any indication of the likely profit (or loss) for the coming year and no earnings value has been entered. It is known that the company is still suffering from trading problems and is relying on its bankers for continuing support. The possible liquidity shortfall can be estimated as follows.

Example

	(£'000)	(£'000)
Current assets:		
Debtors	5,702	
Cash at bank	8,726	14,428
Current liabilities:		
Capital commitments	131	
Loans due for repayment	0	
Creditors	27,638	27,769
Liquidity deficit		13,341
Expected net earnings next year	0	
Undrawn bank facilities	9,729	9,729
Liquidity shortfall		**3,612**

A company can be profitable but still incur (future) liquidity problems. Once again a review of the financial statements can reveal a story. In the next example, the company reported net earnings after tax of £1.3 million but, as a banker with privileged information may gain, the next year disclosed a loss. Given this information, the extent of the short-term liquidity problem is revealed.

Example

	(£'000)	(£'000)
Current assets:		
Debtors	6,005	
Cash at bank	911	6,916
Current liabilities:		
Capital commitments	0	
Loans due for repayment	1,116	
Creditors	6,362	7,478
Liquidity deficit		562
Undrawn bank facilities	0	
Expected net loss next year	2,494	2,494
Liquidity shortfall		**3,056**

These 'approximate' estimates of liquidity do not take the place of detailed projections that the company has raised, but they do show that financial statements can be made to adapt to future analyses and they also offer a working tool as a guide when more appropriate financial information is not available.

Four

Alternative sources
of finance

4.1 Factoring and invoice discounting

Perhaps the most important aspect of factoring or invoice discounting is that it ring-fences the lender's debtor balances to the money advanced. Typically up to 80% of a previously approved debt is advanced to the borrower within two or three working days to be used as working capital in the business. All debts have to be approved as suitable for financing by the lender. If the debt has been factored, the lender will have acquired a good title from the borrower and will be collecting the amount outstanding in its own name. If the debt has been invoice discounted, the title remains with the borrower who collects the amount owing.

As the **factor** will be administering the borrower's portfolio of sales ledger debts and collecting the amounts when due directly from the borrower's customers, the customers will know that the transaction is being factored and this may give rise to some doubt as to the borrower's financial worthiness. The portfolio being factored may either be the borrower's complete sales ledger or only debt selected by the lender as being creditworthy to finance. If any debt is not paid, according to the agreement between the borrower and lender, the lender may have recourse to the borrower for restitution of the amount(s) unpaid by the customer(s).

The risks to the (bank) lender are twofold: that a customer fails to pay and recourse to the borrower is not available; that the borrower may not be able to repay on recourse. The lender will be relying on each individual debtor for repayment in the first instance and it will be important to initiate a rapid response to collect overdue debt should there be any delay in settling the amount(s) due.

The lender should also be monitoring the borrower's account for two reasons: the business may have other financial difficulties outside of its debtors' ledger that could prevent it from meeting its liabilities under the factoring agreement. Examples could be poor quality controls leading to goods being returned, production problems leading to lost orders or default in repaying another loan. If customers become aware of this there may be added difficulty in collecting debt. Alternatively, the business may suffer a downturn in trading. This will be reflected in future in lower sales, less debtors and, ultimately, in a reduced cash flow.

Where **invoice discounting** is adopted, the borrower continues to operate the business' sales ledger and notifies the invoice discounter (the lender) when each sale is invoiced. The lender discounts the invoice amount at the agreed percentage of face value of the invoice and remits the money to the borrower. The customer settles directly with the discounter and the role of the discounter is hidden. Any invoices that are overdue for payment are immediately charged back to the business. Recourse may or may not apply, as before. The risk to the lender is that the borrower will not repay the amounts advanced.

The following table provides a summary of the characteristics of each service:

Facility steps	Factor	Invoice discounter
Ownership of the debts	Yes	No
Trader raises invoices to customer	Receives copy invoice	Receives copy invoice
Trader receives % of invoice value	Pays the trader	Pays the trader
The customer settles the invoice	Receives money direct	Awaits payment
Trader repays the loan	–	Receives repayment
Balance of the debt	Pays balance to trader	–
If the customer is a late payer	Chases the money due	Trader chases customer
Treatment of bad debts	Liable if no recourse	Recourse to trader
Charges payable by the trader	Interest on the advance Ledger administration fee Turnover management fees Money transmission fees Possibly arrangement fee	Interest on the advance Turnover management fees Money transmission fees Possibly arrangement fee

The lender will be examining the sales ledger of the trader for 'unsuitable' debt to eliminate them from the financing agreement. Elimination may be due to: the debt size (too small); debt frequency (occasional rather than regular); debt age profile (too old and potentially liable to offer a poor recovery); the type of business of the customer (too risky or too specialist); the makeup of the sales ledger overall (if a large proportion of outstanding debt relates to a few large customers, they may only be accepted up to a maximum figure outstanding at any one time).

Once the agreement with the trader has been running successfully for a period, the lender can be asked to increase the percentage of ledger balances being advanced. This is usually done through a separate top-up loan, perhaps effectively financing 100% of the debts, that will run coincidentally with the factored or discounted advances.

Although the lender can operate factoring or invoice discounting for any sales ledger size, it is usually the case that, where total debts regularly outstanding are below £100,000, the operational costs for the trader of invoice discounting will be prohibitive relative to the usefulness of the facility. A higher figure will apply for factoring but, in mitigation, the trader will not have any operational costs attributable to staffing, maintaining the sales ledger and chasing overdue debts.

Factors and invoice discounters operate in a highly competitive market. They frequently charge a variable interest rate rivalling the margins on overdrafts quoted for the best corporate clients. The size and quality of the sales ledger of the trader will determine how fine a turnover percentage fee will be charged, ranging from about 0.2% pa up to 1%, and several percentage points higher for smaller debt portfolios. Sometimes the arrangement fee may be waived. The factor's management fee will be regularly reviewed and calculated according to the lending bank's work involved. There will be a regular review by the lender of the conduct of the account and the other fees being levied.

The usefulness of this type of lending service may be apparent where a business is expanding rapidly and effectively outgrows its available capital employed. The balance sheet may have only limited equity capital and asset backing as security on which to base a more conventional loan, and the bank may not be willing to see the overdraft facility continue to increase beyond a certain size. A rapid injection of additional cash could be needed to finance the business's continued and profitable growth.

Subject to an agreed overall credit exposure, an invoice discounting facility expands automatically to meet further increase in sales and debtor balances. This will take the pressure off the overdraft facility limit and enable the business to finance several times its net worth. As profits catch up with the burgeoning cash flow, the business should, in time, be able to refinance itself on more conventional and less expensive credit lines. Consider a notional example of a discounting facility in operation.

£'000	Mth 1	Mth 2	Mth 3	Mth 4	Mth 5	Mth 6
Value of debts	200	300	400	300	200	200
70% discounted	140	210	280	210	140	140
30% not discounted	0	0	60	90	120	90
Total cash received	140	210	340	300	260	230
Compared with:						
No discounting	0	0	200	300	400	300
Difference	+140	+210	+140	0	−140	−70
Difference (cumulative)	+140	+350	+490	+490	+350	+280

It has been assumed in the example that all debts would normally be collected two months after invoicing. Note that a downturn in growth will lead to a reduced discounting facility as the debtors' portfolio matches the run down of sales. Were the table to extend to months 7 and 8, each would have shown a negative cash flow of 140, so that by the end of month 8 the cumulative difference in cash flow would equate to zero. In practice, of course, sales would continue after month 7. The average value of debts outstanding per month in the example was 200 and the average difference cumulatively was 280: not a bad increase in working capital over the period relative to the value of the debtors ledger.

Debts cannot be factored where they are subject to a fixed charge in favour of another party that is not the factor involved. Debts being collected and factored usually have a floating charge placed on them and, where a fixed and floating charge is held by other lender(s) there should be an agreement in place to determine the rights of the various lending parties on the assets of the business. Factoring can be beneficial to companies based overseas who are exporting into the UK and collecting UK debts, as well as for UK exporters collecting currency debts from overseas, where the exchange risk can be minimized to a few days rather than weeks or months for the UK company to collect its receivables.

4.2 Asset finance

There are a number of different ways to finance the acquisition of individual assets, each tailored to offer specific services within the basic lending format. The options are:

♦ hire purchase;
♦ lease purchase;
♦ contract purchase;
♦ contract hire;

♦ operating lease;
♦ finance lease;
♦ general asset-based lending.

Hire purchase finance is a rental agreement allowing the hirer to purchase the asset for a nominal sum at the end of the rental period. Depending on the extent of the indebtedness, if the rental payments are not met the lender can repossess the asset or sue for the balance due by the company under the agreement (The Consumer Credit Act 1974 et seq). A percentage down payment is required and this may be supplemented by any allowance given for a traded-in asset. The hire purchase interest is then added and the balance owing is repaid in equal instalments over the agreed term. The purchaser has the benefit of tax allowances from day one and can charge the interest cost against profits. VAT is payable at outset by the purchaser but can only be recovered on a subsequent disposal in the case of motor cars, if there is no private use.

The lender will be accepting the credit risk of the purchaser; therefore all the usual credit checks should be done. As there will be a front-end deposit paid, initially the size of the debt will probably be covered by the resale value of the asset. The type of asset will determine the period of the hire purchase agreement; computers and vehicles are likely to have a three-year maximum period and assets holding their value better will be on a longer period. Care is needed on specialized plant that has to be built to order and may therefore hold little residual value to other parties.

Lease purchase gives the lessee (the user) possession and use of the asset for a period of time through paying rentals, but it does not give title to the asset, although there can be an option at the end of the lease period to acquire the asset for a nominal sum or to re-lease at a nominal cost over additional years. The lessor (providing and financing the asset) retains title over the leasing period(s) and claims tax relief as the asset's owner. The lessee charges the rental amounts against its corporate tax liability.

The lease agreement will stipulate the penalties the lessee will pay for incomplete performance and the lessor can repossess the asset for non-compliance of the terms after the due notice period has expired. The bank lessor will usually have several companies with different year-ends to own the asset(s) in order to obtain the earliest tax allowances. Banks will probably prefer a leasing deal to a hire purchase commitment due to the greater flexibility it offers for re-possession of the asset in the event of default. It is also beneficial to offset the profits earned from other banking activities against the tax allowances claimed on the cost of the asset that is leased.

Contract purchase is similar to lease purchase but the company is contracted to acquire the asset at the end of the lease period. The asset is not shown in the balance sheet of the prospective purchaser but a 'Note to the accounts' will indicate the contract liability to be paid. Ownership is achieved at the end of the lease period. The lessor gains tax relief as the asset's owner. The lessee cannot reclaim VAT on a subsequent sale. The bank lessor may appreciate the fact that the asset will definitely be taken over by the lessee but this agreement option favours the lessee only if the asset is likely to be used for quite a number of years.

Contract hire, unlike contract purchase, potentially favours the lessor in that at the end of the lease period the lessor will have to sell the asset. This could result in a favourable re-sale price and profit for the lessor if the residual value has been correctly judged (or if the asset has been fully depreciated in the contract terms so that any residual value amounts to a profit). There is the danger, however, that technological advances can cause the asset (eg computers) to be obsolete long before the end of the hire period so that the calculated residual value no longer exists, resulting in an end-term loss for the lessor. The bank lessor would be wise to write off the asset's full value by the end of the original lease.

Finance leases give the lessee substantially all the risks and rewards (ie the risks of maintenance and insurance and the rewards of usage) associated with ownership of the asset and, as such, the asset should be capitalized in the balance sheet of the lessee. Legal title of the asset, however, remains with the lessor. The definition accepted for 'substantially all the risks and rewards' is taken as 90% or more of the present value (calculated using the interest rate specified in the lease agreement) of all lease payments (including any initial payment) of the fair value of the leased asset. The lessee pays the lessor rental for the cost of the asset and its accompanying finance charges. The lessee does not (directly) take over ownership of the lease at the end of the lease period and usually the asset is replaced (if required) through a new lease.

Operating leases give the lessor ownership of the asset with all the standard tax allowance advantages. The lessee pays a rental and does not capitalize the asset in its balance sheet since the period of the lease is deemed to be substantially less than the useful economic life of the asset. The lessee does not (directly) take over ownership of the lease at the end of the lease period and an ancillary lease can be agreed at nominal rental cost. An operating lease is defined as a lease other than a finance lease. The bank lessor acts as owner and financier to either the finance or operating lease agreement and the asset usually reverts to the supplier of the asset on expiry of the lease period(s) for disposal. As financier, the bank is ambivalent regarding whether the deal is a finance lease or an operating lease, since the risks involved are identical.

General asset-based lending is usually part of a larger financing package to purchase assets such as raw materials, unsold stocks or to re-finance existing plant and machinery. The 'pool' of assets provides the security, supported by the credit standing of the company. No specific reliance is placed on trading prospects and cash flow.

The table below summarizes the more usual aspects of each form of asset finance, although care should be taken not to be too strict on demarcation since individual contracts may have their own options as choices.

Traders position	Hire purchase	Lease purchase	Contract purchase	Contract hire	Operating lease	Finance lease	Asset lending
Ownership	At end of agreement	Optional at end	At end of agreement	No	No	No, option to release	Yes, at start
Capitalized	Yes	No	No	No	No	Yes	Yes
Maintenance	No	Yes	Yes	Yes	Optional	Optional	No
Tax offset allowed	On interest	On interest	On interest	On instalments	On instalments	On instalments	On interest
VAT payable	At outset	At outset	At outset	On each instalment	On each instalment	On each Instalment	On asset cost
VAT recovery	On asset cost	On asset cost	No	On payments	On payments	On payments	On asset cost

Lenders position	Hire purchase	Lease purchase	Contract purchase	Contract hire	Operating lease	Finance lease	Asset lending
During the agreement	Owns the asset	Owns the asset	Owns the asset	Owns the asset	Owns the asset	Owns the asset	May be secured
Interest rate	Fixed	Fixed or variable	Fixed	Fixed	Fixed	Fixed or variable	Fixed or variable
Repayments	Fixed	Flexible	Flexible	Fixed	Flexible	Flexible	Flexible
Payments	N/a	N/a	N/a	Cost plus interest	Cost less end value	Cost plus interest	Cost of loan
On end sale	Trader owns	To 3rd party	Trader owns	To 3rd party	To 3rd party	To 3rd party	Trader owns
Security	The asset	The asset	The asset	The asset	The asset	The asset	The asset

4.3 International trade finance

Small businesses with occasional sales to customers abroad will probably invoice in sterling and ask for payment in advance by post, by credit card or by funds cleared through their bank. Electronic banking provides two main types of services: balance and transaction reporting (BTR) and electronic funds transfer (EFT). In the UK, information is limited to cleared or closing balances of the previous day and a forecast for the end of the current day that includes low value UK settlements through the Bankers Automated Clearing System (BACS) but excludes any Clearing House Automated Payments System (CHAPS) transfers.

Overseas transfer settlements may be done by telegraphic transfer (TT), the banks' Society for Worldwide Inter-bank Financial Telecommunications (SWIFT) clearing system, or through other systems such as Western Union Quick Pay clearing, the Trans-European Automated Real-time Gross Settlement (TARGET) for euro payments, or the Clearing House Inter-Bank Payment System (CHIPS) for US Dollars. The choice will depend on relevant rapidity and cost: credit cards are relatively slow and expensive for large transfers, whereas SWIFT is quick but costly for small sums.

As the transactions build up in amount and quantity it may be pertinent to set up a currency bank account abroad for collections and payments. Depending on which overseas country is involved, it is usually beneficial to choose an international home bank with branches in that country rather than a local bank with no direct connections to the home bank. The reason for this is that the local bank will probably run cheques through its local clearing bank for subsequent clearance by its international branch, creating additional bank charges en-route and a time lag of up to two weeks before good value is received at home.

There are three principal payment methods for multiple trading overseas: by open account, documentary collection and through documentary credit. **Open account** is easy to operate and may be conducted in sterling or in currencies. It is risky in that there is no control over the goods or their security and no guarantee of payment. It involves the trading parties dealing with each other on credit terms and completing deals by agreed settlement dates. Failure to do so leaves the injured party the right to sue for the debt and/or restitution of the goods. This payment method is usually chosen where both parties are well known to each other and willing to accept the risk.

Documentary collection is where settlement is effected through a bill of exchange (or similar draft) either for immediate payment (on sight) or at some stated future date (a term draft). A bill of exchange is defined in Bills of Exchange Act 1882 s 3 as:

> *an unconditional order in writing, addressed by one person [the drawer] to another, signed by the person giving it, requiring the person to whom it is addressed [the drawee] to pay on demand or at a fixed or future determinable time, a sum certain in money, to or to the order of, a specified person [the payee] or to bearer.*

The advantage of this method of payment is that the bill can be discounted for cash earlier than its maturity if accepted to do so by the bank. Where the bank signs the bill it is guaranteeing payment thereof and the (now 'avalised') bill may be discounted in the market at a finer (cheaper) interest rate. To avoid misunderstandings there are Uniform Rules for Collections for banks to abide by when collecting settlements.

Documentary credits are letters of credit (L/C) where an issuing bank conditionally or unconditionally guarantees the terms of payment of its customer's (the applicant's) debt to a named third party (the beneficiary), on the presentation of stated documents evidencing the shipment of title of specified goods to the applicant. This may be done in two ways: the issuing bank may undertake to pay the sum due to the beneficiary, or to accept bills drawn by the beneficiary, providing the terms of the L/C are complied with; the issuing bank may alternatively instruct a confirming bank of its choosing (usually situated in the country of the beneficiary) to raise the conditional payment undertaking with an advising bank appointed by the beneficiary. The undertaking may be specified as revocable or irrevocable.

There is a Uniform Customs and Practice for Documentary Credits updated every few years to account for changes in banking practices, giving internationally accepted rules and definitions governing the liabilities and duties of all parties to such credits. Part of this agreement is embodied in the Uniform Rules for Bank-to-Bank Reimbursements (URBBR) relating to documentary credits.

The steps of a typical transaction would be as follows.

1. An overseas importer asks its own bank to guarantee payment (by issuing an irrevocable L/C pertaining to the goods).

2. That importer asks the confirming bank to contact the UK exporter as its advising bank to ensure that the sales contract terms and details are in order so that they can confirm the credit.

3. The exporter will check the documentary details of the transaction, send them back to its advising bank and ship the goods to the importer.

4. The advising bank then sends the documents stating the amount due to the overseas confirming bank, which sends them on to the importer.

5. When the goods are delivered the exporter tenders the documents for release of the goods.

The transaction does not necessarily require a bill of exchange if the overseas issuing bank guarantees payment, in which case it is called a 'deferred payment credit'.

The UK exporter has to take account of: the potential risks when trading with the buyer of the goods; the country risk where the goods are being shipped to; the period of transit of the goods. It will be important to know the credit status of the buyer and the country in question and any regulatory controls that may prevent payment (the exporter's bank may assist in this respect). Export credit and transit insurance may be available. Value Added Tax is raised in the country of shipment and the rules are complex but, broadly speaking, if the invoice shows the required details of the transaction, it will be eligible to be classed as an Input (a purchase) or an Output (a sale or supply) for the respective parties.

Where a credit insurance policy supports the transaction, the bank may finance up to 95% of the value of the deal. Exports of small value may be accommodated under the bank's own block policy cover, usually with recourse if the terms of the policy are not adhered to. Alternatively, the credit standing of the borrower may be sufficiently high to obtain a blanket line of credit, part of which may be used to support its overseas trading. The Export Credit Guarantee Department (ECGD) used to cover short term export risks but this is now done by NCM Limited.

An **acceptance credit** is where a bank has discounted a trade bill of exchange to raise immediate funds for the customer; that is, the exporter draws a bill of exchange supporting the trade on its own bank that the bank endorses and accepts liability for. The bill then becomes a 'bank bill' that can be discounted in the money market at a fine rate for immediate cash. Most bills are of three to six months duration and for individual sums representing the value of the underlying transaction, usually in excess of £50,000.

4.4 Forfaiting

It has been mentioned that a trade bill of exchange (ie a bill of exchange supporting a trade) can be accepted and guaranteed (or avalised) by a bank for payment of a (customer's) debt. If there is an extended credit period, typically spanning from one to seven years, the exporter may wish to pass on all the risks and responsibility for collection of the debt to a forfaiting financier in return for immediate cash. In essence, the buyer (the forfaiter) foregoes the legal right to claim upon any previous owner of the debt; the bill is non-recourse. In addition to trade bills, most forms of debt (eg trade receivables and promissory notes) may be forfaited. A promissory note is defined in Bills of Exchange Act 1882 s 83 as:

> an unconditional promise in writing made by one person to another, signed by the maker, engaging to pay, on demand or at a fixed or determinable future time, a sum certain in money, to, or to the order of, a specified person or to bearer.

Unless the importer is of undoubted standing, the forfaiter will be relying on the unconditional guarantee (aval) of the bank accepting the bill for eventual payment. As the aval is written (ie 'per aval' in the case of a promissory note, or 'per aval for [the drawee]' for bills of exchange) directly on the bill or note and signed by the availing party it is preferable to a formal guarantee being separately raised. The creditworthiness of the underlying bank will have to be acceptable to the forfaiter. The fixed cost of the discounting is set in advance over the life of the credit. This form of credit is prevalent in assisting the exporter to finance the sale of capital goods.

4.5 Term lending

Term lending is any credit offered that is not an overdraft but which, by definition, is repayable on demand. Facilities classified as short-term are usually for three or six months (but can be one, two or twelve months) duration and are based on LIBOR (the London inter-bank offered rate, ie the rate of interest at which top creditworthy banks in London offer to lend each other money in a particular currency for a particular period; similarly LIBID is the London inter-bank bid rate). Medium term facilities are greater than one year and can go up to five or possibly seven years. Facilities that are long-term are above seven years and typically mature at between ten and thirty years. Bank lending for property purchase may extend to 25 years while commercial loans usually mature within 15 years, or exceptionally 20 years, unless they are bond issues.

Short term facilities

LIBOR-based facilities are market-driven; the interest rate on LIBOR-based loans is fixed until maturity and paid at maturity and is an accurate reflection of the average going rate for money in the inter-bank market at the time at which it is set. On the other hand, money drawn by way of overdraft borrowed on current account usually has its rate of interest calculated on a day-by-day basis by reference to the base rate set by the Bank of England in response to overall economic policy guidelines laid down by the Treasury. Some banks charge overdrafts instead by reference to a preset, fixed, borrowing rate. In this respect, the preset rate may be more or less profitable to the bank concerned depending on the volatility of base rate and whether the preset rate accurately mirrors these changes.

The borrower will pay the set LIBOR rate at each maturity date plus the bank's lending margin agreed between the two parties plus any 'mandatory liquid assets' (MLA) costs of the bank over the borrowing period. The MLA costs vary from bank to bank and reflect the costs of the bank in adhering to the reserves ratios set by the Bank of England. The facility can be drawn in currencies and the principal can be rolled over into a similar or different maturity period according to the terms laid down in the lending agreement.

A company having the option to borrow on overdraft or by short term LIBOR will choose the former if it believes that interest rates will fall, in order to gain advantage of the prospective drop in interest rates and vice versa. Note, however, that the LIBOR market may be presuming the same thing and may be mirroring the fall already when quoting its LIBOR rate for the next (lending) period. As has been described in 4.3, if there is an option to borrow by discounting a bill of exchange, this will be another way to set in advance the borrowing cost although, in this case, the cost of borrowing will be paid at the outset of the discounting period.

The prospective borrower has a further choice to make when requiring a short term facility: unlike an overdraft, if the requirement unexpectedly dematerialises part way through the borrowing period there is no possibility of repaying the fixed term loan early and thereby saving on the interest cost. The company could mitigate the cost through placing the surplus funds on deposit. A clear indication of need throughout the borrowing period, therefore, is a prerequisite when activating term borrowing. Short-term borrowing is best adopted principally for ongoing working capital purposes or to meet occasional cash flow shortages.

Medium-term facilities

A so-called '**evergreen**' facility will typically be a credit line for three years that is automatically rolled over after two years for a further year, which is then repeated at each subsequent anniversary. In this manner, the company will be drawing on a facility that will have, at any one point in time, between two to three years until expiry. There will be a caveat in the agreement that the facility can be refused future rollovers if a default occurs by the borrower or, perhaps, if the lender considers at its sole discretion that repayment of the facility is in jeopardy.

Considering the position of the bank as lender, by granting an evergreen facility the bank will not be earning a lending margin that it might normally expect to achieve from a medium-term loan, since the margin will be built up through a number of shorter-term rollovers with no repayment of principal unless the borrower decides not to renew the full amount. Conversely, were the borrowing to be drawn as a medium term loan, the bank could expect to receive regular repayments of capital as well as interest. If the company is a good credit risk the bank might well prefer to have the facility constantly fully drawn.

A medium term loan often incorporates terms specifying that the lending margin will be x% during the first three years, say, and x+1% during the final two years, to recognize that the commitment and the lending risk over five years is potentially more risky than over three years. This may be correct in theory but, in practice, it lends itself to the company repaying the facility early after three years to be replaced by a cheaper two-year credit. If the company is deemed an above-average risk, the bank, if it lends medium-term at all, would be prudent to offer a **programmed loan** facility that regularly reduces the debt at each payment date and charges a fixed interest margin to reflect the higher risk.

The availability of medium-term loans should be offered principally to finance capital assets that have a limited life where their purchase would otherwise reduce the day-to-day working capital of the business to the detriment of trading. The running cost and repayment liabilities should be met comfortably out of retained profits and the use of the money should give the company additional earnings that exceed the overall cost of the facility during its life. Whether or not the bank takes security for the loan should be judged on a case-by-case basis, similarly to short-term credit. This aspect is discussed further in Chapter 5. For sizeable corporations the facility agreement will set out conditions of default and operating ratios to which the company must adhere. Smaller companies may be asked, in addition, for some form of formal security.

Long-term facilities

In one sense, the request for long-term funds from a bank that principally accepts short-term deposits is an anachronism. If long-term financing is required, it should be provided through money from sources that accept long-term investment risk, such as equity capital or specialist finance units that can better match these assets with long-term liabilities. Borrowing short to lend long for a clearing bank is fraught with risks, because if short-term deposits are withdrawn or increase in cost, they may not be easily replaced and, if they are, their cost may exceed the income arising from the long-term loans. Having said that, non-speculative property purchases financed by short-term deposits have been the safest areas for lending in recent times. The reason has been that, on a long-term view and speaking generally, property values have risen sufficiently during the life of the debt to repay the borrowing without difficulty when realising the asset.

When lending long-term the bank should take particular care that the borrower will be able to:

♦ service the loan and effect repayment (out of future cash flow or realization of the asset being offered as security);
♦ offer good legal title to the property (and/or whatever is being taken as security);
♦ confirm that value of the security will not deteriorate over the life of the loan (and monitoring of its value will not be onerous);
♦ prove that realization of the security will be relatively straightforward, whatever event may occur in the future to take this step;
♦ bear the costs of setting up the facility, including legal and valuation fees.
♦ give evidence that adequate and appropriate security is, in fact, being taken.

Where the security taken is not a first charge on asset(s), its valuation is much diminished. Precise valuation criteria will vary from bank to bank but a typical calculation would be as follows.

Stage one

Property asset:	Open market valuation (OMV)
(or the asset's cost if this is lower)	
Value for the first charge:	70% of OMV

Stage two

Property asset:	OMV, or cost if lower
Deduct	Value of the prior (first etc) charge
	= Net value of the asset
Value for the second charge:	45% of the net value of the asset

4.6 Debt securities

Debt raised by a commercial entity may be in bearer or registered form. If the debt is payable to bearer it is usually a negotiable instrument traded over a clearing system such as Euroclear, where good title can be transferred by delivery and the document is usually held for safe keeping by a custodian. A registered debt, on the other hand, is not a document of title and the register of holders confers ownership. The security can raise short-, medium-, or long-term money. Maturities of up to one year are usually in bearer form for ease of negotiability and are called **commercial paper**; if longer than one year, the security is called a **bond** or a **note**.

Commercial paper

Public companies of good credit standing will issue short-term commercial paper typically between one and three months maturity in order to gain direct access to funds that might otherwise be more expensive to raise conventionally by a formal overdraft or loan through a bank. There will be an investment house or bank(s) through which an issue programme will be managed. Where the issue is made in the euro-market (defined as the market constituting the European financial centres that deal in negotiable corporate loans of the currency of a country outside of that country) the issue will be of **euro-commercial paper** (ECP) and is in most cases issued at a discount to its face value rather than by offering an interest rate coupon. Trading in this paper is directly between buyer and seller and not through a central exchange.

Bonds and notes

Commercial companies wishing to borrow over long periods will raise the money through bond issues. The credit standing of the (publicly quoted) company will be sufficient for investors to see that placing their money with the company will provide them with a regular fixed return over the investment period. The investors will require certain covenants to assure them that they can claim repayment or take security in the event that the company falls on adverse times. A **bond** is an interest in a negotiable loan. Bonds issued in registered form in the UK are called **loan stock** or **debenture stock** (debentures for short). A **eurobond**, as partially explained earlier, is usually a bearer bond issued as a marketable loan that has a nominal value expressed in the currency of one country but issued outside of that country. A **note** is synonymous with a bond but is usually used in the context to describe a repayment period of less than five years from issue.

A **debenture** is a document acknowledging a debt and is a negotiable loan issued by a company that charges some or all of its assets as security for the payment of interest and the repayment of principal. A **mortgage debenture** is where there is a significant fixed charge over the asset(s). An **unsecured debenture** is where no asset is charged and this is usually called **unsecured loan stock**. For a company to have access to the public debt market in the UK and issue debentures, it must be a public limited company (plc).

General characteristics of debt securities

A company wishing to raise a loan of significant size, of a set amount, with a medium or long-term maturity, will do so through a domestic or eurobond issue. This is usually syndicated at the outset to a number of managing banks, that for negotiated fees, will then market the bonds in smaller packages to other bank and investment house participants. In the UK, the issue will be offered on a private basis to prospective buyers or, if it is offered to the public, the issue will have to be made through a formal prospectus. Where the issue is substantial and so offers good marketability, it may be listed on one or more European Stock Exchanges.

Debt securities may offer a zero, fixed, or a floating interest rate. Some securities may be convertible into (equity) shares. The advantage of a **convertible** security is that the borrowing company can issue the debt at a lower fixed interest cost through offering, at the outset, added value in the form of a set conversion rate into equity shares to apply at a stated future date(s). The debt security may be **subordinated** to other debt issues, in which case the interest rate coupon will be higher than those debt issues that offer greater security to the holder in the event of a default. The debt may have a 'bullet' (ie repayment in full at maturity), a 'balloon' (repayment of principal with an incremental value added) maturity profile, or be issued at a 'discount' for repayment at face value.

Security debt may be issued on a **high yield** basis, where the company has no positive cash flow due to it being a start-up business, or where it is in a development phase offering investors in the equity a potentially highly successful investment but the equity will raise insufficient funds without an element of debt input. The debt typically may have a maturity of five to ten years and will have a Stock Exchange listing. High yield debt is usually subordinated to bank debt. The advantage of high yield debt to the issuing company is that the operating covenants offered will be less onerous than for a bank loan but the disadvantage is that it will be more costly than conventional borrowing. The covenants will be reactive: if an event occurs, it will trigger a reaction (eg default) but if the company trades within the agreed guidelines (eg operating ratios), the company may do what it likes, for as long as it likes, within the life of the debt.

Senior debt of a company being part of a consolidated group is usually issued by those companies holding the significant assets of the group and thereby offering the greatest balance sheet security. **Mezzanine debt** is the generic term for debt that is subordinated to bank and secured loans but that ranks above the equity in the company.

Similar to the risk applied to forfeiting, where the default risk of an international bank can be less than that of a sovereign state, **debt issued by international trading corporations** may offer a lower risk to holders than debt issued by a domestic bank. The company will, in this case, be able to issue debt at very fine borrowing rates, be free from reliance on an individual bank's lending policy, have less onerous lending covenants to adhere to and be able to spread its borrowings over several markets. Conversely, the company will be more strictly controlled regarding its disclosure of financial information than if it borrowed privately from a bank; it will be subject to independent credit status checks; debt managers will require up-front (multiple) fees for their services and, once issued, the terms of issuing debt securities are not easy to change without incurring higher costs.

Documentation of debt securities is mostly standardized, eg there will be an offer circular, a placing (or underwriting) agreement and an agency agreement with the trustee (for UK security holders) or agent (for Euromarket security holders). The clausing will be similar to bank loan agreements and will cover: the legal requirements of issue; representations and warranties (to the underwriters etc); indemnities (against any breach of representations and warranties); covenants (such as a negative pledge that prevents the raising of security for future, specified, debt); tax grossing-up procedures (so that the issuer has responsibility for any overseas withholding of taxes, and events of default (particularly the non-payment of interest or principal, cross-defaults, and breach of the issue terms). Issues with maturities of less than one year will waive most of these clauses.

4.7 Equity finance

Equity capital may be defined as capital invested for the medium to long-term in a business where there is no prior limitation to participate in a distribution of future profits. It will comprise title to the capital remaining after accounting for all third party liabilities. This capital will be reflected in, but not necessarily shown by, the company's balance sheet as, for instance, where the book value of assets is stated at historical cost rather than at their current market value. Investment may be for the medium-term, as with venture capital, where the investors wish for an exit from their investment by a certain period. Investment may be long-term and this implies that it is the capital required to operate the company on an ongoing basis, consisting of permanent (share) capital along with less permanent and future distributable (retained profits) capital. Future income may arise from profitable operation of the business or from a sale of business assets.

A public or private issue of shares can be the cheapest method of raising finance: in return for the chance to participate in increasing future profits of the company the equity shareholder will be able to vote on the right to receive dividend payments and, in turn, in respect of public limited companies, this can lead to an increased market value of the shares held. For the company, the level of future distributions each year by way of dividends will be optional, depending on profits earned, and should be at a lower cost (as represented by the dividend yield) than servicing the interest on an equivalent amount of debt. For the lending bank, the greater the proportionate element of equity capital in issue relative to its bank debt, the lower the credit risk to the bank.

There may be several types of equity debt in issue: **deferred** shares bear a restriction on a profit distribution unless other classes of shares are paid dividends of specified amounts; **ordinary** shares will have the right to any amount of annual dividends to be declared and will have the right to any surplus assets after all other classes of liability have been repaid unless this right is given to any deferred shares in existence; **participating preference** shares carry the right to receive all or part of the declared ordinary dividend but will stand prior to ordinary shares if the company is wound up; **preference** shares are entitled to the subsequent payment of earlier years' dividends that have accrued but have not been paid due to insufficient distributable profits being available (and are usually called cumulative preference shares), while non-cumulative preference shares do not. A company's Articles of Association describe the rights of each class of share issued.

There may be sub-classes of shares issued for specific purposes, each having its own rights and obligations. For example, ordinary shares may have full voting rights but 'A' ordinary shares none. The latter form is not now recommended for public company shares but it has been evident in the past where a few minority shareholders have wished to retain control over the company. Preference shares have also become less popular in favour of holding loan stock offering a higher income yield, but they are still issued when venture capital is being raised and the venture capital investor(s) want part of their investment held in slightly greater security. Preference shares may also have the right to be redeemable or convertible into ordinary shares, based on a formula laid down at the time of their issue to apply at a specified date(s) in the future. The formula will take into account subsequent changes to the number of ordinary shares in issue eg if the company has a one-for-one scrip issue, the formula will halve the conversion factor to retain the status quo.

Public companies that wish to have their ordinary shares, preference shares and/or debt securities publicly quoted must obtain an official listing in the UK and adhere to the minimum standards set out under the Financial Services and Markets Act 2000 (part VI). Up to 30 April 2000, the London Stock Exchange was the nominated UK Listing Authority but since then this role has been taken over by the Financial Services Authority (FSA). The form of issue may be a **public offer for subscription**, a (more selective) **placement**, that might result where an asset or company is purchased and new shares are issued as vendor consideration, an **intermediaries offer** via brokers to a wider market than with a placing or a **rights issue** or **open offer** to shareholders, the difference being that the number of shares offered in the former case is in proportion to existing shares held whereas the latter has no such restriction.

Equity finance is used partially or wholly as part of consideration for the acquisition of another private or public company. Some shareholders may prefer to continue to hold an equity interest in the acquiring company for their own tax or investment reasons, rather than taking the consideration tendered wholly in cash and/or loan stock. The Companies Act 1985 gave companies the right to purchase their own shares (via a Special Resolution) and, as from 1 December 2003, shares of listed companies may be held in treasury for subsequent disposal, cancellation or re-issue. While held in treasury no dividends can accrue on these shares.

A rights issue will primarily aim to re-capitalize the company. The value of the company pre-rights will be the same overall as that post-rights. That is, the number of shares in issue multiplied by their pre-rights price, plus the number of rights shares at their rights price, will be added together and divided by the number of post-rights shares in issue, so giving the shares a post-rights initial value. The rights issue may be underwritten. If it is not underwritten, the issue is most likely to be at a **deep discount** to its pre-rights market price in order to ensure that all the shares on offer are taken up. This will have the advantage of saving on underwriting fees, but the disadvantage of reducing the sum available from the issue.

A **public offer** for shares may be fixed at the outset of the offer or may be part of a **book-building** exercise by the advising banks. The banks will underwrite the issue but leave open the size and/or the offer price, both of which would be set after soundings of the response from potential investors had been collated and agreed as acceptable with the issuing company.

4.8 Franchising

Franchising may be defined as the exclusive right given to a number of operatives [the franchisees] in a certain area to exploit a business idea or trade or service, that is given by the owner [the franchisor] of that idea, trade or service, in return for payment. An increasing number of start-up businesses, and some established concerns, have insufficient working capital to exploit a new product or idea and are resorting to franchising their operations to gain a rapid, large scale, exposure in the market at minimal cost and effort of their own. The franchisor will set the ground rules of the franchise and thereby hold a great deal of control, including the appointment and location of each franchisee.

The franchisee will be paying an up-front fee (and possibly an annual refresher) to the franchisor, in return for exclusive area rights to operate the franchise and probably to receive prior training, along with the benefit of national advertising and ongoing central advice. The right of exclusivity, however, only applies to the area specified by the original appointment and does not apply where a franchisee subsequently, independently, encroaches on another franchise area.

Bank lending to franchisees is considered a lower risk than if the franchisee were operating independently. The reasons are that the franchisee has been previously vetted as suitable for trading in this manner (and possibly will have conducted a successful 'pilot' exercise)' there will be central assistance at hand from the franchisor in case of need, the business being franchised out will have had a successful track record in other areas; and the franchisee failure rate will have already been established, unless the franchise operation is completely new.

4.9 Other sources of finance

Where it is difficult to export hard currency for the payment of goods due to exchange control regulations or for other reasons, it is sometimes useful to consider trade barter of goods to finance the deal. Machinery parts, for example, may be swapped for a like value of steel. The risks are high unless the two parties each have an acceptable credit rating and/or are known to each other. The risks include a loss in value of one part of the deal, unexpected duties may have to be paid to release the goods or the goods may be susceptible to deterioration, particularly in the case of perishables.

4.10 Small Firms Loans Guarantee Scheme

The SFLGS makes it possible for small businesses with a workable business proposal but lacking security to borrow money from approved (mostly bank) lenders. It is administered by the Small Business Service (SBS), a Government agency of the Department of Trade and Industry (DTI). The scheme has been running for a number of years and subsequent amendments have been brought in periodically, the most recent being to widen the eligibility of businesses. Not all banks and other financial lenders offer SFLGS and it has been alleged that many banks prefer to provide their own products rather than offer the scheme.

The **lenders** that do supply SFLGS loans make all the commercial decisions regarding the credit risk of the potential borrower and the viability of the loan proposition, as well as stipulating the terms of any loan (ie the interest rate cost to the borrower, any security required and any arrangement fee). The SBS will then confirm and guarantee the loan. This guarantee amounts to 75% of the amount outstanding and is due at the time the borrower defaults on the loan repayments (prior to 1 April 2003 some loans were issued with an 85% guarantee). For supplying the guarantee, the SBS will receive from the borrower a 2% annual premium calculated on the loan amount outstanding each year. The premium may be consolidated into the loan subject up to the maximum advance eligible.

The **potential borrower** should expect to be asked to supply a business plan, financial forecasts, an estimate of the finance required, a risk evaluation of the business and proof of personal commitment to the project. There will also be regular monitoring of the business until the loan has been fully repaid. It will be important for the potential borrower to accept that, should a default arise, the liability will be for the full amount outstanding, and not just the 25% outside of the SFLGS guarantee.

The **aim** of this scheme is to aid business development; this may include research and development work, financing a project, starting up a new business, expanding an existing business or generally to improve efficiency. Specific uses not allowed are buying a company's shares or a partnership, replacement of an existing loan or overdraft, the financing of interest payments, repayment of another loan or direct aid for exporting. Other exclusions are loans for: agriculture and horticulture; self-employed artists; financial services and insurance; postal and medical services; gambling; intermediary and ticket agencies; formal education; fisheries; forestry; real estate; sporting organizations; publicly-owned bodies; tied public houses; transport.

The SLFGS is **governed** under the European Community (EC) rules on state aid. This restricts the maximum amount that one organization can borrow over any consecutive three year period. The SBS will check each applicant's eligibility in case earlier state aid restricts the maximum loan that may be granted. The maximum loan otherwise is £250,000 where no other state aid is involved and the minimum loan is £5,000. This top limit is restricted to £100,000 for successful businesses having traded for less than two years. So-called 'connected borrowers' must be included when calculating the maximum loan, such associated companies being companies with common directorships and shareholders owning 20% or more of the company.

The **commercial terms** available allow loans supported by the scheme to have a maturity of from two to ten years. Some lenders allow small borrowings up to £30,000 to incorporate capital repayment holidays within the life of the debt of up to a maximum two years at one time, while other lenders require the repayment holiday to be taken in periods of no more than three months.

4.11 Government and private sector grants

Many grants and loans for business are EC regulated and form part of assistance to regenerate specific areas of social and economic deprivation within national boundaries. The larger programmes typically cover a period of three to five years before they are reviewed for continuation or otherwise. Each government is charged with operating and, on behalf of the EC, monitoring the success of each programme. The detailed scope of this assistance is beyond the remit of this text but there are approximately 212 grants, 164 loans and 25 awards available under the definition of 'business development' alone. Many applications for commercial companies cover information technology, research and development, premises, plant and machinery, business start-up and training purposes.

Five

Security awareness

Security in this chapter concerns lending that is backed by values in varying form of rights over physical assets. The aim of the lender faced wIth a loan default will be to realize the asset backing for monetary value as soon as possible and to eliminate debt to the bank as far as possible.

A lender with a potential lending opportunity should ask the following.

- Is security needed?
- What type of security is available?
- How easy is it to take security?
- How relevant is the asset as security?
- What is the value of the security?
- How can the security be perfected?
- Does the security need monitoring?
- How easily can the security be realized?
- What security should be asked for to facilitate the loan requested?

5.1 The need for security

The need for security can be evident when the borrower defaults on the agreed repayments and it is too late to ask for additional collateral to support the loan before the company becomes insolvent. Small businesses can incur a rapid change of fortune that even regular monitoring by the lender cannot foresee quickly enough. Large businesses will have a portfolio of borrowings and attaching to each facility will be the respective rights of the lender over specific or general assets of the business. In this instance, when a large company defaults, there will be little or no room for each lender to change its security position.

An example of the former would be where the bank held a floating charge over company assets with the right to appoint a receiver upon insolvency and thereby remain in control of the assets, rather than their title reverting to an administrator appointed by the Court. An example of the latter would be where the bank is participating in a syndicated loan and the security obligations and rights are preset in the syndication agreement, with the syndication managers acting for the consensus of bank participants.

Consider two similar public companies, each offering business space to let. Salient financial figures reveal the following:

2003 £ million	Company A	Company B
Turnover	3.7	5.1
Pre-tax operating profit/loss (–)	0.7	–3.4
Total bank borrowings	11.4	3.4
Shareholders equity funds	19.8	7.3
Money on deposit	5.3	4.6
Properties	29.2	5.1
Turnover return on equity funds	19%	70%
Gearing: borrowings to equity funds	58%	47%
Asset backing: properties to equity funds	1.47	times 0.70

Company A is profitable, holds the greater asset backing and is not over-geared with debt. Company B is not profitable (reasons to be enquired about) and has the poorer property asset backing. Extracts from the notes to the accounts relating to security taken show the following.

Company A

> 'All bank loans are secured by first charges on all of the group's freehold and leasehold properties ... by debentures (given by the holding company) and by guarantees given by all companies in the group.'

Company B

> 'The bank loans and overdrafts are secured against legal mortgages over properties owned by the company's subsidiaries and ... other loans are secured by cash deposits.'

The call for security is indicated in several ways.

1. Each group consists of a holding company with investments in subsidiaries operating in their own right and holding their own property assets. There is need to take security from the individual operating companies and the notes of each company show this to be the case.

    Were the security to be wholly based on the holding company, any subsidiary could trade out its property assets without repaying the attendant loan, leaving the bank to rely on the shares in the subsidiary company (held by the parent company) that may well not have any remaining asset backing for its balance sheet borrowings.

2. As operations rely on developing, renting and realising properties, the major assets of each company will be changing and security taken must allow for these events. Neither company specifically states that floating charges have been taken, but it is very likely that these have been incorporated, particularly where properties are in course of construction.

3. Company A retains its money deposits in the holding company while Company B's money deposits are spread over its subsidiaries. The security taken should allow for potential claim on these funds. Company B does not specifically state this to be the case.

4. The security shown to support Company A's advances is the more comprehensive on the face of it since the lender to Company B appears to be relying heavily on the charges taken against properties. The trading position of Company B would also appear to be the more precarious at the date of the balance sheet.

5.2 Definitions

A **surety** is a person whose property is charged as direct security or who acts as guarantor for another's financial obligations. In relation to a charge on property, a **chargee** is the person entitled to use the property when there is default in meeting the obligation that the charge was created to secure.

A **fixed legal charge** on property has to be recognized by anyone subsequently acquiring title to the asset or any interest in it. An **equitable fixed legal charge** may be ignored by any subsequent acquirer of a legal title or interest, if acquired in good faith and for value, providing there was no actual or constructive notice of the existence of the equitable interest at the time of acquisition.

A **floating charge** given by a company on a class of its assets confers on the chargee (ie the bank lender) the right to take all the assets of that class owned by the company at the time when the charge crystallizes for payment of the secured debt. The chargee is entitled to appropriate the property on a default in meeting the obligation that the charge was created to secure and has the power of sale, where the charge is given by deed (Section 101, Law of Property Act 1925). A floating charge has no right to possession of the charged property and it normally crystallizes when the chargee appoints a receiver (see later), under the charge contract, after the company has failed to pay the secured debt when due.

A **legal mortgage** on property transfers legal title to the mortgagee (nee chargee) on condition that it will be returned when the obligation is met without recourse to the charged property. An **equitable mortgage** is where there is only an equitable interest in the property and/or there is an enforceable contract to create a legal mortgage. A **debenture** is a document acknowledging a debt and, specifically, is a written contract by which a company gives a charge on its property as security for payment of a debt owed to, say, a bank.

A **guarantee** is a legal promise by the guarantor (who gives the guarantee) to make good any failure by the principal debtor (the borrower) to meet financial obligations owed to the principal creditor (the lender). To be legally enforceable the guarantor (or agent thereof) must sign a written memorandum of the promise. A **pledge** of goods for a financial obligation gives possession of the goods to the creditor, on condition that possession will be returned when the obligation is met. A **lien** arises when the possessor of goods for a service has the right to hold them until payment is made for that service.

Where a company grants a floating charge, provision may be made for a **receiver** to be appointed by the chargee in order to sell (as the company's agent) the charged assets and meet the company's obligations to the chargee (ie the bank). If the appointment is created under a floating, or a fixed and floating, charge on substantially the whole of a company's assets, the receiver is an **administrative receiver** under the terms of the Insolvency Act 1986.

An **administrator** is appointed by the court in response to a petition brought by the company itself, its directors, or by a creditor, to try and formulate a plan to deal with the company debts without the company being put into liquidation. Where the court orders a company to be wound up, the official receiver attached to the court becomes the company's **liquidator** under the terms of the Insolvency Act 1986 or, if substantial assets are to be administered, an insolvency practitioner is appointed liquidator. If the realizable assets of the company will not meet the expenses of liquidation, and the company's affairs do not require further investigation, the official receiver will apply to the Registrar of Companies for the company to be dissolved.

The Enterprise Act 2002 s 248 replaces the Insolvency Act 1986 Part 11 and consolidates all Statute law on administration. In particular, companies and/or creditors are able to appoint an administrator themselves rather than apply to the court. A court application, however, will still be necessary where the company is being wound up voluntarily, through an application to the court by the holder(s) of a floating charge or if an administrative receiver has been appointed and the court is satisfied that such an order would discharge, avoid or otherwise invalidate the floating charge.

5.3 What type of security is available?

The question is really in two parts: what security is available now and what is likely to be available in the future? Taking a fixed legal charge over the assets in question will satisfy the former and taking a floating legal charge on all assets of the company/group can cover the latter. A charge gives a creditor a security interest in property/assets without the transfer of possession. There are only four principal types of security recognized by English law: the mortgage; the equitable charge; the pledge; the contractual lien. The use of different types of security may be summarized generally as follows.

Assets:	Security available
Freehold/leasehold property	Fixed & floating charge: – on registered or unregistered title; – by a legal or equitable charge; ranking as a first or second (etc) charge.
Plant/machinery (fixed in place)	Fixed legal or equitable first charge.
Other assets present & future eg book debts; uncalled capital; goodwill.	Fixed equitable first charge held at present or in the future.
Eg fixtures/fittings; equipment; book debts; stock; intellectual rights; motor vehicles; moveable plant.	First floating charge; held at present or in the future.
Revenue stream	Prior rights thereto by contract.
Contracts	Stand-in performance.
Trading risks (overseas)	Insurance policies.
Obligations/indebtedness (generally)	Third party guarantees; pledge; lien; company debenture.
Independent assets eg quoted investments; life policies.	The assets themselves with transfer documents signed but not dated.

Security may also be available outside the ownership of the company, such as with private limited companies where the principal/majority shareholder/owners can be called upon to agree to a first (or second, if a building society or other lender already holds a first) charge on their residence or other properties. This is frequently done where the company rents the premises from the owner. If the business is not a company, the bank lender will look to all the assets of the business owner/borrower/shareholder held in his/her name.

5.4 Rights of the chargee

There can be a **legal chargee**, who is given legal title to the property or land and has an immediate right of possession. An **equitable chargee** has no right to possession unless it is in the charge contract but if in doubt, on application, the Court can appoint a receiver to take possession under its jurisdiction pending Court authority to sell the property and settle the debt. A legal chargee/mortgagee may take possession simply by choice and, in so doing, accepts responsibility as a mortgagee in possession, but an equitable mortgagee must show good reason why the court should comply with the equitable mortgagee's request and take possession through its receiver.

The receiver is neutral and their task is to administer property for the benefit of all parties to the proceedings; the chargee wishes the property to be administered solely for its own benefit. This can be done by adding a clause in an equitable charge (such as a floating charge) giving the right for the chargee to appoint a receiver to possess the charged property and sell it for the chargee's benefit.

A chargee who does take possession of the charged property must account to the surety (ie the person providing third party security or an indemnity for performance of the obligation) for all rents and profits that the surety would have received but for the default of the chargee. This also means that the chargee exercising possession of a business will stand in the place of the mortgagor and be accountable to the owner of the equity for all existing or likely business receipts.

Where the charged property consists of land that has been leased, the safest way to receive the rent is for the equitable or legal chargee to appoint a receiver of income, under the Law of Property Act 1925, providing the chargee can exercise a power of sale. A receiver of income is then deemed to be the agent of the surety.

A contract creating a charge as collateral security for an obligation does not give the right to sue the surety for performance of the obligation. The chargee's right would be against the charged property and not against the chargor personally in the absence of contract terms to the contrary. Enforcement of the secured obligation would otherwise be by an ordinary action for recovery of the debt. When the surety's rights are ended (foreclosed), the chargee cannot sue under the charge contract to recover the debt, unless the right of possession of the charged property is given up, but if the property had been sold (not foreclosed) the chargee has the right to sue.

5.5 Floating charges

Whether a charge is fixed or floating

Whether a charge is a fixed or a floating charge is a matter of effect. Referring to the case of re Yorkshire Woolcombers Association Ltd [1903] Vaughan Williams LJ reported:

> 'if a contract of charge contemplates that the company will deal with the assets covered by the charge without reference to the chargee then it is likely to be a floating charge, whereas if the assets can be dealt with only after being released from the charge by the chargee then it is likely to be a fixed charge'.

Romer LJ stated (inter alia) in the same case:

> '...if a charge has three characteristics...it is a floating charge: **if** it is a charge on a class of assets of a company present and future...**if** that class is one which, in the ordinary course of the business of the company, would be changing from time to time...**if** you find that by the charge it is contemplated that, until some future step is taken by or on behalf of those interested in the charge, the company may carry on its business in the ordinary way as far as concerns the particular class of assets being dealt with...'

The assumption (by banks and others) that a fixed charge over the book debts of a company is effective (as, for instance, against the claims of a Receiver in insolvency) was confirmed by the New Zealand case of *Re New Bullas Trading Ltd* [1994] but overruled by the decision of the Judicial Committee of the Privy Council on 5 June 2001, following an appeal by the receivers (Agnew and Bearsley) appointed over *Brumark Investments Ltd (in liquidation)* [2001]. The receivers claimed that the proceeds of collected book debts were subject to a fixed charge where the lender had been in full control of sales invoices and their collection (refer *Agnew and Bearsley v Commissioners of Inland Revenue* [2001]).

The Judicial Committee, whose decision is non-binding in English law, held otherwise: that the company (Brumark) was in control of the process of extinguishing the book debts, since the proceeds were effectively under the control of, and available for use by, the chargor in the ordinary course of its business, through their collection and the ordinary operation of the overdraft account. The borrower had been free to deal with uncollected book debts and this was inconsistent with the nature of a fixed charge; therefore the proceeds were available for use by the company. This decision meant that banks could not automatically claim funds from unpaid sales invoices.

The most recent judgment of whether a fixed or a floating charge is evident has been made by the Court of Appeal in *National Westminster Bank Plc v Spectrum Plus*

Ltd (26 May 2004, also reported in the Times, 4 June 2004). This has overturned the Judicial Committee ruling and the judgment in *Siebe Gorman & Co Ltd v Barclays Bank Ltd* [1979] and has approved the finding of both the *Brumark* and *Agnew* cases that *New Bullas* was wrongly overruled. *Spectrum*, of course, may yet be appealed to the House of Lords but, for the present, the judgment stands as follows.

In *re Spectrum,* a fixed charge was created over book debts by a debenture that imposed restrictions on the use of the proceeds of the book debts: the debts were not to be disposed of prior to collection but were to be paid into an account at the chargee bank on collection that was subject to a floating charge. The crucial issue was whether the restriction on the chargor's potential use of those proceeds was sufficient in law to create a fixed charge on the debts.

The Court of Appeal in 2004 reasoned, however, that the payment of the proceeds of the receivables to an account at the chargee bank effectively transferred the chargor's proprietary interest in the proceeds to the bank. It would reduce the chargor's indebtedness to the bank and thereby falls within the definition of a fixed charge, regardless of whether or not there are terms governing the chargor's dealings on the account. The reasoning of the *Brumark* case is reinstated (and supports, but is preferred to, the judgment in *New Bullas*): that the essential characteristic of a floating charge on book debts is the unrestricted right of the chargor to collect and make use of the proceeds of those debts prior to crystallization. The terms of the *Spectrum* debenture were sufficient to create a fixed charge on the receivables.

It should be noted that the *Spectrum* judgment would not necessarily apply to securitization transactions where the relevant chargor is a Special Purpose Vehicle and book debt proceeds are not paid into an account with the chargee bank; neither would it apply to lending transactions where the depositary bank is not the chargee bank or trustee for the lenders. It was clear in *re Spectrum* that, where the proceeds of book debts are paid into a customer's account with the bank, title to those proceeds passes absolutely to the bank and the bank's obligation to the customer, as a result of receiving those proceeds, depends upon the terms of the contract between them (in this case to repay borrowings under an overdraft facility). The charge is a fixed charge because the book debts should not be disposed of prior to collection and, on collection, the proceeds should be paid to the bank itself.

Recent changes introduced by the Enterprise Act 2002 have had an impact on the nature of floating charges since certain claims now take priority over a floating charge (but not a fixed charge). The Enterprise Act 2002 s 251 has abolished the Crown's preference for debts due to the Inland Revenue, to Customs and Excise and for social security contributions (but not other preferential debts). Holders of floating charges created after 15 September 2003 now face their claims' priority being subject to part of the charges' proceeds being allocated to the benefit of all unsecured creditors.

A floating charge in general confers on the chargee the right to take all the assets of that type owned by the company, at the time when the charge crystallizes for payment of the secured debt. Usually a floating charge crystallizes when the company has failed to pay a due secured debt and the chargee appoints a receiver under the charge contract. Prior to crystallization, the company may fully deal with the assets of the charged class in the normal course of business without reference to the chargee. On crystallization, a floating charge becomes a fixed equitable charge on the specific assets of the charged class owned by the company at that time.

A floating charge crystallizes when a receiver is appointed, when the company goes into liquidation, when it ceases business, when the chargee gives notice within the terms of the charge contract that the charge is converted into a fixed charge, if the company deals with charged assets otherwise than as carrying on its business or on the occurrence of any other event specified in the charge contract to be an event of crystallization.

These events may typically include: the chargee converting the charge into a fixed charge; a levy of execution or distress made on the company assets; another chargee appointing a receiver; a creditor petitioning for the company to be wound up by the court. The prime condition to be satisfied is that the debt secured by the charge has not been paid when due. In relation to a bank overdraft that is repayable on demand, the demand must have been made and not met. The Insolvency Act 1986 section 122 defines various grounds as evidence to support a winding up:

- the company fails to comply with a written statutory demand for payment of a debt exceeding £750;
- execution of a judgement is made against the company anywhere in the UK fails wholly or partly;
- if it is proven to the satisfaction of the court that the company is unable to pay its debts as they fall due;
- if it is proven that the company's assets are less than its liabilities, taking into account prospective and contingent liabilities.

There appears to be some doubt whether a second floating charge created by a company that crystallizes before a first floating charge will give it priority over subsequent crystallization of the first charge (refer *Griffiths v Yorkshire Bank Plc* [1994]) and (*re Household Products Co Ltd and Federal Business Development Bank* [Ontario 1981]).

Before a floating charge crystallizes, it does confer on the chargee an interest in, and rights over, the assets in the class charged. These include an interest in land and it makes no difference that it is a contingent or future interest. A bank has the right to retain money paid into an overdrawn account where it holds a floating charge on that debt and can obtain an injunction to prevent the company (otherwise than in the normal course of business) from dealing in assets held under a floating charge, or it can ask the court to appoint a receiver if an event (whether or not in the normal course of business) threatens the security held under the charge.

Under a composite fixed and floating charge, the chargee may take the property subject to fixed charges and treat the remainder as subject to the floating charge available for payment of any preferential creditors and liquidation expenses. In the case of *Evans v Rival Granite Quarries Ltd* [1910 Court of Appeal] a floating charge was determined not to be a charge on an individual asset until the charge crystallises. As Buckly LJ said:

> 'the nature of the security is a mortgage presently affecting all the items expressed to be included in it, but not specifically affecting any item until the happening of the event which causes the security to crystallize as regards all the items'.

Avoiding a floating charge

Creation of a so-called fixed charge on a company's book debts avoiding the Insolvency Act 1986 s 40 (but still allowing the company to use the money collected and remain under a floating charge if the chargee did not specifically direct the debts to incur a fixed charge) failed, under a subsequent ruling of the Privy Council in *Agnew v Commissioner of Inland Revenue* [2001], where it was determined that the assignment and collection of book debts are just alternative ways of turning a debt into money, so a charge contract allowing either method of realization without the chargee's permission must create a floating and not a fixed charge.

The Insolvency Act 1986 sets out the situations when a floating charge can be avoided. An administrator may avoid it if the charge was created at any time within a period of twelve months before the date of the petition on which the administration order was made or during the period when the petition was pending. The same time period before the commencement of winding-up is given to a liquidator and applies to persons not connected with the company. Charges given to persons connected with the company have a period of two years. Connected persons are a director or shadow director of the company, an associate of either of these persons, or an associate of the company itself (as defined, but including family relatives, business partners and companies under their control).

Section 245 of the Act is intended to prevent an unsecured creditor of a company obtaining a floating charge to secure the existing debt and thereby gain an advantage over other unsecured creditors. Thus, when a company is being wound up, the property secured by a floating charge that can be avoided under this section of the Act cannot be utilized by, or on behalf of, the chargee to pay anything other than, (inter alia) at the time of or after the creation of the charge:

- the value of money paid or goods or services supplied to the company;
- the value of the discharge or reduction of any debt of the company;
- any interest becoming due on either of the above sums under the terms of the agreement.

The value of goods or services is the amount of money at the time of supply that could reasonably be expected to be obtained in the ordinary course of business on the same terms as were supplied to the company.

Where a bank obtains a floating charge over an insolvent company's property as 'continuing security for all present or future indebtedness to the bank on current account' then each payment out of the account after the charge is given is money paid to the company in consideration for the charge. If the account is overdrawn at the time the charge is given, then payments into the account are presumed to pay off the existing overdraft on a first-in-first-out basis (*Devaynes v Noble, Clayton's Case* [1816]) and the bank is left with the debt incurred after the charge was created.

5.6 How easy is it to take security?

It should be mentioned that the bank must initially ascertain that the company, by its Articles and directors' resolution, has sufficient powers to borrow, give security and not these lay down who may execute charges.

Where the asset available to be charged to secure a loan is situated abroad, this can raise problems relating to legal jurisdiction/procedures and the management of the asset to be realized, the possibility of local taxes liability, exchange controls and currency risks. If the asset is a ship, an aircraft or container/pallet, there will be the problem of tracing and sequestrating the asset. Fortunately, to provide protection where there is no possession, there are by statute Government administered registers to record non-possessory charges for; registered (since 1925 et seq) and unregistered (1972) land; ships (1995); trade marks (1994) and designs (1949); patents (1977); aircraft/hovercraft (1972).

Security on **land** is through registering the encumbrance at the District Land Registry or, if the property is unregistered, through the bank physically holding all the deeds of title in its own safe custody. The bank will hold the registered land certificate with a written undertaking from the company to execute a formal mortgage if ever the bank requires. Alternatively, with the certificate, the bank may prefer to lodge a completed form of mortgage with the company's request not to register the mortgage but to have discretion to do so at any time.

In each case, the charge must be registered with the Registrar of Companies within twenty-one days of creation otherwise the charge is void against a liquidator or other creditors of the company. Immediately prior to registration, the bank should make a search at Companies House to ensure that no prior charge is in existence. Charges requiring registration relate to the issue of debentures on uncalled share capital of the company, land and any interest therein, on the company's book debts, a floating charge on the company's property, a charge on calls made but not paid and on a charge created or evidenced by an instrument that on execution would require registration as a bill of sale.

Quoted stocks and shares are easy to take as security and will be held by the bank in safe custody, together with a signed but undated transfer of title in order that, should the bank have to realize the investment, it can do so without further referral to the company for authorization. In case the company is holding the shares as trustee, a fact that might not be known by the bank, a legal mortgage is also best taken on the investments.

Life policies on key directors/owners in force for the period of the bank facility are also easy to take as security and will be lodged with the bank. The life company needs to be notified of the bank's interest should a future claim arise. The bank should have the option to repudiate the loan agreement secured by the policies in the event that the assurance company fails to pay under the policy where the assured has provided material falsehoods as to insurability. There is an insurable interest where a creditor insures the life of the debtor.

Security of **documents of title to goods** will be by way of a pledge and the physical assets will be held through bills of lading and/or trade invoices and/or warehouse receipts giving title of the goods to the bank. The bank should put the goods into its own name and have this acknowledged by the warehouse keeper since a warehouse receipt is not by itself negotiable. The customer will be required to sign a letter of pledge and give authorization for the warehouse keeper to hold the goods to the bank's order. The bank should also insure the goods.

5.7 How relevant is the asset as security?

It is important for the priority of charges to be evident. If the chargee has a legal charge there is still recourse to the property if the underlying obligation secured by the charge is not met. If the chargee has an equitable charge, the property remains charged only if the new owner had notice of the charge at the time of acquiring the property. If the first charge is a legal charge then there is recourse to the property in priority to a second charge. Again, if the first charge is a legal charge, there is priority only if, at the time the second charge was created, the second chargee had notice of the first chargee's interest. If there are two equitable charges over the same property, priority is by order of creation.

The type of security available determines its relevancy. A personal guarantee offers no control on the guarantor's assets. Shares in an unquoted company, apart from the difficulty of valuation, may be impossible to sell and there may be restrictive conditions as to a future disposal in the company's Articles. A whole life policy may prove valueless if the assured commits suicide. Even a freehold building may have its drawbacks if it has dangerous asbestos in its structure. A leasehold building may have onerous restitution of condition liabilities and restrictive operating clauses: the property will be subject to rent reviews, the lease has a finite period to run and, if the bank takes possession, there is the problem of obtaining a new tenant.

5.8 What is the value of the security?

Real estate may have several valuations raised by qualified valuers. The company may have a **going-concern** valuation of its assets when it is trading, a **market valuation** on properties and assets suggesting what these assets might attract at a public sale, and a **bricks and mortar valuation** of the property as it stands. There may also be an **insurance valuation** in case of loss and rebuild. The bank will wish for a conservative bricks and mortar valuation since, if the security has to be possessed to repay the bank debt, the indicative option left will be to sell the property as rapidly as possible. Note that there is no obligation on the bank to sell at other than the best offer received at the time.

Land by itself can reduce in value, depending on the purpose for which it is to be used and possibly subject to changes in the use of surrounding plots. A compulsory purchase order may, or may not, be equivalent to a bricks and mortar valuation. Farmland value will vary according to the grading of the soil and market value for farm properties generally. Buildings on the land can deteriorate and require maintenance. If they have been built or adapted for a specific use, their value will be less than a multi-purpose property. Rental values will be subject to market demand for letting and the perception of what yield investors require before investing.

Quoted stocks and shares will have a present value that can be easily realized, subject to selling charges, but their value will change according to market buying and selling, demand by the public and the marketability of the shares. In this latter respect, dealing in the shares of major companies will be much easier than for small companies where the number of shares in issue can be relatively small. Any share valuation must allow for potential falls in market values.

Endowment policies raised on the lives of key directors will have day-to-day guaranteed surrender values. As it may take time for probate to be obtained in the event of death, the bank should allow for the loss of loan interest from the surrender value as a deduction prior to repayment. A whole life policy will only raise a value for security purposes on death. In either case, the bank may have the liability of paying premiums on the policy if the customer refuses to pay to safeguard the security cover.

Director/owner **guarantees** are taken, in part, to formalize the personal commitment to the company and be preventative of diminution to the company's net worth in case excessive dividends are declared. In terms of their intrinsic value, this may be substantive or otherwise. It may prove difficult and costly to claim under a guarantee and they should not be considered prime security.

Imported **trade goods** will have an invoice value but this may not be achievable in the event of possession and subsequent physical sale, particularly in the case of perishable goods. The value of exported trade goods will depend on the creditworthiness of the overseas importer or, if title is by irrevocable documentary credit or avalised bill of exchange, the standing of the importer's bank.

5.9 How can the security be perfected?

A bank usually takes a charge on all of a company's assets through a fixed charge on specified fixed assets and a floating charge on the company's whole undertaking and property outside the fixed charge. A receiver appointed under this charge is an administrative receiver (Insolvency Act 1986) who realizes the charged assets for the sole benefit of the named creditor(s) holding the charge. In practice, this means the company's assets are sold to satisfy any preferential debts first, followed by secured debts and then the amounts due to other creditor(s). The alternative for the holder of a floating charge is to have an administrator appointed by the court.

The charge on company assets must be registered with the Registrar of Companies at Companies House and care should be taken to view the register to ensure that no previously unknown prior charges have been lodged that will affect the current charge. Great care has to be exercised when taking security to prevent loss in favour of the rights of a company liquidator or of failing to prove that the taking of a guarantee was valid.

Bank charge forms are standardized and reflect the individual wording chosen by each bank. Some clauses will be common to all forms. Typical examples are:

- **continuing security**, allowing the security to remain after the original borrowing has been repaid;
- **all moneys**, allowing the bank to demand repayment now and in the future of all amounts outstanding;
- **prior charges**, allowing the bank to close a debtor's account and credit future receipts into a new account to retain priority for the original secured debt (refer re *Clayton's Case*);
- **additional security**, allowing the bank to add further security or dispose of existing security without impairing the original charge;
- **successor**, allowing the bank to transfer security to a third party, such as when debts are being securitized and sold on;
- **conclusive evidence**, specifying the exact amount of debt charged.

5.10 Does the security need monitoring?

The reason for taking security is to have a tangible asset that can be easily and quickly realized in the event that the loan is not repaid. For the loan to be fully repaid the security must exceed the principal value of the loan amount outstanding, together with the costs of realizing the security and recovery of the interest charge, and any further fees due as a result of the loan default. The amount of default interest charged should be set in the loan agreement together with the fact that it is to incur interest on interest at stated compounded dates. Regular monitoring of the security (at least annually for well-maintained accounts and more frequently where the account or the security holds a greater credit risk) is a necessity for the bank to ensure that the required margin of value over the outstanding debt is retained.

Land and buildings have proved to be the most reliable forms of security that retains (or improves) in value. Valuation of this type of asset is not an exact science, particularly for commercial properties and, depending on the type of property, a loan to bricks and mortar first charge value of between 60% and 80% is the most usual guideline. A subsequent 'desk valuation' without personal inspection may suffice for monitoring, with a formal updating every few years or when the customer requests additional facilities or incurs financial difficulties.

Plant and equipment (including motor vehicles) can have a security value between 10% and 25% of their book figures, depending on whether they are moveable or immoveable and standard or specially built machines. The bank should review the break-up value of the customer's balance sheet annually and allow for significant changes to the assets owned. **Stock** can have an overall average value of between 30% and 35% of its book value, with finished or near-finished stock offering a higher percentage than this and raw materials a lower percentage. **Trade book debts** may be valued at between 65% and 70% of their pre-VAT invoiced amounts, subject to a lower percentage where the portfolio holds a significant amount of overdue debts.

The monitoring of **quoted stocks and shares** can readily be done by reference to the prices reported in the daily or official press. In this instance, the security agreement should have a clause granting the bank the right to ask for additional collateral in case of need to safeguard against any major fall in share prices. Endowment policies should be monitored for the payment of premiums as the guaranteed surrender values will not reduce but rather rise automatically as more premiums are paid.

5.11 How easily can the security be realized?

A legal chargee has an immediate right of possession of the charged property whether or not the surety has defaulted, unless there is an agreement to the contrary. The surety is the person who has provided the security or indemnity for the performance of the obligation. If no right of sale is granted by the charge contract, the chargee may apply to the Court for an order to sell the charged property. A chargee entering into possession becomes the owner of the business and is accountable to the owner(s) for everything that is or might be received. Any profit made on selling charged property after the secured obligation is met must be held on trust for the surety. The chargee has a duty to take reasonable care to obtain the true market value of the property, limited to the value actually obtained at the time of sale unless varied in the charge contract.

The Law of Property Act 1925 gives a power of sale only where the surety has failed to comply within three months' notice to repay the secured debt, where interest payable on the secured debt remains unpaid two months after becoming due or there has been a breach of a term of the charge contract other than those relating to the repayment of principal or interest. There is also the power for a chargee to appoint a Receiver of Income acting as agent of the surety where the property charged is land under deed that has subsequently been leased and accrues rent.

A creditor given security cannot be forced to utilize that security and may decide to commence an ordinary action for repayment of the debt. Where the charge is given as collateral security for another's obligation, the chargee's right is against the charged property and there is no right to sue the surety for performance of the obligation. If a secured obligation is settled without recourse to the security, then the security contract automatically terminates and the security is said to be discharged. A person whose property has been charged always retains an interest in that property and this interest, or 'equity of redemption', ends when either the obligation is met, the right to redeem is ended by court order, the chargee exercises the power to sell the charged property or the property is sold by court order.

No action can be taken by a creditor to realize any security until the secured obligation becomes due and the discharge has not materialized. The case of *Williams and Glyn's Bank Ltd v Barnes* [1981] concerned the allegation that the bank had unreasonably refused to continue to finance the company and a demand for repayment of the overdraft would put the company into liquidation. Ralph Gibson J said:

> 'where money is lent on overdraft by a bank, and there is no agreed date for repayment, and no special terms which require implication of a further term as to the date of repayment, then it is clear to me that the overdraft is repayable on demand.'

He continued:

> '...when a bank lends money to a customer there is no reason to suppose that, in the absence of agreement to that effect, the bank must regard the fulfilment of the customer's known purpose as the agreed, or only, source of repayment. Borrowing from a bank may be replaced by borrowing from another bank or moneylender. If the borrowing cannot be replaced, because of the parlous state of the borrower's business, or of the market generally, I know of nothing in the ordinary contract of lending which requires the lender to share the borrower's misfortune'.

5.12 What security should be asked for?

Having determined that security is required and having ascertained what security is to hand, the bank will need to weigh up the advantages and disadvantages of each option in relation to the risk involved and the type of borrowing facility to be agreed. Where the risk is other than short-term, a first fixed and floating charge on the assets of the company will provide the best security with the minimum of monitoring. The type of short-term borrowings will indicate what form of security to apply. It may involve one or more of the following representative choices:

- taking the title of goods where overseas trading is done;
- relying on a floating charge where the premises are rented and the plant is being purchased on hire purchase;
- accepting that book debts are ring-fenced with a prior charge to support a factoring or invoice discounting facility;
- agreeing an account set-off where the company holds money on deposit from time to time as well as utilizing borrowings;
- taking security on the cash flow to arise from a major contract to enable the financing of the contract to be completed;
- deciding that a particular customer is undoubted and no formal security is needed other than to put in place agreed operating covenants;
- deciding that the business owner should supply a personal guarantee in addition to security supplied by the company;
- deciding to accept the existing security of a major borrower on a pari passu basis with the other lenders.

5.13 Examples of security clausing of a loan agreement

Each loan agreement will have its particular clausing to meet the circumstances of the customer and the bank. Some examples are shown below and reflect how earlier descriptions given in this section are embodied in a formal facility letter in respect of security and related clauses. Further reference is also made in section 6.12. The empty brackets [ ] indicate where specific details of the company/loan agreement would be inserted.

Legal charge over freehold property

Amounts outstanding under the facility will be secured at all times by a [first] legal mortgage over [ ] properties acceptable to the bank. The bank shall require a valuation of [ ] properties in a form to the bank's satisfaction and undertaken by a valuer that meets the bank's approval, showing the aggregate *[type of value required]* value to be not less than [ ]. The bank reserves the right at any time during the period of the facility to have a *[further]* valuation of the properties undertaken at the company's expense by valuers nominated by the bank and to ask the company to substitute *[alternative/additional]* properties in order to maintain the aforesaid value of the bank's security margin.

The aggregate amount of drawings by the company under the facility from time to time outstanding shall not exceed [70] % of the aggregate value of the properties at such time charged to the bank which value shall be determined by the bank. In the event that such percentage shall be exceeded for any reason the company shall at the bank's request either forthwith deposit with the bank by way of security for such drawings such cash and/or additional security that the bank may require or reduce the drawings outstanding so as to ensure that such percentage shall not exceed the satisfactory required percentage. Should the company fail to provide such security or reduction the bank is irrevocably authorised to realize without the company's prior agreement all or any of the properties to ensure that such excess is eliminated.

Mortgage debenture

Amounts outstanding under the facility are to be secured by a [first] legal charge in a form to the bank's satisfaction over the company's assets and undertaking.

Deed of postponement

The bank shall require the execution in a form to the bank's satisfaction of a deed of postponement under which the charge created by a debenture dated [ ] in favour of [ ]shall rank in priority to the charge referred to in paragraph [ ] up to the principal sum of [ ] together with interest thereon.

Charge over shares

The company will complete to the bank's satisfaction lien and share transfer forms in blank and deliver to the bank the share certificates in respect of the company's holdings of the following shares [ ].

Charge over lease/rental agreements

Amounts outstanding under the facility are to be secured at all times by a first legal charge over leasing and rental agreements current from time to time which must be acceptable to the bank and have outstanding rentals discounted at [ ] % pa of not less than [ ] % of such amounts. The bank reserves the right at any time to require the lessees and hirers under their respective leasing and rental agreements charged to the bank to make payments direct to the bank to an account that will be designated and controlled by us. The company shall have the right at any time to substitute any leasing or rental agreements that are charged to the bank with new leasing or rental agreements.

Guarantees

[The company][and subsidiary companies] 'the guarantors' are to enter into a joint and several guarantee of their obligations to the bank under the terms of this facility letter in a form to the bank's satisfaction. Each guarantor is forthwith to agree with the bank that they will perform and observe all the obligations and liabilities to be undertaken in the facility letter. The said guarantors represent and warrant to the bank by signing the duplicate copy of this letter that the giving of the guarantee to the bank pursuant to the provisions of this paragraph will be within their corporate powers and that all relevant corporate action has been taken or will be taken by each guarantor to enable it legally to execute the said guarantee and that the said guarantee when executed will constitute valid and legally binding obligations on each of them in accordance with its terms.

Set-off clausing

The bank shall open a blocked account in the company's name. The company agrees to maintain at all times in this account a sum not less than the outstanding balance of the loan. [No]/ interest will be payable on the account. The company will not be entitled to payment of the whole or any part of the amounts standing at any time to the credit of the account unless and until the bank shall have received payments of the principal and interest on the loan and then only to the extent of such payments.

The company undertakes that at all times the account will be maintained by the company free of any charge, lien or encumbrance and the company will not assign or otherwise dispose of any legal or equitable interest therein. The company irrevocably authorizes the bank to apply all moneys from time to time standing to the credit of the account towards satisfaction of any liability that may at any time be outstanding under the company's loan facility or to debit the account with the amount of principal or of accrued interest on the loan then due and payable and such amount shall be deemed to have been paid to the bank on account of the principal or interest aforesaid.

In addition to any right of set-off or any similar right to which the bank may be entitled at law or in equity the bank may at any time without notice combine and consolidate all or any of the company's accounts with the bank anywhere and set-off any moneys whatsoever and whether on current deposit or any other account and in whatever currency or currencies against any of the company's liabilities whatsoever in whatever currency that may be owing or incurred by the company to the bank whether alone or jointly with any other person or persons company or companies and whether or not any period of any deposit or by reference to which interest thereon is calculated has expired.

Representations and warranties

The company's acceptance of the loan facility and the company's acceptance of the proceeds of each drawing made hereunder shall constitute the company's continuing representation and warranty that:

- the company has full power, authority and legal right to borrow hereunder and to observe the terms and conditions of this facility and that there is no provision in any corporate document, mortgage, indenture, trust deed, or agreement binding on the company *[and the company's subsidiaries]* or affecting the company's property that would conflict with or prevent the company from accepting the facility on the terms and conditions stated herein, or would prevent the company's performance or observation of any of the terms hereof;
- there are no law suits or other legal proceedings pending or, so far as the company's directors know, threatened before any court, tribunal or administrative agency which in the opinion of the directors will adversely affect in any material respect the consolidated financial condition or operations of the company *[and its subsidiaries]*;
- the company *[and its subsidiaries]* is not in any breach of any other agreement for borrowed money;
- there has been no material change in the assets and undertaking of the company *[and its subsidiaries]* since the date of the company's last published annual audited *[consolidated]* accounts that adversely affects the financial position as therein disclosed.

Undertakings

By the company's acceptance of the facility the company undertakes that during its continuance and until all the company's obligations hereunder have been fully met:

- the company *[and its subsidiaries]* will not without the bank's prior written consent create any pledge, mortgage or other charge over any of the company's assets *[including uncalled capital]* and/or undertaking, property or revenues present and future or permit any lien to arise and that should any such incumbrance be created by operation of law or otherwise the same shall forthwith be discharged;
- the company will not without the bank's prior written consent dispose of the company's interest in *[property]/ [shares]*. In the event of any default the bank may at any time require the company to *[.....]*;

- drawings under the facility will only be made in respect of goods invoiced by the company that are subject to firm orders covering at least [ ] % of invoiced value *[excluding any taxes charged thereon]*. The goods financed by a drawing hereunder will be stored in a separate reserved space of *[the company's warehouse]/[a warehouse acceptable to the bank]* that the company will allow the bank access to at all reasonable times. The bank at any time for any reason shall request the company to facilitate title to the goods to be put in the name of the bank and the company shall not *[unreasonably]* withhold permission to do so;

- the company will provide the bank with the following financial information within *[a reasonable period to be agreed with the bank]*:
  - a copy of the company's annual audited *[consolidated]* accounts;
  - quarterly management reports;
  - monthly list of trade debtors analysed by age;
  - such other information as the bank may from time to time reasonably request in a form to be agreed by the bank.

Net tangible assets

- The company will maintain its *[consolidated]* Net Tangible Assets *[as defined]* at all times at a minimum of *[£]* or *[%]* of the Net Tangible Assets as shown in the company's latest published annual audited accounts, whichever is the higher.

Total borrowings

- The company's Total Borrowings *[as defined]* will not at any time exceed *[%]* of the company's Net Tangible Assets *[and if lesser]* or the aggregate of *[%]* of the *[defined]* value of the company's freehold properties and *[%]* of the company's trade debtors not more than *[90]* days old and *[%]* of the company's book values of stocks and work in progress.

Interest cover

- The company's *[consolidated]* profit before interest charges, taxation and dividends for each annual accounting period will not be less than [ ] times the company's *[consolidated]* interest charge for the period.

Dividend restriction

- The company will not make any payments in respect of dividends *[or management charges]* in excess of *[%]* of the company's Net Profit After Tax in respect of each of the company's annual accounting periods.

Working capital ratio

♦ The company's *[consolidated]* Current Assets *[as defined]* will at all times *[exceed]/[not be less than % of]* the company's *[consolidated]* Current Liabilities *[as defined]*.

Conditions precedent

Before the facility is made available to the company the bank shall have received in a form to the bank's satisfaction:

♦ copy of a resolution of the company's board of directors duly certified as a true copy by the company secretary, accepting the facility on the terms and conditions of this letter, approving the execution and delivery of the agreement constituted by this letter and appointing *[persons]* to sign *[drawdown requests etc]*;

♦ the duly executed *[charge/deed of postponement etc]*;

♦ a certified up-to-date copy of the company's Memorandum and Articles of Association;

♦ specimen signatures of the persons authorized to sign as above;

♦ payment of *[any]* arrangement or commitment fee.

Events of default

The typical events of default for a loan agreement may be summarized:

♦ failing to make any payment on the due date;

♦ if any representations or warranties or documentation provided shall be incorrect in a material respect;

♦ if there is default in the performance of any other term or condition of the facility or any other event occurs in the bank's opinion to place the facility in jeopardy;

♦ if a petition is presented or an administration order is made;

♦ if an order is made or resolution passed to wind up the company other than for purposes of reconstruction or amalgamation on terms previously approved by the bank while the company is solvent;

♦ if a meeting is convened or proposal made to enter into any arrangements or composition for the benefit of creditors;

♦ if an encumbrancer, receiver, administrative receiver, manager or similar officer is appointed over the whole or part of the company's undertaking and assets;

♦ if any mortgage or charge becomes enforceable, whether or not the chargee/mortgagee thereof takes any steps to enforce the same;

- if any indebtedness or obligation for the repayment of any borrowed moneys becomes due and payable prior to the specified maturity date due to any default or is otherwise not paid when due;
- if the company suspends or threatens to suspend its business or a substantial part thereof, or suspends payment of debts within the meaning of the Insolvency Act 1986 section 123 or re-enactment thereof;
- if there is a *[material]* change in ownership of the company that has not previously been approved by the bank;
- if the company ceases to be a {*wholly owned*} subsidiary of [ ] or if the company ceases to wholly own [ ] subsidiaries;
- the company will immediately notify the bank in writing *[address]* of the occurrence of any event of default and at any time after the occurrence thereof the bank, whether or not notified by the company, may by notice in writing *[address]* declare that all amounts due under the facility are immediately due and payable and such declaration shall be effective from the date of such occurrence or such other date as the bank may specify in the said notice.

Note that many of the above clauses will incorporate wording to include guarantors of the company's obligations.

Other clauses

The loan agreement will include wording as to:

- the definition of terms;
- treatment of costs in the event of default;
- calculation of mandatory reserve assets liabilities;
- changes in (taxation etc) circumstances;
- loan repayment and prepayment and cancellation terms;
- arrangement fees and commitment commission;
- minimum utilization terms;
- interest margins;
- drawdown options;
- currency options;
- facility availability;
- general conditions as to legal jurisdiction etc.

Six

Stewardship: monitoring and control of lending

Monitoring of lending is a key element of a bank's duties. After the lending bank has given approval for a new or additional credit facility for the company, and the documentation and any security has been put in place, it is not appropriate for the bank to claim to have fully investigated the lending proposition and so wait for the company to fulfil its commitments. While the company may try hard to do so, its trading environment is susceptible to adverse external influences or the company may make poor operating judgements even after an exemplary track record. The bank should bear in mind general external commercial and internal influences not recognized at the time of the original assessment of the company and how they are likely to affect the risk of non-repayment of both the amount borrowed and its servicing costs. Some of these influences are listed below.

External influences	Questions to ask
Changes in interest rates	Will the change affect repayment of the facility?
Changes in fiscal policy	Will they create an adverse trading climate?
Changes in competition	Will this affect turnover and profitability?
Local planning news etc	How will it affect the business?
Governmental controls	Will this lead to unexpected higher expenditure?
Technological advances	Will the company's present markets diminish?
Trading markets	Can any adverse changes be nullified?

Internal influences	Questions to ask
Key staff changes	Will the company change its trading policy?
New products	Will they be a success or require much R & D?
New expansion plans	What will be their net effect on resources?
Loss of customers	How important will this be in sales terms?
Selling price changes	Will their overall effect be beneficial or not?
New marketing policy	What is the assessment of cost to reward?

The aim of the bank will be to recognize, in advance as far as possible, if any of these changes will adversely affect the company's business and, if so, to establish whether the changes will affect the borrowing covenants or lead to a request for additional finance. If the difficulties identified are significant, the next step will be to request a meeting with the company to discuss their effect on the bank's financing and the company's proposed remedial measures.

This degree of advance monitoring requires a full and up-dated understanding of the company's business. It applies to the larger corporation as much as the smaller business. As an example of the former, a certain public company had loan facilities outstanding to a number of major banks. There was public knowledge of difficulties with products that included a particular ingredient. The company drew down all of its then undrawn facilities, with those banks' agreement but without informing them of imminent problems. A short time afterwards, the company disclosed its financial problems to all of the banks. Had they taken a prior view of the circumstances surrounding the company's market products, depending on the terms of each facility, there would have been an opportunity for the bank(s) to reduce or withdraw the availability of part of their commitment.

In one sense, the **control** of lending is more reactive to events compared with a pro-active monitoring of individual customers' accounts. Once an adverse situation has arisen on a customer's account, control action should be initiated to protect the bank from loss. In another sense, control is exercised in a more general way through Head Office directives to concentrate, or otherwise, on certain types of lending when gaining new business or renewing existing borrowing. A classic case of reactive control would be where a significant rise in house prices, coupled with rising interest rates, leads a bank to review the future size of its lending portfolio in property investment for re-sale.

6.1 The purpose of reviewing customers' accounts

The purpose of reviewing customers' accounts is not to assume that they are acting without due consideration to the bank's money, although this may well be the case in certain instances, but to ensure that the account is operated within agreed terms and to give the bank the earliest notification of any event that may impinge on this arrangement.

The Proceeds of Crime Act 2002, effective from February 2003, requires all businesses to report any suspicion of money laundering. The Money Laundering Regulations 2003, effective 1 March 2004, obligate all eligible organizations including banks, providing services in relation to the formation, operation or management of a company, to appoint a Money Laundering Reporting Officer and to establish appropriate internal reporting procedures:

- to properly identify customers using large amounts of cash;
- to copy the identification documents;
- to maintain records relating to the transactions.

This includes reporting suspicious transactions and, if a payment of more than Euro 15,000 is involved, satisfactory evidence of bona fides must be obtained from the customer otherwise the transaction will be terminated. The regulations set out the framework without guidance on its implementation, ie what constitutes 'suspicion' and what precise measures must be taken to gather customer information.

The frequency of reviewing a customer's account will depend on the circumstances of the individual case. Accounts may be reviewed annually where there have been no problems for some time and where the bank can assume, based on experience, that any financial difficulty or changing circumstances will be promptly notified by the company. Accounts that have had or are having cash flow problems may require monthly trading figures to be sent regularly and promptly to the bank for its monitoring. In more extreme cases, the operation of the account may be monitored weekly or daily.

6.2 Information sources for review

The immediate sources of information on progress of customer's financial affairs will be the transactions going through the account(s) maintained. This will include the transactions of the day as well as items in immediate transit that are not yet cleared. Small private companies may have only a cheque account and perhaps a deposit account, while larger companies with subsidiaries will run concurrent accounts in sterling and currencies that are cleared daily to a net balance, requiring central funding or depositing in the overnight money market.

The bank's computer system will highlight for further examination any anomalies arising in the conduct of the customer's account. Further reference to this is discussed in 6.3. The bank should have noted, on opening the account, any internal money management system in use by the company and have judged its working capability. In turn, this will indicate any areas of financial control for the bank to monitor and, if necessary, discuss with the customer. For example, the company may rely on financing a branch through an imprest system, by repaying in arrears the previous month's expenses as a float for the following month. If the following month's costs are higher than the float, the account will become overdrawn which may, or may not, have been authorized in advance.

The bank should receive anually the trading accounts of the customer's business for comparison with the previous year, together with any profit and cash flow forecasts that are available. This will provide the financial background for discussion with the customer at the next annual review of the account, offering an opportunity to enquire the state of current trading and to assess whether the bank can be of further service. It may be necessary to visit the company's offices, for example, if a loan is being advanced for the purchase or extension of property or for the acquisition of new capital equipment.

It has been known for a company to request additional overdraft facilities to finance significantly higher raw materials or finished product stocks than in the past, only for the banker to find that the stocks are non-existent and that the money has been spent in other ways. By the time annual accounts have been prepared and issued, it will be too late for the bank to safeguard its lending position.

Information sourced through third parties or publicly reported should be treated with caution in case the truth is misrepresented. A carefully worded enquiry to the company would show that the bank was taking the welfare of the business to heart and, if the enquiry was couched around the possibility of a review of the credit limit (ie 'is the present facility large enough?'), this may counsel the company to act pre-emptively and discuss any problem should cash flow be at a crisis.

6.3 'Out of order' report

A business account may be shown as being out of order from the terms agreed between the customer and the bank for a number of reasons. Probably the most common is when the account has exceeded its authorized credit limit: this may be due to poor cash management or financial circumstances forced on the business. It will be the banker's important task to discover which circumstances apply. Reasons for poor cash management are: inadequate cash flow forecasting; overspending; inaccurate estimation of cash cleared on the account (particularly in respect of currency receipts from overseas); lack of attention to day-to-day cash resources.

Reasons for adverse financial circumstances usually stem from a lower than expected turnover. This may be compounded by a lack of quick remedial action that might include delaying the payment of creditors to curb future expenditure. There may be other reasons for the business having a cash shortfall and exceeding its credit limit: the over-stocking of raw materials; debtors proving slow to settle their accounts; a large bad debt; capital expenditure being met out of working capital; personal drawings or salaries exceeding the business earnings; occasional, sizeable, cost items (eg quarterly rent).

If the cash position can, or will, be remedied within a short time span, then the adverse report may be discounted from further action on condition that the customer recognizes what has happened and agrees on a suitable solution to prevent a recurrence. The banker may simply note minor violations and let the account run its course without further action.

Where there is adverse financial circumstance, an immediate judgement is required from the banker on two counts: what must the customer do to rectify the situation and what immediate action is required from the bank. In both cases, the customer should first be notified (preferably by telephone followed by a confirming letter) of the breach of account terms. If the customer agrees to correct the situation at once, the bank takes no further action; a further review of the position should be made if more time is requested towards resolution. Will acceptance of more time prove the right course or will the financial position get worse?

If the customer cannot immediately restore the account to within its agreed terms, a more thorough examination of the creditworthiness of the business is called for as early as possible. This will have two objectives: to safeguard the bank's position and to discern whether the business can trade out of its predicament. Further action decided may lead the bank to: take a preference over future incoming receipts; create a separate bank account for the future payment of wages; crystallise any floating security that is held. If the business predicament is shown to be temporary, the bank may be willing to advance more credit, suitably secured and priced, with strict monitoring procedures.

If the customer can or will not respond to the banker's enquiries, an unusual situation with larger businesses, the bank may have no option but to take steps to close the account. Before this is initiated, the consequences of all other avenues should be explored: for example, the crystallization of security or the appointment of an administrator may have ramifications on facilities from other banks and perhaps adversely affect the rights of the bank initiating the closure. Care must also be taken regarding litigation should its action be seen to create the collapse of the business (refer ss 5.11 and 6.10).

6.4 Causes and warning signs of trading difficulties

In general, there are three basic types of warning signs for a business before possible failure arises: the first occurs when the business changes a previously successful operating profile; the second can occur when external events prejudice its trading operations; the third may emerge internally when management fails to appreciate the adverse significance of an event.

A **change in operating profile** will lead to additional trading risks. This may take place when a company ventures into a new field or location or when it markets a new product. Unless the project has been thoroughly assessed for both risks and rewards and for financing, it may cause unacceptable financial loss. The bank should be aware of the new business emphasis and make a broad appraisal of monitoring requirement, considering whether to make no change or to raise its monitoring profile during an interim period while the project risks failure.

The bank should already be aware of possible **adverse changes in external events** significant to the wellbeing of the company. An example might be where the franchise of a major part of the business is due for renewal in one year's time: what will happen if this franchise is not renewed; what is the company doing about this risk; are alternative markets and/or products being found? Another example is a shift in public preference to out-of-town hypermarkets from small in-town shops: is the retailing company adapting to this change; how will it affect the bank relationship? If the retailer does nothing, future turnover, earnings and cash flow may suffer – the warning signs are there.

A **failure by management** to appreciate such warning signs can also apply internally when technical, production, or general commercial problems have been unforeseen. These are more difficult for the bank to deduce in advance and in many instances, after a drop in sales or profit has been reported, the bank's enquiry elicits the reason from management. This situation should not be confused with trading at an inadequate level to meet expenditure and the repayment and servicing of debt. With the former, the management has failed to remedy the problem rapidly; with the latter, management has been additionally found at fault in its financial forecasting. The judgement of the bank in its assessment of the capabilities of management has been found lacking and, in the latter example, the bank also failed in its financial monitoring.

A common warning sign of financial difficulties ahead can lie **in overdue trading debts before they become irrecoverable**. Before a debt becomes 'bad', one or more of several errors of judgement must have occurred:

- ♦ when credit to the account was initially granted, was either a poor credit assessment of that customer was made, or no assessment was made at all;
- ♦ the level of credit was too generous or, more likely, subsequent extensions to the limit were allowed without suitable re-appraisal of the creditworthiness of the customer;

♦ regulation of the customer's account by the supplying company has proven inadequate: the terms of trade initially agreed between the parties have not been kept by the customer; the supplier has failed to chase the customer sufficiently to recover overdue amounts within the agreed time period; the supplier has failed to stop all future credit being taken (putting the account on a cash-with-order basis) while setting terms for the gradual recovery of existing overdue sums.

6.5 Default and bank agreements

The bank will have specified all the events of default in the credit agreement made with the customer. Such events will be a mixture of common clauses and clauses relevant to the particular business of the company (refer s 5.13). The more common clauses are:

♦ failure to make payments of interest or of principal specified in the lending agreement by the due date(s);

♦ cross-default by the borrower in making due payments under other lending agreements;

♦ breach of any other clause in the lending agreement, to include non-compliance of covenanted undertakings and failure to adhere to representations made in the lending agreement (eg selling assets);

♦ material adverse changes in the circumstances (the financial condition) of the company *(note: the interpretation of this clause is usually stated to be at the discretion of the bank)*;

♦ statutory defaults, such as insolvency and the breaking of or non-adherence to the of the country under which the agreement is drafted;

♦ changes in control of the company.

A breach of any of these clauses will lead to a demand for repayment of the credit facility and no obligation to make further advances if specified in the original facility. The clauses may also extend to other companies within the group. To avoid breaches of what may be termed 'clerical errors', such as forgetting to make a payment by the due date, a clause is frequently inserted allowing the company a number of days (say seven working days) of grace before the breach is formalised. Where the company has several bank lenders, the terms granted to earlier bank agreements usually become the template for later deals. What may change, however, is the individual cost of money at the time of the agreement when market influence and the borrower's credit rating will act as a guide.

The **cross-default clause** is important to the bank, as it ensures that all banks will be treated as one in the event of failure. The cross-default may be invoked without some of the group banks knowing that default has occurred until later in the proceedings, particularly if it relates to a subsidiary overseas. Corporate borrowers may partially overcome this constraint by compartmentalising the lending to its subsidiaries on a country by country basis, offering security only to bank borrowings in those countries. A material adverse change clause applying to the holding company, however, depending on the wording, may still over-ride the freedom offered by the separation of cross-defaults.

The lending agreement may limit the scope of events of default if mutually agreed between the bank and the borrower. For example, debts below a certain value may be excluded, or actions by overseas regulators may change the interpretation of the borrowing. In this latter case, it is usual to renegotiate (or even repay) the loan agreement rather than invoke a default. Occasionally one bank in a syndicate that is in a different category of risk to other group banks may be allowed special consideration and priority over some security, providing all banks agree. Default of this bank's lending terms will not apply to other lenders to the company.

The **change of control** clause safeguards the bank(s) from a takeover of the company by another entity which would change the lending risk basis without the bank(s) being able to rescind their existing loan agreements. In turn, this may assist the management in resisting a takeover battle and losing control of the company. In practice, the successful company in a takeover will often re-negotiate the existing lending terms applicable and/or substitute its own bank(s) in place of those original banks. This usually means that banks being retained will do so at a lower margin than before and with different lending covenants.

6.6 Default and the bank's remedies

When a company is in default the bank should first act within its individual powers to minimize any potential loss. This may include setting off account balances in credit against the borrower's lending facilities in default, providing both accounts are in the same name and held by the same bank and that the lending agreement provides the means to the set-off, ie that the loan is now due and payable (refer s 5.13).

Secondly, the bank will look to all external remedies to prevent the loss of any assets controlled by the defaulting company. This will frequently take the form of a freezing order by way of a **pre-judgment attachment** (formerly known as Mareva injunctions) effected as an execution judgment by attachment on the assets of the defaulting party (the defendant), agreed by the court in favour of the bank (the plaintiff). Proof is required that there is a real risk of failing to satisfy the claim by making available the assets that are held by the defendant in the country.

Thirdly, the bank will act to recover funds now in jeopardy of being fully repaid. The court may decide, at its discretion, that if the remedy of claiming damages will be inadequate, or if the loan agreement terms offer a more suitable remedy to settle the claim, an order for **specific performance** of the loan agreement may be granted. There may also be the need for a **prohibitory injunction** to prevent the defaulting company from performing acts in breach of the agreed lending covenants. The bank has the option to **sue** in Court for damages and the recovery of monies owing arising from the breach of covenants, as well as rescinding the loan agreement. In practice, there will be clauses in the loan agreement stating what (compounded) interest rate will apply as damages.

Fourthly, the debtor company may offer terms for an agreed settlement of the outstanding debt in order to remain in business. The threat of legal action often gains a response and it is less costly than the bank resorting to court proceedings for recovery of the loan. The procedure of restructuring the company's total debts eliminates the need to appoint an administrator over the company's assets and thereby enforce liquidation. Choosing to let the company continue to trade and thereby, in time, repay a greater part of the outstanding debt must be weighed against the possibility that the company will eventually fail or that it will take so long to repay monies due that the bank(s) would have been better off cutting their losses early for a lower repayment sum and using the proceeds to offer interest-earning loans to other businesses.

Each **restructuring agreement** will be tailored to the individual characteristics of the company in distress. It effectively means that a completely revised business plan and cash flow forecast will have to be drawn up (by the lead bank/s) to be agreed by the debtor company and all participating banks. Invariably, it will include an element of the bank(s) writing off part of their original debt and, perhaps, taking equity shares in exchange. The security taken and lending covenants will be stringent, as will future monitoring of the bank account and trading against the forecast returns. There will be a period of freezing the lending status quo of all banks prior to negotiating an on-going lending settlement. This will be managed by the lead bank(s), that will periodically report to all the other banks on the progress of negotiations, the current trading situation of the company and the choices the banks have in order to raise a settlement agreeable to all parties.

In re-structuring, the banks will take a greater interest in company policy and in the treatment of trade creditors to prevent any action on their part that might prejudice the company's future operations. Part of the bank debt (and possibly the debt of some major trade creditors) may be formalized into bonds (refer s 7.5) with prior repayment rights. The agreement will include measures on how the banks will be repaid over time. Some banks may wish to remain as principal banks to the company while others may wish to withdraw their support as early as possible. The former banks may agree to allow early repayment to the latter banks, but at a cost.

6.7 Cross-firing

This is the name given where a customer exploits the time taken to clear funds through an account and the bank honours cheques that have been deliberately drawn on the account by the customer before they are cleared; the customer knows that there would otherwise be insufficient funds to meet the cheques' presentation but has no prior approval from the bank for an overdraft on the account. When the cheques are presented for payment, (usually) two days later, the money has been banked elsewhere and the original account becomes overdrawn. Such misuse of the bank account must be systematic and accounts may be used at different banks or branches of a bank, or even in conjunction with different accomplices; the bank must also continue to allow sums to be paid from cheques banked before they are cleared. This cross-firing will fail if either the customer stops replacing the money withdrawn by new cheques or if the bank stops paying money away against funds that continually remain uncleared.

Where many banking and cheque transactions are made into and out of an account daily, it may be difficult to ascertain whether cross-firing is being applied. The best check may be to monitor the amount and regularity of uncleared effects. If the customer wishes to make a singular fraudulent withdrawal, an approximately identical amount has to be continually replaced and this should be easily spotted. If the customer wishes to increase his deception, the total of uncleared amounts will balloon and there will be a noticeable increase in turnover through the account as well. As the restitution of uncleared balances must be effected within the presentation time window, the relative incidence of cheque bankings to payments may present a pattern that can be recognized as cross-firing.

If the account shows round-sum bankings and cheque withdrawals, this may be a sign either of trading weakness and/or cross-firing. Trading weakness may arise if the business cannot settle with trade creditors fully on time or through poor credit management in failing to collect the full amount of due trade debtor balances. Cross-firing does not require round-sum transactions these are frequently seen where the customer want to maintain an easy record of the amounts involved. Where the payee and the drawer of cheques are identical, this may indicate either cross-firing or simple reimbursement of one account of the customer from another that is in credit. The frequency and size of these transactions will offer a clue to which explanation is correct.

6.8 Overtrading

Overtrading has been defined as expansion of a business without sufficient financial support. Expansion usually results in an increase in sales, although there can be start-up businesses that incur costs and run out of money (ie capital) prior to commencing trading. Overtrading may only occur for a short period or it may prove endemic. An example of the former would be where staffing, production and stocks are increased in anticipation of higher sales, so that when the additional sales eventually materialise, the positive cash flow of the business is restored. An example of the latter would be where an anticipated increase in sales does not materialise and the business is over-geared for the size of trading being attained and the available financial resources invested in the business.

It can be difficult to recognize when a business is overtrading before it runs into significant cash flow problems. An approximate test as to whether a manufacturing company is overtrading might be as follows.

Test A

1   Estimate the present average monthly level of sales.

2   Take the expected average present gross profit percent on sales.

3   Estimate the annual cost of indirect expenses and convert to a monthly basis.

4   The net profit will be (1) x (2) + (3); convert to an annual basis.

5   Deduct from the net profit any capital expenditure (less sale proceeds) expected during the year.

6   Deduct also any total of irrecoverable VAT for the year.

7   The result will be the financial resources being generated by the business in a full year.

8   Compare step (7) with the cash resources of the business (ie present cash in hand and available bank facilities not yet drawn). If the resources are inadequate then the business is overtrading relative to the financial support that is available.

In some cases, the present average gross profit percentage is not available and to take an historic figure from the previous year's statutory accounts would be misleading. If so, Step 2 may be substituted by the following.

2a   Calculate the present monthly direct cost of labour and overheads.

2b   Calculate the estimated cost of materials necessary for the forecast level of sales.

Then continue with step 3 as before.

Note: the reason for estimating some costs annually and converting them to a monthly basis is to allow for expenses that occur less frequently than monthly. A broad estimate of irrecoverable VAT is to calculate (the current rate of 17.5%) VAT on total sales and deduct from this the VAT on total expenses after ignoring non-VATable expenses (ie wages, salaries, rent and rates, insurance and loan interest).

It will be crucial for a business not to overtrade and so raise the spectre of insolvency. It is equally important for the bank to recognize in good time whether such a situation is likely to arise and to broach alternative remedies to the company concerned. The test steps shown above, while estimating many figures on a present day basis, still rely on historic expense forecasts. The additional trading may refer to a new project for which no historic returns are available. How can it be seen whether the new project will lead to overtrading? Consider the following test.

Test B

1   What current numbers of units are being produced and what is their budgeted cost of production?

2   How many production units are proposed for sale, including the projected expansion, over a measured future period?

3   What will be the revised overheads of production [ie (1) + (2)]?

4   What is the forecast level of unit sales over the same period?

5   Are steps (2) and (4) compatible? Assuming this is so ...

6   How much additional financing will step (3) require (including any additional labour and capital equipment) and over what period before receipts from the additional sales are received?

7   Does the business have additional finance readily at hand?

8   If there is a financial shortfall the company will be overtrading. Will this be for a short period until sales receipts increase, or will the shortfall require additional financial support?

9   What will be the position of the bank if a request for additional credit is made?

The bank should already know whether the management of the company is capable of trading over a period when it is difficult to match cash flow with outgoings. The individual circumstances of each company will vary but a typical 'action plan', listing a suggested order of assessment for the company to relieve a financial position brought about by overtrading, is as follows.

Action plan

1 Reduce production to volumes that can be quickly sold.

2 This may lead to putting production staff on short time (if the situation is deemed temporary) or making redundancies.

3 Cancel outstanding capital equipment replacement programmes.

4 If there is a turnover deficiency (where the overtrading has been due to expanding production capacity), try to increase immediate sales without unduly prejudicing existing profit margins or, if the problem is a surfeit of orders, extend the period of supply and, in an extreme case, consider sub-contracting production.

5 Review all expenditure budgets for cuts to improve cash flow.

6 Accelerate recovery of sales debts and pay creditors later.

7 Limit the retention of stocks to a critical minimum and endeavour to order replacement stocks on short time delivery.

8 Upgrade monitoring of cash flow to a daily need (if required).

9 Consider the injection of additional permanent (shares) or working (loans from the directors and/or the company's bank) capital AND agree In advance with the bank how the new funds will be used.

Similar tests apply to service companies. For retail businesses the critical evaluation will be to achieve the correct balance between sales and stock and not to overspend in areas that may not prove rewarding such as marketing. Other companies operating in the service sector will have to confirm the correct balance between expensive staffing and business won. In each case, the bank will be forewarned if frequent excess borrowings are seen over the previously agreed credit limit or if the customer takes sales receipts in cash to settle bills without paying the funds first into the bank.

The bank has to be aware of any resilience of management to change past practices and it should not necessarily accept the likely response that financial difficulties are temporary and the company will trade itself out of its predicament. This is rarely the case where there are unrecognized fundamental problems and a willingness to change past practices will be accepted. Too many companies have been milked of profits through owners removing capital in the form of excessive salaries or dividends. When trading returns and cash flow drops, there can be resistance to reinvest such money into the business if it is easier for the bank to meet the shortfall. The bank must look at each new application for support as a new proposal and judge the situation at the present time on its own merits.

6.9 Temporary difficulties

If the situation of overtrading is not easy to discern, consider the position of a business that is in temporary difficulties; is the trading difficulty temporary or not? If it is temporary, then the bank should be aware that support now is critical towards the company's future profitability and at the same time it releases the bank from placing the company in liquidation when loans may be fully repaid. Equally, for the bank to put new funds at the disposal of the company may exacerbate the loss incurred. How can this dilemma be resolved?

Some general rules of engagement can be laid down as follows.

- ♦ What was the reason for the difficulties in the first place?
- ♦ What did management do about it and was it successful?
- ♦ Will the difficulties resolve themselves naturally?
- ♦ Can the difficulties be easily combated by internal measures?
- ♦ What will be the cost of these measures relative to the reward?

If the difficulties are externally driven then the question to answer is whether they will be resolved rapidly or remain for a period, in which case can the company survive over this time? If management recognizes the problem(s), is it raising pertinent solutions for adoption? If the problems are more far-reaching, what is the time scale for their resolution and what is the cost of financing? The bank should initially be sympathetic about assisting the company unless its management have reneged on its agreed commitments. After all, the bank agreed to lend to the company at its initial assessment. There is the celebrated case not made public of the clearing bank that changed its mind six times before allowing the public company in question to fall into liquidation; this demonstrates commitment to the customer but a failure to take a decision.

6.10 Unpaid cheques and control action

The short answer for any bank is never to refuse to meet a cheque of acceptable amount presented for payment outside the agreed limit of the company's credit, without first asking the customer for an explanation. This assumes that the customer can be contacted that day for an explanation and that all previous conduct of the account has been exemplary. If there have been previous problems for the customer in meeting presented cheques and/or problems for the bank in obtaining suitable explanations regarding conduct, the customer has presumably been forewarned that a credit limit is final and that cheques over this limit will be peremptorily refused.

The bank should be aware that to refuse a cheque on unclear grounds may lead to the company losing public credit status and possibly being drawn into liquidation that, in turn, may be the prelude to legal action for compensation. In these circumstances, the bank should review the past conduct of the account and make a fresh appraisal of the conditions of support. This may lead to taking additional security for increasing the credit limit, providing advice on the future running of the account or limiting the credit made available with a programme of redemption of outstanding loan balances. Having to refuse payment of a cheque, unless the reason is clerical, is a major step towards reappraisal of the customer company as a credit risk (refer s 6.3).

How does the bank know whether an unpaid cheque or failure to meet a loan repayment is the precursor of worse financial difficulties for the company, without enquiring why the situation has arisen? The bank will fail in its obligations if it looks only to its security and does not enquire further the financial position of the company. The initial requirement is to have an up-to-date financial position to hand as soon as possible. After this, a meeting with management is essential to offer explanation for the previously supplied financial data, after which the management should be asked what they intend to do to rectify the situation and what revised forecasts of trading are to hand. If these are acceptable to the bank they should be regularly monitored thereafter.

6.11 Management information

The tests of good management of a business are:
- ♦ the extent of, and how quick, financial information is supplied;
- ♦ what the information conveys;
- ♦ whether the necessary action is subsequently initiated.

Computer programmes off-the-shelf offer ready-made data that frequently is not user-friendly to the company in question. Larger companies have their own systems but have a similar weakness if the information becomes too verbose and levels of control flounder under bureaucracy.

Each business has its own critical measures of monitoring. A so-called 'cash cow' such as a hypermarket chain will look to receive an optimum cash return on space and selling and at what profit margins. A construction company will be looking to tender at the right margin to make a profit but to curb operating costs where the contract is placed at a fixed price. In an ideal world each bank loan should be supported by company budget and trading forecasts that are regularly monitored by the bank in order that variances can be quickly picked up and mutually resolved.

Monitoring takes time, which is costly even if computer generated. Usually only companies in difficulty receive regular monitoring and are in receipt of weekly or monthly returns of critical financial information like sales achieved, the orders in hand and the total and age of trade debtor balances. Larger companies will be constrained by covenants to control the total of borrowings relative to the net (equity) worth of the business. Each facet of information is important for the bank to assess constantly its lending risk and not only to rely on loose annual verbal sales forecasts by company management.

The decisive action for the bank when fully monitoring an account is to get as much up-to-date information as possible on trading in advance of the supply of any historic accounting information or explanations given by management. This means assessing the general trading environment of the company and benchmarking similar companies trading in the same field. Ideally, a peer company should be asked what they think of the company: this question is the most frequently requested by investors before investing equity in a business, and it could equally apply to a lending bank, subject always to relevant confidentiality constraints.

6.12 Covenants in facility agreements

Covenants are undertakings drawn up by the lender(s), and accepted by the borrower to adhere to certain obligations for the duration of the loan agreement. In principle, they safeguard the lender(s) from acts that the borrower may initiate to reduce security for the loan (refer s 5.13). This security may be tangible (ie a debenture) or an operating restriction. Common clauses are:

♦ a negative pledge – restricting the company from granting security over its assets to third parties;
♦ to maintain the assets of the company – by not disposing them without prior approval and ensuring that they are fully insured against loss;
♦ to maintain the net worth of the company – by limiting its borrowings to a set figure and/or restricting the amount of dividends that may be declared to its shareholders;
♦ to maintain its identity as to the type of business to be conducted and/or the type of companies it may acquire;
♦ to maintain its individuality against a takeover or amalgamation when control may become invested in others;
♦ financial covenants.

The drafting of the negative pledge clause will be important, since the company will be wishing to restrict its influence on existing prior charges or of future short/medium term loans having a lien on certain assets (eg hire purchase agreements; import/export arrangements; title retention; account set-offs and sale and leaseback arrangements). Any covenants must be clear whether they are to apply at one regular date or for each trading day.

The financial covenants set can vary according to the standing of the borrowing company. There are usually clauses restricting the total amount of borrowings (relative to the overall net worth of the business), a minimum level of earnings to interest payable on the outstanding loans, and possibly a minimum ratio of current assets to current liabilities. The definition of borrowings is usually extensive, embracing lease and hire purchase obligations, contingent liabilities such as guarantees and indemnities, and other deferred indebtedness such as pension obligation.

6.13 Settlement risk

There is settlement risk when forward financial commitments are entertained. The risks associated with foreign exchange dealings and interest rate exposures are discussed in Chapter 7. Other risks abound: settlement may seem simple enough between one bank situated in the Far East and another in Europe, but if one market closes before another market opens there is potentially a period of risk within each deal is not covered for changes in pricing.

The situation may also arise internally, where one branch overseas commits itself to large foreign exchange deals or commitments that are not covered elsewhere within the bank. In this case, the branch may instigate a rollover position to cover its unauthorized dealings. Internal audit procedures and authorizations may be inadequate initially to prevent a build up of the now loss-making liability. Bank headquarters are asked for more capital to support the unauthorized operation and eventually the adverse settlement position becomes known and the bank concerned incurs large losses in closing it.

It is difficult to account for collusion within a bank to cover unauthorized dealings other than to monitor all outstanding (exchange or loan) positions at the end of each day and to regulate the extent of the size of dealings during that day. Dual responsibility is probably the best initial form of defence and astute monitoring is the second best, after initiating comprehensive operating control procedures.

6.14 Proceeds of crime and money laundering

The Proceeds of Crime Act 2002, effective from 24 February 2003, and the Money Laundering Regulations 2003, effective from 1 March 2004, have given banks and other organizations (as defined) extensive legal obligations with which to comply. Failing to report knowledge or suspicion of money laundering is punishable by a jail sentence of up to five years. If assistance has been given in any way supporting the offence, the jail term may extend to 14 years. It is an offence to disclose information that may prejudice an investigation where there is suspicion that a report has been made to the National Crime Intelligence Service.

The three main money laundering offences are:
- concealment;
- making arrangements for using or possessing criminal property;
- acquiring criminal property.

Criminal property (ie cash or other tangible or intangible property) covers any benefit from criminal conduct where the alleged offender knows or suspects that it has been obtained by dishonest means. Banks and other financial institutions have been subject to money laundering obligations for some years and the new legislation extends this to non-financial organizations. There is no de minimis threshold for reporting suspicions: any suspicion must be reported to the appointed Money Laundering Reporting Officer. It is unclear at present whether one can validly claim that one did not believe that a disclosure would prejudice an investigation.

Many banks have had to upgrade their existing monitoring procedures and ensure that staff have sufficient training and awareness to identify and report any suspicious activity. Essentially, there is a need to know your existing customer sufficiently and to vet adequately all new customers. In practical terms, illegal money may arise in an account either for the use of the recipient or to be transferred away to another haven for which purpose the bank, by acting as agent of the transferor, will add some credence. In the first case the bank has to know its customers well enough to be able to judge whether a particular deal is within the normal trading of that business; in the latter case, the detection relies largely on inspection of the unusual transfer by the bank.

Seven

Identifying and managing risk

The three most significant risks and those that businesses feel least able to manage are:

(1)   increased competition;

(2)   adverse changes in customer demand;

(3)   reduced productivity due to staff absenteeism and turnover.

The most manageable are financial and hazard risks.

Source: *Financial Times report 2004*/Marsh McLennan research; 950 European companies with turnover between Euro36-360 million).

There are many types of risk. For the lending banker risk rests on the probability of failure or loss associated with a particular course of action that results in an undesirable event. Evaluating the event will take into account its probability and the extent of its effect. Banks should not be willing to accommodate high risk within a lending proposition. Every bank must make its own judgement regarding the degree of risk it is willing to countenance.

Where companies, established to transact sophisticated treasury functions, ask their bank(s) to take the counter-party risk, these banks would be highly exposed if they failed to match open currency or interest rate positions through the market by offsetting positions with the appropriate derivative instruments. A derivative is widely defined as something that arises from another source; in banking terminology, it means a financial instrument that is derived from the value and type of trading risk involved. The various financial instruments are explained in 7.2 et seq.

7.1 Value at Risk

The measurement of risk most commonly used today by the major banks is called Value-at-Risk (**VaR** for short) and is believed to have first been adopted by JP Morgan in the 1990's. Each bank operates with a changing portfolio of trading instruments that hold different risks and they need to raise a method of calculating levels of risk that management is prepared to accept. These calculations incorporate a mixture of views on interest rates, equity share prices, currency rates, loan creditworthiness, commodity prices and other (macro-economic) factors. The potential loss in currency value of trading positions due to adverse market movements is calculated over different periods of time and for assumed different confidence levels.

The most frequent time period taken is one day, on the basis that the bank can re-set the risk exposure next day by trading out of its position, either by closing the open position(s) to realize the loss or by hedging (ie protecting) the exposure forward into another time period and taking the view that the loss position will reverse. This latter option is rarely chosen in practice because major dealing losses have previously arisen through bank dealers continually carrying forward their (unauthorized) loss positions, accumulating enormous proportions without apparent market recovery.

Having calculated the risk of loss for each time period, the next step is to choose an acceptable confidence level. This may be stated as a 99% (or whatever figure is chosen) probability that under normal market conditions there is only a 1% (ie remainder) chance for a loss to occur that is greater than the currency value proposed as acceptable for the bank. As might be expected, the higher the VaR currency value, the greater the risk for the bank. It is important for the bank to monitor its own VaR constantly and dealing losses recently publicized have accumulated in size largely due to poor internal monitoring procedures and controls.

VaR has limitations when used to predict future losses: when trading markets are volatile, the risk to reward ratio increases. If a one-day scenario is computed, this will not account for dealing positions longer than one day or, indeed, for dealings in a fluctuating market during that day. The calculations are only as good as the basic programming material assumed and it is difficult to predict with accuracy by how much, and when, world economies will react to changing circumstances. It has been mentioned that the matching of exposures, whether currency exchange rates or interest rates, is a key measure towards limiting risk. It should be remembered that for every bank deal there must be another source taking the counter-view and that this is an inherent risk.

7.2 Financing risk

The company risks, at any one time, being unable to finance trading from commercial sources or at a cost that uses up most of its earnings after tax and provides an inadequate return for its shareholders/owners. This risk includes the potential inability to re-finance existing debt when it matures or is repaid. From the company's point of view, there is some merit in having more than one funding source, providing the finance required can support the business operating with two banks.

The advantages are a greater likelihood of competition giving the best financing terms for the company and possibly greater choice of financial products. The disadvantages are that two bank relationships may prove difficult if the company offers security and/or requires financial support at a time of need (one bank may be sympathetic and the other bank not). Larger corporations, due to the size of operations, will have several banks providing banking services, not least since every bank will set each customer a maximum credit limit as a matter of prudence.

7.3 Currency risk

Taking a simple example, a customer expects to receive US$100 in six months' time and asks its bank to sell the equivalent amount of US$ today for delivery in six months' time and to loan it the proceeds in £ now. The present exchange rate is US$100 = £60. The customer either expects US$ meanwhile to lose value (in which case conversion of US$100 in six months' time will be less than £60) or wishes to receive the cash now for use in its business.

The bank has lent the customer £60 and has a future liability of paying the market US$100 in six months' time. The customer has to repay £60 after six months', when it will receive US$100. The risk of the bank is:

♦ that the loan outstanding to the customer of £60 for six months will not be repaid;

♦ there is a **forward liability** to pay the market US$100 in six months' time.

Since there is a currency mismatch, the bank does not wish to take this risk. The bank therefore buys US$100 for delivery in six months' time from the market (ie another bank) to match the transaction. The cost to the bank will be the supply of £60 to lend plus the two currency deals. The customer will have to pay the borrowing cost and the equivalent currency deal cost. Interest spreads and dealing margins have been ignored.

The bank could have decided that US$100 today would be worth (in today's sterling terms) only US$90 in six months' time. It may decide not to buy US$100 forward for delivery in six months' time but to take the risk of exchange rates moving in its favour to buy dollars at the 'spot' (ie immediate delivery) price ruling in six months time. This exposure will have to be within the limits put on each bank by the Bank of England for their own dealings.

There are other choices open to the customer and the bank: instead of selling dollars forward, an **option** (to deal for forward delivery) could have been taken to sell in six months' time at the prevailing currency rate now. An option has the advantage of being exercised or abandoned by the purchaser. The option will be taken up if a profit ensues and US$100 costs less than £60 for the bank; otherwise, the converse will apply.

A 'call option' gives the right to purchase currency and a 'put option', the right to sell the currency. If the purchaser is dealing in a volatile currency with significant fluctuations in exchange rates to the home currency, a 'cylinder option' may be taken out. This sets dealing limits both above and below the present spot rate at which the option will be exercised (within the cylinder price limits) and limits the attaching risks of profit and loss.

Similar to an option is a more recent addition to the derivatives market called a **covered warrant**. The warrant is 'covered' in that no short selling (without the underlying asset as backing) is permitted. It gives the holder the right, but not the obligation, to buy or sell a currency (or asset, share or index) at a predetermined price on or before a fixed (expiry) date in the future. Such warrants issued by banks and other financial institutions are negotiable and usually have a longer maturity (up to two years) than options. The underlying asset is the security for the deal and there is a conversion ratio (ie warrants per single asset). The offer (purchase) and bid (sale) price spreads can be wide and the possible risk/reward ratio is therefore highly geared.

7.4 Interest rate risk

Fluctuations can occur in interest rates and there are instruments to counter this risk. A **forward-forward** deal commences on one forward date and ends on another forward date. When a borrowing (or deposit) deal is known to arise in the near future, it can be useful to lock in the interest rate based on the market's current interest rate structure, rather than have the uncertainty of waiting until the date the deal commences. The lending bank will incur interest rate risk exposure up to the time that the deal matures.

An alternative instrument to use would be a **forward rate agreement** (FRA). The FRA is purchased immediately and fixes in advance the cost of the forward borrowing (or the deposit). In this case, however, the deal is done at the market interest rate ruling on that future day and the FRA settles separately the interest rate difference between the FRA striking price and the overall rate. The FRA is a known contingent risk in that it is off-balance sheet and does not crystallize until activated; the risk can be recalculated at any time and the agreement, although binding, has yet to materialize. If a bank has surplus funds and expects interest rates to fall, it could buy an FRA and make a profit if interest rates fall below the FRA rate. If interest rates rise above the FRA rate, however, a loss would be incurred.

7.5 Other trading instruments to reduce risks

Some trading instruments have multiple uses: for currency, interest rate or commodity dealings. A **futures contract** is similar to an FRA. It is formalized by having standard specifications and terminology and can only be dealt through a recognized exchange market. Such contracts have the benefit of being able to be traded at any intervening time up to their maturity date. They are quoted at an index shown as '100 minus the agreed interest rate'. There is, in most cases, a notional delivery date and, when delivery is due, an exchange delivery settlement price is set, eg 100 minus the BBA (British Bankers Association) three months' LIBOR (London Inter-bank Offered Rate). The calculations are similar for currency deals.

A bank can **hedge** its FRA exposure through using the futures market, rather than using a forward-forward deal, because the former will incur virtually no risk since it will be settled through the relevant exchange body rather than another market dealer. The exchange partly covers itself against risk by asking that all dealers put up an initial (partial) margin as collateral against adverse market rate movements that might give rise to a default. There is also a variation margin that is paid daily to mirror that day's dealing profit or loss, so leaving the original exposure on the deal intact. There can be a counter-party risk to the bank where it has allowed the counter-party to settle its daily variation margin through a separate credit facility. Note also that if the bank wishes to cover its risk position after having sold an FRA, it must sell a corresponding futures contract, since the sale of the FRA will be profitable if interest rates rise, in which case the price of the equivalent future contract would fall and the bank would have sold the contract at the higher price.

An ideal instrument for hedging interest rate or currency risk is a **swap**. An **interest rate swap** contract commits two parties to exchange two streams of interest or currency payments over an agreed period, calculated to apply to a common, but notional, principal amount. One party agrees to remit a flow of cash payments, equivalent to a fixed interest rate on the principal sum, to the other party, who will in turn make cash payments back to the original party equivalent to a floating interest rate on the same principal sum. The dates of the payments swap need not be coincidental but the maturity date of the agreement will match. A 'basis swap' is similar, except that this swap is between two floating rate calculations with different reference rates, eg six month LIBOR and 30-day commercial paper. Other references used are 'fixed-fixed' and 'fixed-floating' rates.

A **currency swap** contract involves two different currencies, but in this case the notional principal amounts are physically exchanged on maturity. The basis contracts can be fixed-floating, fixed-fixed or floating-floating. The swap may also be a combined interest rate and currency deal. A 'differential swap' is where a reference interest rate in one currency is applied to a notional principal of another currency. The two swap parties may be bank-to-bank or corporations with a bank intermediary. The risks of the bank are related to the counter-party(s).

Swaps are widely used for hedging interest rate and currency rate risks where there is volatility of rates or where multinational corporations wish to partially or wholly eliminate the effect of changes in rates on their trading returns. They do not incur an up-front investment of funds and they offer good market liquidity for trading in a competitive environment.

A **credit default swap** (CDS) is being increasingly used in the bond (refer 7.6) and loan markets for the management of risk. As the name implies, should a borrower default on its loan, the bank or banks syndicated to the lending will be repaid in full from the counter-party, usually an insurance company. CDSs are negotiable in the market and have the advantage that the borrower does not know its borrowing has been underwritten for risk by the lender. They may lead the bank(s) buying CDSs to be less concerned about taking lending decisions where they know that the risk of default has already been covered. The cost of the cover will also reduce the profit margin taken on the loan.

To put risk management into perspective, not all risks relate to trading deals and not all risks have to be covered against loss. When dealing in foreign currencies, there will be an economic factor generally affecting a company's trade that could be partially or wholly hedged. How much turnover should be hedged and over what period? To what extent should future profits be safeguarded? A good example to consider is the cross-border motor vehicle industry.

Similar questions may be asked when embarking on a long-term project involving other currencies. Assumptions made at the time may be entirely altered when the project comes to fruition. To what extent should tender prices reflect hedged currencies? The construction industry is exemplary in this case. There are also accounting risk variations that occur: the balance sheet value of a deal in mid-term may differ from its risk at both inception and maturity. This aspect has been discussed in Chapter 3.

Interest rate risks are usually covered externally through the use of derivatives, as has been described. There are alternative methods to cover certain internal risks: group deposits and borrowings (in like currencies) may be netted out daily; bank accounts may be structured so as to minimize surplus balances and overdrafts; assets and liabilities may be closely matched by value, by currencies and by maturities; company cash flow requirements may be better matched to production and trade cycles; the company's terms of trade may be modified (eg taking advantage of discounts offered for early settlement or settling in local currencies by borrowing at beneficial interest rates).

7.6 Securitization

Securitization is the financing of a pool of assets (or business interests) through a **special purpose vehicle** ('SPV', ie a company set up specifically for this purpose), where the cash flow from those assets is used to service and repay the financiers. Typically, a block of outstanding mortgages is packaged together and is sold by the holding bank or building society to the SPV, which raises finance for the purchase through a bond issue. The vendor bank is, in effect, selling the future income and profit from these assets (after taking front-end fees and interest margins for its actions as principal to the individual transactions) for a present value that can be used to finance new deals.

The agreement between the bank and the SPV may grant the bank the right to any residual surplus after all the individual mortgages (or other assets) have been repaid, but importantly, there is no recourse to the bank in the event of a shortfall in repayments. Similarly, the SPV is not liable should the originating bank be subject to adverse credit events. This enables the bonds secured by the underlying assets to be rated higher than unsecured debt of the originating bank.

An originating bank uses securitization towards more efficient use of capital; an originating commercial company uses it to lower its weighted average cost of capital and to diversify its sources of finance with access to the capital markets. Further advantages are possible: it may allow a company to increase borrowings without affecting its balance sheet gearing ratio. An example would be for a company to enter into a sale and leaseback of its properties rather than borrowing on-balance sheet against these assets. The borrowing company will also be able to achieve a lower financing cost, since the assets held as security and the arising cash flow will be ring-fenced.

Many different types of asset can be securitized. The asset may be in the form of a set of crystallized debts (running mortgage agreements) or in assets that are cash producing (ranging from complete company businesses to property leases and trading concessions). The cash flow must be predictive and ongoing (early termination options will limit the reward for the SPV, which might find itself left with realized assets but ongoing financing debt). Sophisticated potential default modeling can be used, combined with derivatives, to reduce or eliminate risk. The Basel 2 Accord is likely to accelerate the use of securitization by banks.

7.7 Bonds

A **bond** is a security issued when a marketable loan is raised and it evidences title to the debt, together with the issue terms including interest payments and repayment of the principal sum. Bonds are usually issued in bearer form where possession confers ownership, or they may be registered, when they are more correctly called a bearer debenture. A bond issued for less than five years may be called a **note** (or a promissory note, as defined in the Bills of Exchange Act 1882). Eurobonds are bearer bonds issued on the international market in various currencies, whereas domestic bonds are issued in individual countries. The market prices of issued bonds reflect the credit standing of the issuer, which may be a government or a public corporation.

A bank's near-liquid earning assets will include a portfolio of bonds, subject to the general risk of changing yields as well as the standing of the issuer. If a government is the issuer, the economic and fiscal policies of that government will influence demand for the bond issue (whether UK gilt-edged securities or USA Treasury Notes). Government bonds have good marketability due to the size of the issues, regardless of the ruling interest rate yields, but corporation bonds stand a much greater risk of difficulty of realization and capital loss if the issuer's creditworthiness is suspect at the time of sale. A well-publicized example was the loss suffered by the Abbey National Bank in realizing its portfolio of relatively high-risk international corporate bonds in 2003.

Certain types of bonds have specific characteristics: a **floating rate note** (FRN) has a fixed interest margin over a variable interest rate that is based on a known quoted market pricing, such as three or six months' LIBOR. Regular interest payments are made until maturity of the FRN that is usually issued initially for a longer period than its cousin, the **certificate of deposit** (CD). Both FRNs and CDs are fully negotiable. There is also a market in **bond futures**, where a seller must deliver to the buyer an agreed amount of bond at an agreed time for an agreed price.

A bank may wish to borrow from the market while holding security in the form of government or high credit quality commercial bonds. The security could be sold to realize cash, otherwise the bank may enter into a **(sale and) repurchase agreement** (a 'repo') with a counter-party to sell the security, and at the same time, buy back the same security at a subsequent date at an agreed price. It is equivalent to borrowing cash against collateral and offers a further instrument to improve market liquidity. The borrowing bank's risk is of performance at maturity.

The market in derivatives is constantly being developed further. As long as a counter-party can be found as risk-taker, new products will appear. A recent development in the bond market has been the introduction of a **credit-spread warrant**. This is effectively a call option, giving the right for an investor to purchase a bond on a future date at a fixed price. The recipient of the funds will be the issuing company; the warrant holds the right of purchase of the bond. The warrants will be negotiable through the investment bank managing the issue. The bank will hope to deal in the warrants in the market at a profit. The aim is to lock in the purchase price of the bond immediately, in case the price margin (the spread) that the company has to pay for the funds (over a benchmark swaps interest rate) widens and the price becomes more expensive.

One final point to note about external currency trading: 'spot' settlement is made two working days in the future but it is still the base point for forward trades. A 'forward outright' is an outright purchase, or sale of one currency for another, for settlement on a fixed date in the future other than the spot date. Banks deal with one another in 'forward swaps', that is, the forward outright price less the current swap price.

The relative characteristics and risks of the various forms of derivatives discussed are summarized in the following table.

Instrument	Maturity (typical)	Negotiable	Risk factor basis
Overdraft	On demand; to 1 yr	No	Creditworthiness
Commercial paper	1 to 6 months	Yes	Issuer
Futures contract	Up to 3 months	Yes	Exchange traded
Bond futures	Up to 3 months	No	Counter-party
'Repo' agreement	Up to 3 months	No	Collateral backed
Bill of exchange	3 or 6 months	Yes	Acceptor
Floating rate note	Up to 6 months	Yes	Issuer
Option	Up to 6 months	Yes	Exchange/issuer
Certificate of deposit	Up to 1 year	Yes	Issuer
Forward-forward	Up to 1 year	No	Counter-party
Forward rate agreement	Up to 1 year	No	Contingent/issuer
Covered warrant	Up to 2 years	Yes	Exchange/issuer
Swap	3 months to 10+ yrs	No	Counter-party
Loan	Variable 1-10+ yrs	No	Creditworthiness
Bonds	Can be up to 30 yrs	Yes	Credit standing

7.8 Ratings services

There are subscription services available to assist lenders and investors in evaluating the risks of individual companies, sectors and countries. A credit rating indicates the likelihood of default on its financial obligations. Three well-known services are Standard & Poors, Moodys and Fitch Ratings. Their evaluation procedures are broadly similar, offering some 20 valuation gradings, and are based on a mixture of public information and personal interviews with corporate managements. A final assessment grades each company and this grade, with subsequent changes, is largely relied on to price the public funding programmes for those companies by investment banks.

The risk evaluation covers an assessment of the corporation's: strategy; management; competitors; suppliers; customers; gearing; capital spending programmes; banking relationships; the regulatory environment. It builds up a medium-term earnings model (say three years) that is then subjected to discounted cash flow value analysis and compared with price:earnings ratios, efficiency valuations and profit margins of peer groups. This is brought together into a final single rating.

Since public companies must provide a statement for the public at the earliest opportunity to the Stock Exchange of any news that is share price sensitive, it is not necessarily the case that the ratings services will be evaluating companies in advance of important news or that their evaluation will be accurate. Their value lies in the reasons behind a grading change, the benchmarking of companies to their peer groups and, particularly, when assessing sovereign risks.

7.9 Bank relationships

The relationship between a bank and its customer is contractual: that of (lending) debtor and creditor (or vice versa if taking deposits) and of agent and principal (in collecting and paying cheques). The lending banker may have a primary or secondary relationship with the company: the primary relationship would be where the bank acts as the company's daily transaction bank and is a major source of finance to the company; a secondary relationship is one where the bank joins a loans syndicate in a minor role and leaves management to the principal managers of the facility. In this case, the bank will be relying to a degree on the prime banker(s) for assessing the credit risk and the pricing of the loan deal. For this service, the secondary bank will earn a lower fee.

Whether or not a bank is a prime or a secondary source for the company, a risk evaluation is still required and it might be said that the risk position of a secondary source bank is inferior should a default occur. It will have limited input to the terms of any restructuring of debt and possibly limited access to the available security. The prime source bank will have daily knowledge of the financial conduct of the company through its bank accounts and should be in a better position to redeem a deteriorating financial situation early, where possible.

The bank, through its staff representative(s), should:

- ♦ be knowledgeable of the business of the company and up-to-date with all published news relating to the company;
- ♦ be able to ask one or two pertinent questions about the company's trading;
- ♦ know the responsibilities of the people that are to be seen;
- ♦ have a common outside interest as a talking point;
- ♦ be knowledgeable of all current banking products, even if one's own bank does not offer some of these services;
- ♦ be knowledgeable of current banking trends, loan pricing, news;
- ♦ hold a view on future monetary economics: interest rates; currency trends; fiscal assumptions; recent public news of relevance;
- ♦ try and have at least one new product to hand to offer the company with reasons why this should be considered;
- ♦ maintain a regular contact with key personnel in the company;
- ♦ prepare a (short) list of relevant questions to ask at the meeting;
- ♦ ask if the company has a financial problem requiring assistance;
- ♦ let the company executive have his/her say in the conversation;
- ♦ try and leave with a return commitment to provide advice.

It will be much harder to raise a new customer than to retain an existing banking relationship. The bank representative should:

- ♦ not duck the question if the bank cannot deliver;
- ♦ be accurate regarding what the bank can deliver (in terms of pricing etc);
- ♦ discuss in detail why there have been any changes in bank policy;
- ♦ emphasise what bank products are currently good value and why;
- ♦ provide a speedy reply to questions raised that cannot be immediately answered;
- ♦ set up a dialogue with the bank's in-house specialist provider, if appropriate.

As banks try to raise more and more cross-selling opportunities and their risk exposure to each company grows, it will be increasingly important to have an in-depth knowledge of what and how the company is doing. A close relationship between bank and company will support this ideal. A benefit of the joint relationship is the monitoring of the company's treasury dealings. Some questions to answer are as follows.

- ♦ Are all operating accounts cleared daily, with the net position deposited overnight?
- ♦ What is the return on average surplus funds and could the money have been utilised to greater benefit in/outside the business?
- ♦ If currencies are dealt in, how much percentage cash flow risk is hedged?
- ♦ In what instruments is the company dealing? Could more appropriate treasury instruments be suggested?

- ◆ When facility rollovers arise, does the company test the market for the best rates and maturities?
- ◆ What treasury objectives are in place? How frequently is treasury policy revised?

A model treasury policy must incorporate at least the following characteristics.

Characteristics	Action
Objectives	How is the management of risk to be applied?
Responsibilities	Are all relevant management roles defined?
Identification	Risks relating to currencies; interest rates; refinancing; liquidity; counter-party; macro exposure & investment.
Tolerance	How much risk is to be allowed?
Controls	Is the monitoring of controls adequate?
Reporting	Does this include performance measurement?

7.10 Derivative examples

In practice, financial calculators will be used with built-in programmes, but it might be useful for descriptive purposes to go back to basics without going into higher mathematics and formulae.

Example 1: Simple interest

A deposit of £100 is made at 4% pa interest for 91 days.

The proceeds after 91 days will be £100 plus interest:

$$100 + [100 \times (4/100) \times (91/365)] = £100.99$$

Example 2: Compound interest

A deposit of £100 is made at 4% pa interest for 365 days and reinvested for a further 365 days until maturity in two years time.

The proceeds in two years will be as follows.

After year one:	$100 + [100 \times (1 + 4/100)] = £104.00$
After year two:	$104 \times (1 + 4/100)] = £108.16$

Example 3: Daily compounding

A deposit of £100 earns interest at 4% pa for 365 days compounded daily.

The effective interest rate is:

100 x {[1 + (4/100)/365] to the power of 365} – 1 = 4.08%

Example 4: Future value to present value

A deposit earns interest for 91 days at 4% pa and has a future value of £100.

Its present value is:

100/[(1 + (4/100) x 91/365] = £99.01

Check: £99.01 invested for 91 days at 4% pa will earn interest of £ 0.99

added to the initial deposit of £99.01 = £100 after 91 days.

Example 5: Internal rate of return

The internal rate of return (IRR) is used to calculate the internal (ie the company's) value of a set of future investment or project cash flows and is the single discounted overall annual percentage rate that, when applied to each individual cash flow, will give a present day value of zero. The present day (ie the first) figure in the cash flow will be negative since it represents the original investment cost. Subsequent cash flow figures will be positive, representing the future income returns, or negative if there is additional expenditure. The IRR return is then compared with the target return set by the company to decide whether the investment is to proceed.

Start of year	Initial investment	Cash flow annually	Net flow	Discount-ing factor	Present value
1	2,000		–2,000	1.000	–2,000
2	0	500	+500	0.9091	+455
3	0	500	+500	0.8264	+413
4	0	600	+600	0.7513	+451
5	0	600	+600	0.6830	+410
6		440	+437	0.6209	+271

In this example the discounting factor (the IRR) is 10% pa. The present day value of 600 at the beginning of year 4 (ie end of year 3) discounts back to a present value of 451. The sum of the present day values, after allowing for the initial investment, is zero. The calculation principle is that given by Example 4.

Example 6: Annuities

An annuity calculates the value (ie the yield) of a series of cash flows that can be purchased by an initial investment. The yield is the IRR. Example 5 provides an example and answers the question: what is the present value of the cash flows in years 2 through to 6 using an interest rate yield of 10% pa? The answer is the sum of each year's present value, ie £2,000.

Example 7: Trading strategies and risk

A bank will quote for a deal by offering two prices: a BID, at which level it is prepared to buy, and an OFFER, at which level it is prepared to sell. The higher rate is the dealing rate offered to the customer to buy, and the lower rate is the dealing rate the customer would get by selling to the bank. As described earlier, a CALL is to buy in a deal and a PUT is to sell. This applies throughout market dealing, even though a call on an FRA is equivalent to a put on an interest rate futures contract.

A company holds currency A and wishes to hedge against currency B. Its options are as follows.

(1) Do nothing and assume that currency A will appreciate against currency B, taking the risk of an adverse movement between the currencies (that currency A will depreciate against currency B).

(2) Sell currency A forward to lock in the present cross-exchange rates (and lose the opportunity of currency A appreciating against currency B).

(3) Buy a put option in currency A, taking the view that currency A will appreciate without the risk of being wrong.

The company has also borrowed funds that will require rolling over for another term. There are three similar choices open to the company.

(1) To wait until the rollover date and take the interest rate ruling at that time on the borrowing.

(2) To buy an FRA to fix in advance the cost of the borrowing.

(3) To buy an agreed amount of an FRA, in a stated currency, at an agreed interest rate, for an agreed maturity, on an agreed delivery date. This is called an **interest rate guarantee** (IRG) and fixes the maximum cost of the future borrowing (or, if selling, fixes the minimum return on a future deposit).

Example 8: Forward-forward

The company has a 'gap' in its cash flow in three months' time but will reinstate its positive cash flow in six months' time. Borrowing is required from month 3 to month 6. Opportunity is taken advantageously of borrowing interest rates currently available in the market. The borrower:

(1)   pays LIBOR + 1% (say) to the lending bank;

(2)   receives LIBOR (say) under the FRA;

(3)   pays the fixed FRA rate under the FRA agreement.

The net cost to the company will be the 1% LIBOR differential plus the cost of the FRA that will be known at outset. The company has hedged its interest cost exposure through an FRA. There is no exchange of principal.

Example 9: Interest rate swap

The company in Example 8 might also have hedged its exposure through taking up an interest rate swap. In this case, the interest flows (not the principal) are exchanged and in practice, the flows are netted out where they coincide at an exchange date. The fixed and floating rate exchanges may be at different payment intervals. For example, the company will:

(1)   borrow funds and pay interest (say) every three months at a cost based on three months' LIBOR + the lending margin;

(2)   receive from the counter-party interest on the borrowing at an agreed fixed interest rate throughout the term of the borrowing;

(3)   pay the counter-party the agreed fixed swap rate on the deal.

In Example 8 the settlement was at the beginning of the deal and quoted on a discount basis. For a swap, the settlement is done at the end of each relevant payment period.

Example 10: Currency swap

Similar to an interest rate swap, a currency swap exchanges cash flows in two different currencies, usually with the added exchange of the principal amounts of the currencies at a pre-agreed rate, set at inception of the deal, that is reversed at maturity. This exchange of principal, however, can be notional between the parties. The value of each currency at commencement of the exchange must be identical. In this example, the company has borrowed in currency A at a fixed interest rate and wishes to swap this into currency B at a floating rate. The steps are as follows.

(1)   The exchange rate between currencies A and B is set at outset between the parties and the notional or actual exchange of principal is made.

(2) The interest rate payments relating to each currency principal are swapped and paid over, each in their chosen currencies, between the parties at their pre-arranged interest dates.

(3) At maturity, the reverse notional (or actual) exchange of principal is made at the currency rates set at inception.

Note that the appropriate value of each different cash flow is its net present value (calculated on a discounted cash flow basis) converted at the spot exchange rate.

Appendix A

Example of a business plan with an investment proposal

Acknowledgement

The example shown below was first published in 'Financial planning for the small- and medium-sized enterprise', Peter Lyons, (2002, Butterworths LexisNexis, Tolley's Businesswise publications, 2nd edition) ISBN 0 7545 17853.

Note: The text contained within square brackets should be adjusted to specific case requirements.

This example of a business plan and investment proposal is not related to any known publication or company or type of business described and any such similarity is purely coincidental.

<u>**Business plan**</u>

<u>**and**</u>

<u>**Investment proposal**</u>

New Magazine Limited

Location

Date

[Disclaimer:

This business plan and investment proposal has been commissioned by and raised for the sole use of New Magazine Limited who have given instructions for its preparation from the information and explanations they have provided and no warranty expressed or implied is given to any other party for any actions taken or conclusions drawn therefrom. This document does not constitute an offer of securities under The Public Offer of Securities Regulations 1995 as amended and subsequently re-enacted by reason of paragraph 7 sub-section (2) (d): that any securities which constitute an offer will be made to a restricted circle of persons whom the offeror reasonably believes to be sufficiently knowledgeable to understand the risks involved in accepting the offer. Unquoted businesses carry a high risk of failure and such investments may be difficult to repay.]

Prepared by: Name

Address

New Magazine Limited

Contents	Page

Investment proposal

New Magazine Limited

Investment proposal

The launch of a new nationally distributed magazine is proposed to fill a gap in the market catering for young adults and families with an interest in **biking**. No other biking magazine currently being published is dedicated to the editorial content now proposed as its prime attraction. It will be called 'On Your Bike' and issued monthly, with a cover price of £2.50, available through the major chains and other national outlets.

An experienced management team has been put together by Twin Wheeler, an entrepreneur with a flair for business development and offering long-standing experience of the biking world. He will be ably assisted by recognized media advertising and distribution companies to ensure that the launch will be professionally managed from the outset.

Equity finance of £25,000 has already been raised and negotiations are in progress to obtain a bank loan of £60,000 for a period of two years to help finance production and trading. As with all new publications, the level of investment in start-up promotion costs will be crucial to the degree of success of the launch.

◆ It is estimated that a further **£100,000 equity (risk) capital** will be needed for this aspect of the operations, perhaps being contributed by up to four investors.

◆ For this cash investment **a 31.25% share of the business is offered**, with projected repayment of the whole investment **at the end of the third trading year**.

◆ After that time profits are forecast to expand further and **at least a dividend of similar amount should be possible to be declared annually** to shareholders.

The investment can be structured for approval under the Enterprise Investment Scheme if investors prefer. Otherwise, shares may be realized through an earlier trade sale or possible market flotation if the business expands sufficiently in the UK and overseas. **Turnover is forecast to exceed £1 million by year four and publication in China is being researched**.

This proposal should be read in conjunction with the business plan that has been formulated and the caveats stated therein that any money invested will be fully at risk of loss if assumptions about the market and the trading projections underlying the business plan do not materialize for whatever reason. Potential investors should be aware that all forecasts given in the business plan and the investment proposal have been put forward on the basis that any person relying on their accuracy and authenticity do so wholly at their own risk. The forecasts, comments and assumptions provided are the personal views of Twin Wheeler who has given and not withdrawn his consent for their publication.

1. Introduction

1.1 The project

New Magazine Limited is a new company raised to publish a nationally distributed magazine to cater for young adults and families in the socio-economic A/B/C1 groups, in the age range of 15 to 35 years old, with an interest in biking. It will be a quality publication, to be issued monthly through newsagents and by individual subscription, with a cover price of £2.50. There is no direct competitor dedicated to bike news with special reference to the niche area of [*put in the target theme*].

1.2 The controlling management and business background

The entrepreneur and major shareholder is Mr Twin Wheeler, aged 50 years, who has had a lifelong interest in bikes. He has built up an extensive list of contacts in the industry and, in 1998, spotted a gap in the magazine market for this type of publication. With the financial help of his family a 'pilot' publication was launched in 1999 named 'Off your Bike'. This was conceptually a success but was backed by limited financial resources, professional editorial and advertising staff and eventually was forced to fold after several issues due to insufficient advertising revenue being generated to spend on promoting the publication. A circulation of 20,000 copies was reached, offering readers 64 magazine pages for a cover price of £2.25. The experience gained from this foray into the market has proven invaluable for the proposed launch. Twin is now well supported by a skilled editorial, administrative and marketing team. A nucleus of equity investment has been raised and it is planned to have this augmented by risk capital from other interested parties. A modest amount of commercial funding is also to be raised.

1.3 The magazine market

There are four bike magazines currently on sale that are likely to be Twin's nearest competitors, the largest by circulation being 'Big Spokes' (c 70,000 copies) but this is a young men's lifestyle publication. 'Medium Rim', the second largest by sales (c 50,000 copies) also focuses on young male readership and mainstream biking. The third publication is 'Small Wheel', having the lowest circulation at c 30,000 per month and offering an emphasis on highbrow features but with little advertising content. Finally there is 'Tiny Saddle' which is available free at garages and covers news on all new bike products. The other publications sell for between £2.50 and £3 per copy. An examination of a recent edition of 'Big Spokes' disclosed that the magazine had 172 pages including 66 pages of advertisements, a proportion of just over 38% of the total page area.

2. Proposed operations

2.1 The concept

It is recognized that to operate successfully there are three key aspects that must be correctly tackled: (a) targeted marketing to gain readership; (b) a sustained distribution network; (c) a growing level of advertising revenue.

(a) Marketing

The marketing campaign is designed to create an awareness of and to stimulate interest in the magazine through strategies that will effectively drive the target readership into the retail environment so that they are induced to buy a copy through a combination of in-store and magazine promotions. The campaign initially will be promoted nationally through in-store displays and modest expenditure on external posters and 'flyer' advertisements in other publications in London & SE England, which houses about one-third of the UK population. Depending on the speed of success, further promotions will prioritize other urban centres.

(b) Distribution network

The distribution network appointed is 'Wheeler Dealers', a company related to Twin Wheeler's family. This company will take one half of the cover price (£1.25) in return for supplying the magazine to at least 8,000 outlets throughout the UK. An initial print run of 80,000 copies will be ordered, 50,000 for the full magazine and 30,000 for a free marketing issue of 24 pages. Cash sales will be received in instalments: 40% in the month after publication; 40% one month later; the balance one month after that, with deductions allowed for unsold copies.

(c) Advertising

It is aimed to sell an initial 14 pages of advertising per issue of circa 96 pages. This is close to a 15% advertising content, for which the standard charge will be pitched at a rate 30% less than the established bike magazines currently offer. The advertising space will be heavily discounted initially and managed through an established agency ['Wheels in Print'] for a commission of 22.5%. National consumer goods companies and bike manufacturers and distributors will be approached for paying space. The terms of trade will be 30 days credit for the national companies and pro forma invoicing to smaller firms. A classified section will be added in due course.

2.2 Resources

The editorial office, administration centre and marketing co-ordination base will be situated at Twin's premises at Wheeler's Heights, The Fens, England. This location offers the added benefit of being situated in a government-assisted area and raises the possibility of start-up grant assistance. Separate premises are likely to be required as the business grows. Printing and distribution, as has been indicated, will be sub-contracted out. Indirect overheads, therefore, during the crucial start-up trading period will be minimal, except for travel costs and the promotional budget. All staff requirements for the first two years are contained in the expenditure budget, with additional article writers being added on a self-employed basis as the publication expands.

2.3 Administration

A local book-keeper will be employed full-time to monitor the day-to-day accounting system and to administer the office and a qualified accountant will serve part-time to control all finances and raise monthly management returns. A 'Venerable' computer accounting system will be used with network access available by the management. A strict budgetary control of expenditure, particularly during the first years of operations, will be established.

2.4 Promotion

It was originally intended to concentrate the marketing effort in London and to aim for an intensive but short run expenditure period. After further research the advice given was to emphasise in-store promotions, generally over a longer period, as being better value for money. Apart from the initial launch budget, future advertising and promotion expenditure will be subject to available resources and revenue achievement.

2.5 Pricing

The news-stand price of £2.50 has been pitched slightly below the average retail price of existing biking publications. It was felt that a much lower price would detract from the quality of the publication and reduce the potential revenue to an unacceptable level.

2.6 Royalty fee

A royalty fee of 5% of the net profit before tax to be earned is proposed payable to Twin Wheeler in recognition of his past development services to the project, with a maximum aggregate payment of £50,000.

3. Funding

3.1 An overview

With 64% of income in the first trading year dependent on advertising revenue and 27% of expenditure expected to be taken up on promotion of the magazine, the extent of its success or otherwise will depend significantly on attaining the former targets within the cost limitations of the latter. Advertising revenue has already been heavily discounted in the first months and, for financial prudence beyond the expectations of the advertising agency, this income projection has been further reduced assuming that not all of the advertising space will be filled. It will be up to the management and the investors how they react to the actual monthly trading results as they occur: whether more or less promotional expenditure is warranted and for what, in order to establish a viable publication circulation.

3.2 Projected cash flow and dividend forecasts

Based on the assumptions given in the various Appendices tables, there is projected a peak funding requirement of circa £160,000 by month three of trading that is eliminated by month 30. It is proposed that investors provide equity capital of £100,000 and Twin Wheeler's family connections £25,000, topped up by a commercial bank loan of £60,000 repayable over two years. For the present, possible grant support has been ignored. Thereafter, monthly cash flow is forecast to be increasingly positive with a first dividend to investors being payable at the end of the third trading year. If all targets are attained, the first dividend can be 100% return, subject to retaining sufficient cash in the business and to corporation tax liability. Future annual dividends may be expected at a similar figure, unless it is decided by the shareholders to expand the magazine into other international markets for greater returns and retain part of the distributable profits for this purpose.

3.3 Future financial requirement

The financial projections have assumed that income will not vary significantly from month to month. In practice, if a range of advertisers can be persuaded to fill the pages of each issue, this will not be a problem. It will be prudent to have some financial resources ready to enable the publication to continue production should income temporarily drop for whatever reason. The cash flows show that the bank facility to be drawn is £60,000, of which no more than about £30,000 will be used and then only during the first six months of trading. This will leave the business with the flexibility of a contingency allowance to meet any unexpected temporary dip in income.

3.4 The risks and rewards – a SWOT analysis

The critical period for operations will be the initial months of trading. Expenditure bills will have to be settled before advertising and retail receipts are received. For example, months two to six are scheduled to generate income of circa £255,000; any shortfall on this total will require further financing or a cutback in expenditure such as the promotion budget.

Strengths

♦ Diligent agency work should attain adequate launch advertising revenue before the bulk of the proposed funding is invested or drawn down.
♦ Much advertising is related to new bike products, a necessary spend if each new model is to generate public awareness and future sales.
♦ Heavy discounting of advertising rates should prove attractive to potential advertisers.
♦ The magazine is aiming both for general and specialist bike readers.

Weaknesses

♦ The saturation point for bike magazine readers is unknown.
♦ Circulation has to attain a critical mass to attract future advertisers.
♦ For the magazine to become established, further investment in promotion may be necessary.

Opportunities

♦ The retail sales circulation figures forecast compared with the size of the overall market are very modest.
♦ The age range of readers targeted is a premium segment of the buying market.
♦ Most expenditure is known in advance, hence the gearing factor to expand profits at a greater rate than expenditure is high.
♦ The budgets set exclude distribution of the magazine in other world markets.

Threats

♦ Existing magazines may try and duplicate the proposed editorial emphasis.
♦ The retail outlets for circulation may be curtailed due to unforeseen external reasons.
♦ Any future imposition of VAT on magazines would adversely affect cash flow.

3.5 Investors' potential returns

Subject to corporation tax due on profits from year three, over the first three years of trading investors are forecast to receive their original investment returned and thereafter similar annual dividends. Allowing for the risks involved, this average return is very generous. It should be possible for investor(s) to apply for immediate personal tax relief on their investment in the company under the Government's Enterprise Investment Scheme and also receive the benefit on disposal of their shares free of capital gains tax. There are other developments in the offing from which investors may gain benefit: in particular, plans are at the formative stage to promote the magazine internationally and through the Internet. Investors will be given news of these opportunities at a later stage.

3.6 The funding package proposed

The funding package example proposed is to increase the share capital in two stages.

No of shares	Twin wheeler	Other directors	New investors	Total
Already in issue	2	0	0	2
Issue shares at par £1	4,718	280	0	4,998
Rights 3 for 5 @ £40	2,832	168	0	3,000
Rights waived	–2,452	–48	+2,500	0
Revised shares in issue	**5,100**	**400**	**2,500**	**8,000**
Proportions owned	*63.75%*	*5.00%*	*31.25%*	
The shareholders pay:				
Shares @ £1	4,720	280	0	5,000
Shares @ £1 + premium £39	15,200	4,800	100,000	120,000
Total investment	**£19,920**	**£5,080**	**£100,000**	**£125,000**

3.7 Profit sensitivities

The preamble to Appendices d and e describes the assumptions made in the various budgets on which the investment returns are based. They have been drawn up with the aim of showing a reasonably conservative trading outlook and the objective is to achieve a much higher profit return than that indicated. As with all new ventures that have to win a foothold in the market, no matter how careful the project plans are laid out and how experienced the management, in practice the financing requirement may or may not prove sufficient and this risk must be understood by potential investors. Appendix f provides a number of changed trading assumptions to the base model and how they could affect the profit to be earned.

Appendix a – the management

Twin Wheeler – Managing Director, age 50

Twin is an entrepreneur with an aptitude for creative writing. He started his career in 1962 as an assistant editor for a local newspaper and was sent round on his bike to provide copy for each weekly issue. In 1968 Twin moved to a magazine publishers and boosted his earnings at the same time by selling bike parts. He was appointed Regional Development Manager of the sports section of the magazine by his publishers in 1975 and later this was to incorporate responsibility for the group's chief overseas representative office in Asia in 1980. Meanwhile his bike parts business had flourished into a chain of six shops, all of them profitable. Early in 1990 Twin resigned from the publishing firm to concentrate on his bike shops. In 1996 he acquired a competitor ['Bikes Downhill'] when they had cash flow difficulties. This business was turned round into profitability within two years and a year later Twin sold his enterprise to an Asian conglomerate and put all the proceeds into trust for his family. He now wishes to use his skills and experience in promoting a new magazine for biking enthusiasts.

Anno Domini *C.V. description ...*	Creative Director	age 47
Justin Scribble *C.V. description ...*	Graphics Editor	age 40
Opti Mystick *C.V. description ...*	Marketing Manager	age 31
Count Ant *C.V. description ...*	Accountant (part-time)	age 52
Miss Itout *C.V. description ...*	Administrator	age 21

Freelance writers to include ...

Appendix b – outline of marketing programme

The marketing strategy to be adopted is to gain acceptance at a wide number and range of 'high street' retail outlets using 'point-of-sale' promotion within those shops to urge the purchase of the magazine itself. In this way, a rapid direct feedback of consumer acceptance at individual retail sources can be monitored and it is believed this will show a better reward on marketing expenditure than through indirect and more expensive static advertising spots. A breakdown of the marketing spend within the projected budget is as follows:

Week	Outlet (codename)	Type	Month 1	Month 2	Month 3	Total
One	Pound	Stand	7,000	0	0	7,000
	Pound	Posters	2,400	0	0	2,400
	Euro	Posters	0	600	3,000	3,600
	General	Leaflets etc	7,000	6,000	6,000	19,000
		Total	**16,400**	**6,600**	**9,000**	**32,000**
Two	Franc	Stand	5,000			5,000
	Mark	Posters	4,000			4,000
	Lira	Posters		1,500		1,500
	Peseta	Posters		1,000		1,000
	General	Leaflets etc	7,000	6,000	6,000	19,000
		Total	**16,000**	**8,500**	**6,000**	**30,500**
Three	Euro	Stand	3,000			3,000
	Dollar	Posters		4,000		4,000
	General	Leaflets etc	6,000	6,000	6,000	18,000
		Total	**9,000**	**10,000**	**6,000**	**25,000**
Four	Franc	Posters		4,000		4,000
	Rand	Posters	5,500			5,500
	Guilder	Posters	3,000			3,000
		Total	**8,500**	**4,000**	**0**	**12,500**
Month	Campaign budget	**Total**	**49,900**	**29,100**	**21,000**	**100,000**

The campaign continues at month four with refresher advertisements. The free issues will be inserts in various existing publications.

Appendix c – research on the expected advertising response

(not shown)

Explanatory notes to Appendix d

It will be sensible to provide an explanation how the profit and loss account and cash flow projections are arrived at, even if most entries may be self-explanatory.

As can be seen, total revenue is made up of the sale of copies (at £1.25 per magazine); advertising revenue and subscriptions income from readers.

Direct costs comprise: advertising commission (at 22.5% of advertising revenue); each month's proportion of readers' annual subscriptions carried forward; printing costs according to the print run number for each edition; estimates of other direct costs.

Indirect costs include: administration expenditure; the promotion budget; quarterly VAT (recovery) and royalty fees payable in arrears.

The first three years trading is set out on an identical pro forma for easy comparison purposes.

The cash flow spreadsheets summarize the profit and loss account figures except that the income and expenditure items, where appropriate, include VAT, with all entries accruing in the months the income will be received or the cost incurred.

The resulting net operating cash flow is then adjusted for non-trading items such as equipment expenditure and the repayments of the bank loan.

Important figures then shown are the cumulative cash flow (giving the maximum amount required to be financed) and the monthly net borrowing requirement (showing how much money will have to be borrowed).

The spreadsheet is completed by an abridged balance sheet, including the cash balance at the end of each month and the profit and loss account that will incorporate the monthly trading profit or loss on a cumulative basis.

The three years' spreadsheets should be read for their contents and for the general form in which the financial projections are set out. The detailed cell workings are not given.

Appendix d – Profit and loss projections: years one to three

New Magazine Limited **Profit and loss account** **Budget year one**

Sheet one	Month 1	Month 2	Month 3	Month 4	Month 5	Month 6	Month 7	Month 8	Month 9	Month 10	Month 11	Month 12	Year one
INCOME													
Print run	50,000	40,000	30,000	30,000	30,000	30,000	30,000	30,000	30,000	30,000	30,000	30,000	390,000
Copies sold (%)	30.0	30.0	35.0	35.0	35.0	35.0	35.0	35.0	35.0	35.0	35.0	35.0	20.0
Retail sales	15,000	12,000	10,500	10,500	10,500	10,500	10,500	10,500	10,500	10,500	10,500	10,500	78,000
Promotion issue – free	30,000	0	0	0	0	0	0	0	0	0	0	0	0
Retail income	1.25	1.25	1.25	1.25	1.25	1.25	1.25	1.25	1.25	1.25	1.25	1.25	1.25
Retail sales revenue (£)	18,750	15,000	13,125	13,125	13,125	13,125	13,125	13,125	13,125	13,125	13,125	13,125	165,000
Copy pages	96	96	96	96	96	96	96	96	96	96	96	96	
Advert pages	14.0	14.0	14.5	14.5	15.0	15.0	15.5	15.5	16.0	16.0	16.0	16.0	
Advertising content (%)	14.6	14.6	15.1	15.1	15.6	15.6	16.1	16.1	16.7	16.7	16.7	16.7	
Advert revenue per page	3,250	3,250	3,250	3,250	3,250	3,250	3,250	3,250	3,250	3,250	3,250	3,250	
Percent of advertising space filled	100	90	80	70	60	60	60	60	60	60	60	60	
Advertising revenue (£)	45,500	40,950	37,700	32,988	29,250	29,250	30,225	30,225	31,200	31,200	31,200	31,200	369,688
Subscriptions (number)	0	75	60	53	53	53	53	53	53	53	53	53	
Subscription revenue (£)	0	1,875	1,500	1,313	1,313	1,313	1,313	1,313	1,313	1,313	1,313	1,313	15,188
TOTAL REVENUE (£)	64,250	57,825	52,325	47,425	43,688	43,688	44,663	44,663	45,638	45,638	45,638	45,638	581,075

179

Sheet one continued	Month 1	Month 2	Month 3	Month 4	Month 5	Month 6	Month 7	Month 8	Month 9	Month 10	Month 11	Month 12	Year one
EXPENDITURE													
Direct costs													
Advertising commission	10,238	9,214	8,483	7,422	6,581	6,581	6,801	6,801	7,020	7,020	7,020	7,020	90,200
Subscriptions carried forward	0	1,719	2,938	3,859	4,672	5,375	5,969	6,453	6,828	7,094	7,250	7,297	59,453
Print costs	17,500	14,000	10,500	10,500	10,500	10,500	10,500	10,500	10,500	10,500	10,500	10,500	136,500
Print cost of promotion issue	15,000	0	0	0	0	0	0	0	0	0	0	0	15,000
Salaries & employers NI:	5,114	5,114	5,476	5,114	5,114	5,476	5,114	5,114	5,476	5,114	5,114	5,476	62,822
Article writers fees	3,000	3,000	3,000	3,000	3,000	3,000	3,000	3,000	3,000	3,000	3,000	3,000	36,000
Photographic library	400	400	400	400	400	400	400	400	400	400	400	400	4,800
Sub-total	**51,252**	**33,447**	**30,796**	**30,296**	**30,268**	**31,333**	**31,784**	**32,268**	**33,225**	**33,128**	**33,284**	**33,693**	**404,775**
Indirect costs													
Directors salaries & NI	2,764	2,764	2,831	2,764	2,764	2,831	2,764	2,764	2,831	2,764	2,764	2,831	33,438
Administration wages & NI	1,935	1,935	2,419	1,935	1,935	2,419	1,935	1,935	2,419	1,935	1,935	2,419	25,156
Accountancy fees	800	800	800	800	800	800	800	800	800	800	800	800	9,600
Travel & sundry costs	600	600	600	600	600	600	600	600	600	600	600	600	7,200
ABC circulation fees	1,006	785	0	0	0	0	0	785	0	0	0	0	2,576
Promotion budget	50,626	31,500	17,874	6,000	6,000	8,000	6,000	6,000	8,000	6,000	6,000	8,000	160,000
Finance costs	1,700	479	458	438	417	396	375	354	333	313	292	271	5,825
VAT recovery	0	0	0	-21,162	0	0	-13,320	0	0	-13,611	0	0	-48,093
Depreciation	250	250	250	250	250	250	250	250	250	250	250	250	3,000
Sub-total	**59,682**	**39,114**	**25,232**	**-8,375**	**12,766**	**15,295**	**-595**	**13,489**	**15,233**	**-949**	**12,641**	**15,170**	**198,702**
NET PROFIT BEFORE TAX	**-46,684**	**-14,736**	**-3,703**	**25,504**	**654**	**-2,940**	**13,474**	**-1,094**	**-2,820**	**13,458**	**-288**	**-3,226**	**-22,402**
Less royalty fee	0	0	0	1,275	33	0	674	0	0	673	0	0	2,654
ADJUSTED NET PROFIT	**-46,684**	**-14,736**	**-3,703**	**24,229**	**621**	**-2,940**	**12,800**	**-1,094**	**-2,820**	**12,785**	**-288**	**-3,226**	**-25,056**

New Magazine Limited   Profit and loss account   Budget year two

Sheet two	Month 1	Month 2	Month 3	Month 4	Month 5	Month 6	Month 7	Month 8	Month 9	Month 10	Month 11	Month 12	Year two
INCOME													
Print run	30,000	30,000	30,000	30,000	30,000	30,000	30,000	30,000	30,000	30,000	30,000	30,000	360,000
Copies sold (%)	35.0	35.0	35.0	35.0	35.0	35.0	35.0	35.0	35.0	35.0	35.0	35.0	20.0
Retail sales	10,500	10,500	10,500	10,500	10,500	10,500	10,500	10,500	10,500	10,500	10,500	10,500	72,000
Promotion issue – free	0	0	0	0	0	0	0	0	0	0	0	0	0
Retail income	1.25	1.25	1.25	1.25	1.25	1.25	1.25	1.25	1.25	1.25	1.25	1.25	1.25
Retail sales revenue (£)	13,125	13,125	13,125	13,125	13,125	13,125	13,125	13,125	13,125	13,125	13,125	13,125	157,500
Copy pages	96	96	96	96	96	96	96	96	96	96	96	96	
Advert pages	16.0	16.0	16.0	16.0	16.0	16.0	16.5	16.5	16.5	16.5	16.5	16.5	
Advertising content (%)	16.7	16.7	16.7	16.7	16.7	16.7	17.2	17.2	17.2	17.2	17.2	17.2	
Advert revenue per page	3,500	3,500	3,500	3,500	3,500	3,500	3,500	3,500	3,500	3,500	3,500	3,500	
Percent of advertising space filled	65	65	65	65	65	65	70	70	70	70	70	70	
Advertising revenue (£)	36,400	36,400	36,400	36,400	36,400	36,400	40,425	40,425	40,425	40,425	40,425	40,425	420,525
Subscriptions (number)	53	53	53	53	53	53	53	53	53	53	53	53	
Subscription revenue (£)	1,313	1,313	1,313	1,313	1,313	1,313	1,313	1,313	1,313	1,313	1,313	1,313	15,750
TOTAL REVENUE (£)	50,838	50,838	50,838	50,838	50,838	50,838	54,863	54,863	54,863	54,863	54,863	54,863	634,200

Sheet two continued	Month 1	Month 2	Month 3	Month 4	Month 5	Month 6	Month 7	Month 8	Month 9	Month 10	Month 11	Month 12	Year two
EXPENDITURE													
Direct costs													
Advertising commission	9,100	9,100	9,100	9,100	9,100	9,100	10,106	10,106	10,106	10,106	10,106	10,106	115,238
Subscriptions carried forward	7,203	7,203	7,203	7,203	7,203	7,203	7,203	7,203	7,203	7,203	7,203	7,203	86,436
Print costs	12,000	12,000	12,000	12,000	12,000	12,000	12,000	12,000	12,000	12,000	12,000	12,000	144,000
Print cost of promotion issue	0	0	0	0	0	0	0	0	0	0	0	0	0
Salaries & employers NI:	5,330	5,330	5,709	5,330	5,330	5,709	5,330	5,330	5,709	5,330	5,330	5,709	65,475
Article writers fees	4,500	4,500	4,500	4,500	4,500	4,500	4,500	4,500	4,500	4,500	4,500	4,500	54,000
Photographic library	500	500	500	500	500	500	500	500	500	500	500	500	6,000
Sub-total	38,633	38,633	39,012	38,633	38,633	39,012	39,639	39,639	40,018	39,639	39,639	40,018	471,149
Indirect costs													
Directors salaries & NI	2,903	2,903	2,972	2,903	2,903	2,972	2,903	2,903	2,972	2,903	2,903	2,972	35,110
Administration wages & NI	1,993	1,993	2,491	1,993	1,993	2,491	1,993	1,993	2,491	1,993	1,993	2,491	25,910
Accountancy fees	880	880	880	880	880	880	880	880	880	880	880	880	10,560
Travel & sundry costs	700	700	700	700	700	700	700	700	700	700	700	700	8,400
ABC circulation fees	0	900	0	0	0	0	0	900	0	0	0	0	1,800
Promotion budget	24,000	6,000	8,000	6,000	6,000	8,000	6,000	6,000	8,000	6,000	6,000	8,000	98,000
Finance costs	250	229	208	188	167	146	125	104	83	63	42	21	1,625
VAT recovery	−8,432	0	0	−16,352	0	0	−16,371	0	0	−16,880	0	0	−58,034
Depreciation	188	188	188	188	188	188	188	188	188	188	188	188	2,250
Sub-total	22,482	13,792	15,439	−3,501	12,830	15,377	−3,582	13,667	15,314	−4,154	12,705	15,252	125,621
NET PROFIT BEFORE TAX	−10,277	−1,588	−3,614	15,706	−625	−3,551	18,806	1,556	−470	19,378	2,518	−408	37,430
Less royalty fee	0	0	0	785	0	0	940	78	0	969	126	0	2,898
ADJUSTED NET PROFIT	−10,277	−1,588	−3,614	14,920	−625	−3,551	17,865	1,478	−470	18,409	2,392	−408	34,532

New Magazine Limited

Profit and loss account

Budget year three

Sheet three	Month 1	Month 2	Month 3	Month 4	Month 5	Month 6	Month 7	Month 8	Month 9	Month 10	Month 11	Month 12	Year three
INCOME													
Print run	30,000	30,000	30,000	30,000	30,000	30,000	30,000	30,000	30,000	30,000	30,000	30,000	360,000
Copies sold (%)	35.0	35.0	35.0	35.0	35.0	35.0	35.0	35.0	35.0	35.0	35.0	35.0	20.0
Retails sales	10,500	10,500	10,500	10,500	10,500	10,500	10,500	10,500	10,500	10,500	10,500	10,500	72,000
Promotion issue – free	0	0	0	0	0	0	0	0	0	0	0	0	0
Retail income	1.25	1.25	1.25	1.25	1.25	1.25	1.25	1.25	1.25	1.25	1.25	1.25	1.25
Retail sales revenue (£)	13,125	13,125	13,125	13,125	13,125	13,125	13,125	13,125	13,125	13,125	13,125	13,125	157,500
Copy pages	96	96	96	96	96	96	96	96	96	96	96	96	
Advert pages	17.0	17.0	17.0	17.0	17.0	17.0	17.5	17.5	17.5	17.5	17.5	17.5	
Advertising content (%)	17.7	17.7	17.7	17.7	17.7	17.7	18.2	18.2	18.2	18.2	18.2	18.2	
Advert revenue per page	3,750	3,750	3,750	3,750	3,750	3,750	4,000	4,000	4,000	4,000	4,000	4,000	
Percent of advertising space filled	75	75	75	75	75	75	80	80	80	80	80	80	
Advertising revenue (£)	47,813	47,813	47,813	47,813	47,813	47,813	56,000	56,000	56,000	56,000	56,000	56,000	566,875
Subscriptions (number)	53	53	53	53	53	53	53	53	53	53	53	53	
Subscription revenue (£)	1,313	1,313	1,313	1,313	1,313	1,313	1,313	1,313	1,313	1,313	1,313	1,313	15,750
TOTAL REVENUE (£)	**62,250**	**62,250**	**62,250**	**62,250**	**62,250**	**62,250**	**70,438**	**70,438**	**70,438**	**70,438**	**70,438**	**70,438**	**796,125**

Sheet three continued	Month 1	Month 2	Month 3	Month 4	Month 5	Month 6	Month 7	Month 8	Month 9	Month 10	Month 11	Month 12	Year three
EXPENDITURE													
Direct costs													
Advertising commission	11,953	11,953	11,953	11,953	11,953	11,953	14,000	14,000	14,000	14,000	14,000	14,000	155,719
Subscriptions carried forward	7,203	7,203	7,203	7,203	7,203	7,203	7,203	7,203	7,203	7,203	7,203	7,203	86,436
Print costs	13,500	13,500	13,500	13,500	13,500	13,500	13,500	13,500	13,500	13,500	13,500	13,500	162,000
Print cost of promotion issue	0	0	0	0	0	0	0	0	0	0	0	0	0
Salaries & employers NI:	5,498	5,498	5,881	5,498	5,498	5,881	5,498	5,498	5,881	5,498	5,498	5,881	67,504
Article writers fees	4,500	4,500	4,500	4,500	4,500	4,500	4,500	4,500	4,500	4,500	4,500	4,500	54,000
Photographic library	500	500	500	500	500	500	500	500	500	500	500	500	6,000
Sub-total	**43,154**	**43,154**	**43,537**	**43,154**	**43,154**	**43,537**	**45,201**	**45,201**	**45,584**	**45,201**	**45,201**	**45,584**	**531,658**
Indirect costs													
Directors salaries & NI	3,048	3,048	3,121	3,048	3,048	3,121	3,048	3,048	3,121	3,048	3,048	3,121	36,866
Administration wages & NI	1,993	1,993	2,491	1,993	1,993	2,491	1,993	1,993	2,491	1,993	1,993	2,491	25,910
Accountancy fees	880	880	880	880	880	880	880	880	880	880	880	880	10,560
Travel & sundry costs	700	700	700	700	700	700	700	700	700	700	700	700	8,400
ABC circulation fees	0	900	0	0	0	0	0	900	0	0	0	0	1,800
Promotion budget	16,000	6,000	8,000	6,000	6,000	8,000	6,000	6,000	8,000	6,000	6,000	8,000	90,000
Finance costs (leased equipment)	3,000	0	0	1,000	1,000	1,000	1,000	1,000	1,000	1,000	1,000	1,000	12,000
VAT recovery	-7,750	0	0	-18,506	0	0	-18,663	0	0	-19,450	0	0	-64,368
Depreciation	188	188	188	188	188	188	188	188	188	188	188	188	2,250
Sub-total	**18,059**	**13,708**	**15,380**	**-4,698**	**13,808**	**16,380**	**-4,855**	**14,708**	**16,380**	**-5,641**	**13,808**	**16,380**	**123,418**
NET PROFIT BEFORE TAX	**1,037**	**5,388**	**3,334**	**23,794**	**5,288**	**2,334**	**30,091**	**10,528**	**8,474**	**30,878**	**11,428**	**8,474**	**141,049**
Less royalty fee	52	269	167	1,190	264	117	1,505	526	424	1,544	571	424	7,052
ADJUSTED NET PROFIT	**985**	**5,118**	**3,167**	**22,604**	**5,023**	**2,217**	**28,587**	**10,002**	**8,051**	**29,334**	**10,857**	**8,051**	**133,996**

Appendix d – Profit and Loss projections: years one to three

New Magazine Limited

Cash flow											Budget year one	
Sheet one	Month 1	Month 2	Month 3	Month 4	Month 5	Month 6	Month 7	Month 8	Month 9	Month 10	Month 11	Month 12	Year one
REVENUE													
Retail sales	0	7,500	13,500	15,000	13,500	13,125	13,125	13,125	13,125	13,125	13,125	13,125	141,375
Advertising sales	0	0	53,463	48,116	44,298	38,760	34,369	34,369	35,514	35,514	36,660	36,660	397,723
Subscriptions	0	1,875	1,500	1,313	1,313	1,313	1,313	1,313	1,313	1,313	1,313	1,313	15,188
REVENUE CASH FLOW	**0**	**9,375**	**68,463**	**64,429**	**59,110**	**53,198**	**48,806**	**48,806**	**49,952**	**49,952**	**51,098**	**51,098**	**554,285**
EXPENDITURE													
Advertising commission	0	12,029	10,826	9,967	8,721	7,733	7,733	7,991	7,991	8,249	8,249	8,249	97,736
Printing costs	0	38,188	16,450	12,338	12,338	12,338	12,338	12,338	12,338	12,338	12,338	12,338	165,675
Salaries	5,114	5,114	5,476	5,114	5,114	5,476	5,114	5,114	5,476	5,114	5,114	5,476	62,822
Article fees etc	0	3,995	3,995	3,995	3,995	3,995	3,995	3,995	3,995	3,995	3,995	3,995	43,945
DIRECT COSTS	**5,114**	**59,326**	**36,748**	**31,414**	**30,168**	**29,542**	**29,180**	**29,438**	**29,800**	**29,695**	**29,695**	**30,057**	**370,178**
Salary & wages	4,700	4,700	5,249	4,700	4,700	5,249	4,700	4,700	5,249	4,700	4,700	5,249	58,594
Other indirect office costs	2,827	2,567	1,645	1,645	1,645	1,645	1,645	2,567	1,645	1,645	1,645	1,645	22,767
Promotion budget	0	59,486	37,013	21,002	7,050	7,050	9,400	7,050	7,050	9,400	7,050	7,050	178,600
INDIRECT COSTS	**7,527**	**66,752**	**43,907**	**27,347**	**13,395**	**13,944**	**15,745**	**14,317**	**13,944**	**15,745**	**13,395**	**13,944**	**259,961**
Royalty fee	0	0	0	1,498	38	0	792	0	0	791	0	0	3,119
EXPENDITURE CASH FLOW	**12,641**	**126,079**	**80,655**	**60,259**	**43,601**	**43,486**	**45,716**	**43,755**	**43,744**	**46,231**	**43,090**	**44,002**	**633,258**
NET OPERATING CASH FLOW	**-12,641**	**-116,704**	**-12,192**	**4,170**	**15,509**	**9,711**	**3,090**	**5,052**	**6,208**	**3,721**	**8,007**	**7,096**	**-78,973**
Equipment expenditure	14,100	0	0	0	0	0	0	0	0	0	0	0	14,100
Bank loan repayments	0	2,500	2,500	2,500	2,500	2,500	2,500	2,500	2,500	2,500	2,500	2,500	27,500
TOTAL NET CASH FLOW per month	**-26,741**	**-119,204**	**-14,692**	**1,670**	**13,009**	**7,211**	**590**	**2,552**	**3,708**	**1,221**	**5,507**	**4,596**	**-120,573**
Cumulative cash flow	-26,741	-145,945	-160,637	-158,967	-145,958	-138,746	-138,156	-135,605	-131,897	-130,676	-125,168	-120,573	

Sheet one continued	Month 1	Month 2	Month 3	Month 4	Month 5	Month 6	Month 7	Month 8	Month 9	Month 10	Month 11	Month 12	Year one
FINANCING													
Investors cash advanced	125,000	0	0	0	0	0	0	0	0	0	0	0	125,000
Bank Loan	60,000	0	0	0	0	0	0	0	0	0	0	0	60,000
Net cash flow													
cumulative	**158,259**	**39,055**	**24,363**	**26,033**	**39,042**	**46,254**	**46,844**	**49,395**	**53,103**	**54,324**	**59,832**	**64,427**	
Bank facility outstanding	60,000	57,500	55,000	52,500	50,000	47,500	45,000	42,500	40,000	37,500	35,000	32,500	
Net borrowing (-)/													
Funds in hand (+)	98,259	-18,445	-30,637	-26,467	-10,958	-1,246	-1,844	6,895	13,103	16,824	24,832	31,927	
BALANCE SHEET													
Fixed assets													
Office/other equipment	12,000	12,000	12,000	12,000	12,000	12,000	12,000	12,000	12,000	12,000	12,000	12,000	
Less depreciation @ 25%	250	500	750	1,000	1,250	1,500	1,750	2,000	2,250	2,500	2,750	3,000	
Net book value	**11,750**	**11,500**	**11,250**	**11,000**	**10,750**	**10,500**	**10,250**	**10,000**	**9,750**	**9,500**	**9,250**	**9,000**	
Current assets													
Debtors	65,071	128,639	119,522	126,896	111,416	101,015	109,194	103,298	96,741	104,055	96,009	87,938	
Cash at bank	158,259	39,055	24,363	26,033	39,042	46,254	46,844	49,395	53,103	54,324	59,832	64,427	
Less current liabilities													
Creditors	-96,764	-58,114	-40,257	-27,322	-26,481	-28,481	-26,701	-26,701	-28,920	-26,920	-26,920	-28,920	
Net current assets	**126,566**	**109,581**	**103,628**	**125,607**	**123,977**	**118,787**	**129,337**	**125,993**	**120,924**	**131,459**	**128,921**	**123,445**	
EMPLOYMENT OF													
CAPITAL	**138,316**	**121,081**	**114,878**	**136,607**	**134,727**	**129,287**	**139,587**	**135,993**	**130,674**	**140,959**	**138,171**	**132,445**	
Bank loan	60,000	57,500	55,000	52,500	50,000	47,500	45,000	42,500	40,000	37,500	35,000	32,500	
Shareholders funds	125,000	125,000	125,000	125,000	125,000	125,000	125,000	125,000	125,000	125,000	125,000	125,000	
Profit and loss account	-46,684	-61,419	-65,122	-40,893	-40,273	-43,213	-30,413	-31,507	-34,326	-21,541	-21,829	-25,055	
CAPITAL EMPLOYED	**138,316**	**121,081**	**114,878**	**136,607**	**134,727**	**129,287**	**139,587**	**135,993**	**130,674**	**140,959**	**138,171**	**132,445**	
Creative Director	2,203	2,203	2,254	2,203	2,203	2,254	2,203	2,203	2,254	2,203	2,203	2,254	26,645
Graphics Editor	1,829	1,829	1,870	1,829	1,829	1,870	1,829	1,829	1,870	1,829	1,829	1,870	22,117
Marketing Manager	1,081	1,081	1,352	1,081	1,081	1,352	1,081	1,081	1,352	1,081	1,081	1,352	14,059

New Magazine Limited

Cash flow

Budget year two

Sheet two	Month 1	Month 2	Month 3	Month 4	Month 5	Month 6	Month 7	Month 8	Month 9	Month 10	Month 11	Month 12	Year two
REVENUE													
Retail sales	13,125	13,125	13,125	13,125	13,125	13,125	13,125	13,125	13,125	13,125	13,125	13,125	157,500
Advertising sales	36,660	36,660	42,770	42,770	42,770	42,770	42,770	42,770	47,499	47,499	47,499	47,499	519,938
Subscriptions	1,313	1,313	1,313	1,313	1,313	1,313	1,313	1,313	1,313	1,313	1,313	1,313	15,750
REVENUE CASH FLOW	**51,098**	**51,098**	**57,208**	**57,208**	**57,208**	**57,208**	**57,208**	**57,208**	**61,937**	**61,937**	**61,937**	**61,937**	**693,188**
EXPENDITURE													
Advertising commission	8,249	10,693	10,693	10,693	10,693	10,693	10,693	11,875	11,875	11,875	11,875	11,875	131,778
Printing costs	12,338	14,100	14,100	14,100	14,100	14,100	14,100	14,100	14,100	14,100	14,100	14,100	167,438
Salaries	5,330	5,330	5,709	5,330	5,330	5,709	5,330	5,330	5,709	5,330	5,330	5,709	65,475
Article fees etc	3,995	5,875	5,875	5,875	5,875	5,875	5,875	5,875	5,875	5,875	5,875	5,875	68,620
DIRECT COSTS	**29,911**	**35,997**	**36,377**	**35,997**	**35,997**	**36,377**	**35,997**	**37,180**	**37,559**	**37,180**	**37,180**	**37,559**	**433,310**
Salary & wages	4,896	4,896	5,464	4,896	4,896	5,464	4,896	4,896	5,464	4,896	4,896	5,464	61,021
Other indirect office costs	1,857	2,914	1,857	1,857	1,857	1,857	1,857	2,914	1,857	1,857	1,857	1,857	24,393
Promotion budget	9,400	28,200	7,050	9,400	7,050	7,050	9,400	7,050	7,050	9,400	7,050	7,050	115,150
INDIRECT COSTS	**16,152**	**36,010**	**14,370**	**16,152**	**13,802**	**14,370**	**16,152**	**14,860**	**14,370**	**16,152**	**13,802**	**14,370**	**200,564**
Royalty fee	0	0	0	923	0	0	1,105	91	0	1,138	148	0	3,405
EXPENDITURE CASH FLOW	**46,063**	**72,007**	**50,747**	**53,072**	**49,800**	**50,747**	**53,255**	**52,131**	**51,929**	**54,471**	**51,130**	**51,929**	**637,280**
NET OPERATING CASH FLOW	**5,034**	**-20,910**	**6,461**	**4,135**	**7,408**	**6,461**	**3,953**	**5,077**	**10,008**	**7,466**	**10,807**	**10,008**	**55,908**
Equipment expenditure	0	0	0	0	0	0	0	0	0	0	0	0	0
Bank Loan repayments	2,500	2,500	2,500	2,500	2,500	2,500	2,500	2,500	2,500	2,500	2,500	2,500	30,000
TOTAL NET CASH FLOW per month	**2,534**	**-23,410**	**3,961**	**1,635**	**4,908**	**3,961**	**1,453**	**2,577**	**7,508**	**4,966**	**8,307**	**7,508**	**25,908**
Cumulative cash flow	-118,038	-141,448	-137,487	-135,852	-130,944	-126,983	-125,530	-122,954	-115,446	-110,479	-102,173	-94,665	

Sheet two continued	Month 1	Month 2	Month 3	Month 4	Month 5	Month 6	Month 7	Month 8	Month 9	Month 10	Month 11	Month 12	Year two
DISTRIBUTIONS													
Investors dividend	0	0	0	0	0	0	0	0	0	0	0	0	0
Bank loan	0	0	0	0	0	0	0	0	0	0	0	0	0
Net cash flow													
cumulative	**66,962**	**43,552**	**47,513**	**49,148**	**54,056**	**58,017**	**59,470**	**62,046**	**69,554**	**74,521**	**82,827**	**90,335**	
Bank facility outstanding	30,000	27,500	25,000	22,500	20,000	17,500	15,000	12,500	10,000	7,500	5,000	2,500	
Net borrowing (–)/													
Funds in hand (+)	36,962	16,052	22,513	26,648	34,056	40,517	44,470	49,546	59,554	67,021	77,827	87,835	
BALANCE SHEET													
Fixed assets													
Office/other equipment	12,000	12,000	12,000	12,000	12,000	12,000	12,000	12,000	12,000	12,000	12,000	12,000	
Less depreciation @ 25%	3,188	3,375	3,563	3,750	3,938	4,125	4,313	4,500	4,688	4,875	5,063	5,250	
Net book value	**8,813**	**8,625**	**8,438**	**8,250**	**8,063**	**7,875**	**7,688**	**7,500**	**7,313**	**7,125**	**6,938**	**6,750**	
Current assets													
Debtors	93,994	95,504	87,617	96,590	88,745	80,920	94,026	90,615	82,324	91,455	83,228	74,999	
Cash at bank	66,962	43,552	47,513	49,148	54,056	58,017	59,470	62,046	69,554	74,521	82,827	90,335	
Less current liabilities													
Creditors	–50,100	–32,100	–34,100	–32,100	–32,100	–34,100	–33,106	–33,106	–35,106	–33,106	–33,106	–35,106	
Net current assets	**110,855**	**106,956**	**101,030**	**113,638**	**110,701**	**104,836**	**120,389**	**119,555**	**116,772**	**132,869**	**132,949**	**130,228**	
EMPLOYMENT OF													
CAPITAL	**119,668**	**115,581**	**109,467**	**121,888**	**118,763**	**112,711**	**128,077**	**127,055**	**124,085**	**139,994**	**139,886**	**136,978**	
Bank loan	30,000	27,500	25,000	22,500	20,000	17,500	15,000	12,500	10,000	7,500	5,000	2,500	
Shareholders funds	125,000	125,000	125,000	125,000	125,000	125,000	125,000	125,000	125,000	125,000	125,000	125,000	
Profit and loss account	–35,332	–36,919	–40,533	–25,612	–26,237	–29,789	–11,923	–10,445	–10,915	7,494	9,886	9,478	
CAPITAL EMPLOYED	**119,668**	**115,581**	**109,467**	**121,888**	**118,763**	**112,711**	**128,077**	**127,055**	**124,085**	**139,994**	**139,886**	**136,978**	
Creative Director	2,292	2,292	2,345	2,292	2,292	2,345	2,292	2,292	2,345	2,292	2,292	2,345	27,711
Graphics Editor	1,903	1,903	1,945	1,903	1,903	1,945	1,903	1,903	1,945	1,903	1,903	1,945	23,001
Marketing Manager	1,136	1,136	1,419	1,136	1,136	1,419	1,136	1,136	1,419	1,136	1,136	1,419	14,762

New Magazine Limited

Cash flow

Budget year three

Sheet three

	Month 1	Month 2	Month 3	Month 4	Month 5	Month 6	Month 7	Month 8	Month 9	Month 10	Month 11	Month 12	Year three
REVENUE													
Retail sales	13,125	13,125	13,125	13,125	13,125	13,125	13,125	13,125	13,125	13,125	13,125	13,125	157,500
Advertising sales	47,499	47,499	56,180	56,180	56,180	56,180	56,180	56,180	65,800	65,800	65,800	65,800	695,277
Subscriptions	1,313	1,313	1,313	1,313	1,313	1,313	1,313	1,313	1,313	1,313	1,313	1,313	15,750
REVENUE CASH FLOW	**61,937**	**61,937**	**70,617**	**70,617**	**70,617**	**70,617**	**70,617**	**70,617**	**80,238**	**80,238**	**80,238**	**80,238**	**868,527**
EXPENDITURE													
Advertising commission	11,875	14,045	14,045	14,045	14,045	14,045	14,045	16,450	16,450	16,450	16,450	16,450	178,394
Printing costs	14,100	15,863	15,863	15,863	15,863	15,863	15,863	15,863	15,863	15,863	15,863	15,863	188,588
Salaries	5,498	5,498	5,881	5,498	5,498	5,881	5,498	5,498	5,881	5,498	5,498	5,881	67,504
Article fees etc	5,875	5,875	5,875	5,875	5,875	5,875	5,875	5,875	5,875	5,875	5,875	5,875	70,500
DIRECT COSTS	**37,348**	**41,280**	**41,663**	**41,280**	**41,280**	**41,663**	**41,280**	**43,685**	**44,068**	**43,685**	**43,685**	**44,068**	**504,986**
Salary & wages	5,041	5,041	5,612	5,041	5,041	5,612	5,041	5,041	5,612	5,041	5,041	5,612	62,776
Other indirect office costs	1,857	2,914	1,857	1,857	1,857	1,857	1,857	2,914	1,857	1,857	1,857	1,857	24,393
Promotion budget	9,400	18,800	7,050	9,400	7,050	7,050	9,400	7,050	7,050	9,400	7,050	7,050	105,750
INDIRECT COSTS	**16,297**	**26,755**	**14,519**	**16,297**	**13,947**	**14,519**	**16,297**	**15,005**	**14,519**	**16,297**	**13,947**	**14,519**	**192,919**
Royalty fee	61	317	196	1,398	311	137	1,768	619	498	1,814	671	498	8,287
EXPENDITURE CASH FLOW	**53,706**	**68,352**	**56,378**	**58,975**	**55,538**	**56,319**	**59,345**	**59,309**	**59,085**	**61,797**	**58,304**	**59,085**	**706,191**
NET OPERATING CASH FLOW	**8,231**	**-6,415**	**14,240**	**11,642**	**15,079**	**14,298**	**11,272**	**11,309**	**21,153**	**18,441**	**21,933**	**21,153**	**162,335**
Equipment expenditure	0	0	0	0	0	0	0	0	0	0	0	0	0
Bank loan repayments	2,500	2,500	2,500	2,500	2,500	2,500	2,500	2,500	2,500	2,500	2,500	2,500	30,000
TOTAL NET CASH FLOW per month	**5,731**	**-8,915**	**11,740**	**9,142**	**12,579**	**11,798**	**8,772**	**8,809**	**18,653**	**15,941**	**19,433**	**18,653**	**132,335**
Cumulative cash flow	*-88,934*	*-97,848*	*-86,109*	*-76,967*	*-64,388*	*-52,589*	*-43,818*	*-35,009*	*-16,356*	*-416*	*19,018*	*37,671*	

Sheet three continued	Month 1	Month 2	Month 3	Month 4	Month 5	Month 6	Month 7	Month 8	Month 9	Month 10	Month 11	Month 12	Year three
DISTRIBUTIONS													
Investors dividend	0	0	0	0	0	0	0	0	0	0	0	–125,000	0
Bank loan	0	0	0	0	0	0	0	0	0	0	0	0	0
Net cash flow													
cumulative	**96,066**	**87,152**	**98,891**	**108,033**	**120,612**	**132,411**	**141,182**	**149,991**	**168,644**	**184,584**	**204,018**	**97,671**	
Bank facility outstanding	0	0	0	0	0	0	0	0	0	0	0	0	0
Net borrowing (–)/													
Funds in hand (+)	*96,066*	*87,152*	*98,891*	*108,033*	*120,612*	*132,411*	*141,182*	*149,991*	*168,644*	*184,584*	*204,018*	*97,671*	*97,671*
BALANCE SHEET													
Fixed assets													
Office/other equipment	12,000	12,000	12,000	12,000	12,000	12,000	12,000	12,000	12,000	12,000	12,000	12,000	12,000
Less depreciation @ 25%	3,188	3,375	3,563	3,750	3,938	4,125	4,313	4,500	4,688	4,875	5,063	5,250	5,250
Net book value	**8,813**	**8,625**	**8,438**	**8,250**	**8,063**	**7,875**	**7,688**	**7,500**	**7,313**	**7,125**	**6,938**	**6,750**	**6,750**
Current assets													
Debtors	77,038	81,258	74,873	86,523	79,156	71,763	91,812	93,192	84,777	96,358	87,969	79,555	79,555
Cash at bank	96,066	87,152	98,891	108,033	120,612	132,411	141,182	149,991	168,644	184,584	204,018	97,671	97,671
Less current liabilities													
Creditors	–46,453	–36,453	–38,453	–36,453	–36,453	–38,453	–38,500	–38,500	–40,500	–38,500	–38,500	–40,500	–40,500
Net current assets	**126,652**	**131,957**	**135,311**	**158,103**	**163,315**	**165,720**	**194,494**	**204,683**	**212,921**	**242,443**	**253,487**	**136,726**	**136,726**
EMPLOYMENT OF CAPITAL	**135,464**	**140,582**	**143,749**	**166,353**	**171,377**	**173,595**	**202,182**	**212,183**	**220,234**	**249,568**	**260,425**	**143,476**	**143,476**
Bank loan	0	0	0	0	0	0	0	0	0	0	0	0	0
Shareholders funds	125,000	125,000	125,000	125,000	125,000	125,000	125,000	125,000	125,000	125,000	125,000	125,000	125,000
Profit and loss account	10,464	15,582	18,749	41,353	46,377	48,595	77,182	87,183	95,234	124,568	135,425	18,476	18,476
CAPITAL EMPLOYED	**135,464**	**140,582**	**143,749**	**166,353**	**171,377**	**173,595**	**202,182**	**212,183**	**220,234**	**249,568**	**260,425**	**143,476**	**143,476**
Creative Director	2,383	2,383	2,438	2,383	2,383	2,438	2,383	2,383	2,438	2,383	2,383	2,438	28,820
Graphics Editor	1,979	1,979	2,023	1,979	1,979	2,023	1,979	1,979	2,023	1,979	1,979	2,023	23,922
Marketing Manager	1,136	1,136	1,419	1,136	1,136	1,419	1,136	1,136	1,419	1,136	1,136	1,419	14,762

Appendix f – Profit sensitivities

A number of different operating scenarios have been calculated from the base model (Example 1) after month 3, together with their effect on trading results.

Examples	Print run	Retail sales	Advert pages	Advert space filled	Promotion budget: Weekly	Promotion budget: Mths 13–25
1 (base)	30,000	10,500	14.5 – 17.5	60–80%	£1,500	£40,000
2	30,000	10,500	14.5 – 17.5	100%	£1,500	£40,000
3	30,000	10,500	14.5 – 17.5	80%	£1,500	£40,000
4	30,000	8,000	14.5	80%	£1,500	£40,000
5	30,000	8,000	14.5	60%	£1,500	£40,000
6	20,000	8,000	14.5	60%	£1,500	£40,000
7	20,000	8,000	14.0	60%	£1,500	£40,000
8	20,000	8,000	14.0	60%	£1,000	Nil

Profit (+) or loss (-) projections before tax

Example	Year one £'000	Year two £'000	Year three £'000
1 (base)	−25	+34	+134
2	+125	+205	+268
3	+42	+100	+148
4	+18	+60	+109
5	−60	−45	−10
6	−30	−5	+33
7	−52	−48	−34
8	−34	−10	−4

The first major assumption has been to write down the projections of advertising space filled by the percentages shown. This is a conservative contingency in case the forecast advertising response proves to be optimistic in any way. Were the agency selling the advertising space to be proved correct, the profits would be shown as in Example 2. Example 3 gives a mid-way drop in advertising revenue expectations and is then modified in Example 4 for (24%) lower retail copies sold.

Example 5 takes the assumptions given in the previous example but drops the advertising space back to a more conservative 60% figure. In practice, if retail sales drop, then the print run would be lowered, as is shown by Example 6, and the number of advertised pages may be curtailed as well (Example 7). If these very much lowered trading scenarios did occur, management would be expected to reduce the future promotion budget to conserve expenditure and an idea of this result is projected in Example 8, that shows, even in this extreme case, a near break-even position by year three. Twin Wheeler wishes to emphasize that it is very unlikely that all the forecast returns will be missed to the degree shown and he is confident the business can ride out any temporary difficulty.

Questions for the lending banker

1)   Is a loan of £60,000 a good risk proposition?

     The loan will be supported by £125,000 of equity capital and only half of the required funds is forecast to be used.

2)   Is it likely that the project will run short of finance and the bank asked for additional funding?

     There is always a risk that income with start-up ventures will take longer to reach their planned turnover.

3)   How easily will repayment be achieved?

     It is projected that the bank credit will not be required after six months; is a two year facility appropriate?

4)   What security should the bank request?

     A first fixed and floating charge over company assets and personal guarantee of the managing director/shareholder.

5)   Would it be preferable to channel a loan under the DTI's Small Firms Loans Guarantee Scheme?

     This would reduce the risk for the bank.

Appendix B

How to read financial statements

It may be helpful if a 'quick guide' is given on how to read the financial statements of a company business. This will not take the place of a full 'due diligence' lending proposal exercise, but it should enable a quick assessment to be made from the figures and questions asked of management, so that any further in-depth appraisal (refer to Chapter 3) can be more appropriately channelled. The 13 steps are as follows.

The balance sheet

1. Book net worth

- ◆ Total the share capital in issue and the retained earnings figures;
- ◆ add to this any 'pseudo capital' eg directors loans and other borrowings of a long-term permanency;
- ◆ deduct any intangible assets eg goodwill or deferred assets in the form of expenditure not yet represented by completed assets;
- ◆ (*optional*) deduct the stated value of brand names and similar items;
- ◆ the result will show the book value of the net worth of the business.

Now analyse how the net worth is made up, ie it will consist of an amount of fixed assets, an amount of net current assets (or liabilities) and other long-term items. Consider how much of net current assets relates to stock (and work-in-progress): is this at a minimum strategic level for trading or is it excessive?

2. Borrowings

+ Total the external short-term and long-term debt outstanding in the form of bank overdrafts, loans and other third party loans;
+ add hire purchase and leasing balances where they are 'on-balance sheet', ignoring any notes showing future leasing commitments;
+ how safe are the borrowings in terms of interest/repayments cover?

View the borrowings as a percentage of net worth: is it high (over 100%), low (less than 50%) or middling, bearing in mind the type of business being transacted and the need or, otherwise, for finance? How many times is the annual interest/repayment cost covered by profits?

3. Total long-term assets compared with total long term debt

+ Long-term assets are taken as tangible fixed assets and investments held not being classified as short-term holdings;
+ long-term debt is external third party borrowings not being classified as current liabilities.

Do long-term assets exceed long-term debt? If not, by how much is the business 'imbalanced' and is this risky? (If long-term assets exceed long-term debt, this means that some long-term assets are being financed by short-term debt and the business is 'borrowing short to invest long-term' with the potential risk of not being able to renew short-term debt and so suffering a cash flow problem).

4. The mix of fixed assets

+ Does the asset base comprise mostly of freeholds and leaseholds?
+ Are the leaseholds short- or long-term? If short-term, is there adequate security of tenure?
+ Does the asset base principally consist of written down plant and machinery?

Freehold assets may hold a current value in excess of their book value. If so, is the net worth of the business properly shown by the balance sheet? Is it good financial management to hold freehold assets rather than use the locked-in funds to increase working capital to earn more profit? Does much plant and machinery have to be expensively replaced soon?

5. Trade debtors compared with trade creditors

+ By how much does one total exceed the other total?
+ Is the business accepting more credit than it is giving (to its suppliers)?

A business will be better placed if it accepts more credit since this will be part of its operating (working) capital from which to earn more profit.

(Note: by converting the annual turnover into a daily amount, we can calculate how many days are represented by outstanding trade debtors. If the standard terms of trade are to give 30 days credit after the month end and customers receive invoices mid-month, this approximates to 45 days outstanding. A higher figure shown than this may suggest relatively poor credit control).

6. Stocks and work-in-progress

♦ Compare the total stock figure with that for purchases made in the year;
♦ how are stocks made up between raw materials and finished products?

If stocks are high relative to purchases in the year, are excess stocks held? If the finished products value is high it may mean that sales are sluggish. The number of times stock is turned over will indicate the business activity. A quick turnover and high activity will indicate good sales demand.

7. Current assets exceeding current liabilities (or vice versa)

♦ The higher the net current asset total then the more financially strong will be the business, providing long-term debt is of modest size;
♦ similarly, a net current liabilities position will indicate the opposite.

To have a positive net current asset position, providing it is not mainly tied up in stocks or the stock value is not affected by seasonal influences, will denote a good cash position and augur well for future expenditure plans.

The profit and loss account

8. The gross profit percentage margin earned on turnover

♦ Is the turnover product mix (if made available) acceptable?
♦ Is the level of turnover acceptable for the cost base and capital employed?
♦ What is the position of the order book? Too few orders may mean too high selling prices; too many orders may mean prices are too low.
♦ How efficient is production? Is there 'slack' to be taken up and can the goods be sold?
♦ Is the gross profit margin acceptable for the type of business run?
♦ What effect is competition having on the business?
♦ What is the state of labour relations, recruitment and staffing levels?
♦ Are the earnings retained in the business sufficient, or is the business over-trading?

What are the trends shown by these figures? They should be evaluated in the context of the type of business, the current state of its financial health and the bank's reasons for assessing the business.

9. Net profit earned before tax and exceptional items

- ♦ Taxation is not directly controllable but it may be minimized;
- ♦ exceptional items should not be accounted as part of on-going trading;
- ♦ is the reported net profit sufficient reward earned by the business?

Has tax planning been effective in reducing the aggregate tax rate borne? The reason for any exceptional items should be enquired after. What has been the trend of net profit? What factors have influenced it?

Other factors

10. Cash flow

- ♦ Take the retained earnings from the profit and loss account;
- ♦ add to this the depreciation/amortization deducted from the profit;
- ♦ add any cash invested by way of internal or external receipts;
- ♦ deduct the total of capital expenditure on assets less sales proceeds;
- ♦ deduct any non-recurring exceptional expenditure;
- ♦ the resulting figure will be the cash flow arising for the year.

The business may show a profit being earned but a negative generation of cash due to non-operational payments exceeding receipts. Will this recur? It should be assessed whether the cash flow being generated is adequate to finance the future operational plans for the business.

11. Notes to the accounts

- ♦ Examine each note to the financial statements to see whether it portrays items that must be taken into account, either to affect that year's results or future trading projections.

It is important to appraise the effect on cash flow of any future liabilities such as the cost of future leasing and capital expenditure commitments.

12. The trend shown by the operating results for the year(s)

- ♦ Assessing the trends shown by comparative figures for earlier years must complement a single profit and loss account and balance sheet.

13. Lending risks

♦ Taking all the above information the lending risk can now be judged.

Appendix C

Corporate lending case studies

The following examples have been chosen to illustrate particular aspects of bank lending assessments. All the companies are publicly quoted and the financial information has been taken from their published financial statements as issued at that time. It is assumed that the assessor at this stage does not know any subsequent or privileged information. Selected information is shown, as appropriate. Company quotes are in italics.

Case one – an industrial manufacturing conglomerate

The group is involved in electronics, printing tapes and construction (62% of turnover), energy and data cabling (17%), automotive (11%) and medical products (10%). The group had a difficult trading year up to 31 March 2003. Turnover was virtually static and continuing operations before exceptional items showed a small profit before tax of £2.7 million.

The American acquisition made two years earlier, incurring a large goodwill element in the purchase price, required a goodwill impairment charge against profits of £12 million apart from a normal amortization charge of £5.1 million, suggesting that in hindsight the group either overpaid for the acquisition or purchased with poor timing in relation to the subsequent trading results of this entity. Other exceptional charges totalling £5.3 million related to a structural cost reduction programme implemented at the European subsidiaries, involving redundancies, recommissioning of plant and machinery and writing down fixed assets. This programme will continue in the following year.

The paper division of the group was sold in 1999 but led to post-acquisition liability claims from the acquirer. Subsequent agreement between the parties has raised an exceptional charge of £5.8 million against profits, but half of the funds previously put in escrow, amounting to £13.1 million, have now been released. Future payments included in provisions for liabilities are expected to arise of £1 million over each of the next five years. All American claims by former paper mill employees as to asbestos exposure have so far been cleared without foundation.

> 'One of the principal business risks to the company is a significant global economic downturn that is both severe, unforeseen and prolonged. Principal risks to the business are reviewed on a regular basis by senior management.'

Salient financial figures reported

Group profit and loss account	£ million	Trend
Turnover	187	−4%
Pre-tax profit	2.7	−53%
After charging:		
depreciation	7.8	+16%
goodwill amortization	2.2	+5%
interest payable	1.1	+9%
Before charging:		
exceptional items	22.9	+79%
Taxation	1.5	−35%
Earnings available for distribution	1.2	−66%
Group balance sheet		
Goodwill	24.9	−42%
Freehold/long leasehold (cost)	27.2	−1%
Plant & machinery etc	106.3	+6%
Less depreciation on tangible assets	68.8	+13%
Fixed assets at book values	**89.6**	**−18%**
Trade debtors less creditors	16.0	−15%
Other debtors less creditors	−13.1	−52%
Stocks	19.3	−18%
Cash at bank	13.0	−10%
Cash escrow fund	13.4	−51%
Bank borrowings unsecured	−3.5	−40%
Net current assets	**45.1**	**−12%**
Bank loans unsecured	−25.2	-8%
Taxation & other provisions	−18.6	−6%
Liabilities due after one year	**−43.8**	**−7%**
Share capital & reserves	**90.9**	**−20%**

Extracts from the financial statements

Profit and loss account

1. *'Analyses of operating profits/losses and net assets by market segment are not available. A geographic analysis of net assets is not provided as, in the opinion of the directors, such disclosure would seriously prejudice the group's interests'.*

2. The current year tax charge of £1.5 million is the equivalent of a 56% tax charge on group profits (in spite of tax losses of £20.2 million) due to 'exceptional permanent differences' arising on overseas operations.

3. Non-exceptional profit before tax and interest, at £3.8 million, covers bank interest payable 3.5 times.

4. Research and development expenditure during the year (not shown in the table) amounted to £3.4 million, unchanged on the previous year.

5. *'The impact on profit from the fall in sales was partly offset by cost savings achieved through the reorganization programme. Prospects for the industrial division remain mixed ... that for the cable industry remain dull ... the short-term outlook for automotive is weak ... but there are solid growth prospects for medical.'*

Balance sheet

6. Borrowings at the year-end totalled £28.7 million (mostly US$, Euro and Swissfr, to mirror asset exposures) of which 90% were at floating interest rates. No bank borrowings have a maturity exceeding two years. Committed borrowings totalled £34 million plus £10 million uncommitted. A £30 million committed facility is due to expire on 30 April 2004. All borrowings are unsecured. There are cross-guarantees between the parent company and its UK subsidiaries in respect of bank and other financial obligations.

7. *'After making enquiries, the directors have a reasonable expectation that the group has adequate resources to continue in operational existence for the foreseeable future. For this reason they continue to adopt the going concern basis in preparing the financial statements.'*

8. The UK defined benefit pension schemes were last reassessed in April 2000. The results of revaluations due in April 2003 are not yet available, but *'it is expected that the annual pension charge to the profit and loss account ... in respect of the UK defined benefit schemes will increase significantly'.* (Contributions in respect of the USA schemes *'are not expected to increase significantly'* and the French and Italian schemes' liabilities of £2.5 million are already accounted for in the financial statements of the group.

9. Capital commitments contracted but not yet provided total £2.4million.

10 'Group accounts do not include a separate profit and loss account for the parent company as permitted by section 230 of the Companies Act 1985. The parent company loss for the year ... is £54.4 million after including a £56 million charge for fixed assets impairment and goodwill ... that has no impact on the consolidated profit and loss account or on cash.'

11 The average cost per group employee, excluding redundancy payments, was £30,119 compared with £31,808 for the previous year, representing a saving of £4.6 million.

The company has approached you to participate in the syndicate of banks being asked to renew the £30 million credit facility due on 30 April 2004. What is your decision?

Suggested comments

12 **Overview:** the company has a poor trading outlook overall and it is crucial for its future viability that the reorganization of costs already commenced is speedily completed and that any loss-making divisions not of group strategic importance and with poor chances of a rapid trading turnaround are put up for sale, in order that resources can be concentrated on more important group activities. If there are loss-making divisions, these should be critically appraised for a likely seasonality or economic upturn. If the answer to this appraisal is affirmative, the lending banks should be asked to support their retention. The prime action now is to renew, if possible, the £30 million syndicated facility (on the assumption that company cash flow forecasts suggest this size of facility is adequate for future working capital).

13 **Profitability:** ignoring exceptional costs, to earn a pre-tax profit return on turnover of just 1.4% is pretty appalling, even allowing that an industrial conglomerate is unlikely to have all its operations pulling the same way at the same time. In 1999 the group had sales of £512 million and a pre-tax profit of £62 million with shareholders' funds of £230 million. The lending bank should critically examine the strategic policy of the group to see if further measures should be implemented to ensure a recovery in earnings.

14 **Cash flow:** even with the current very low earnings the present interest cover on the cost of borrowings is fairly good. Trade debtors exceed trade creditors and the total of net current assets, including stocks, is positive. There are worrying factors: the trading outlook is not good; more exceptional costs may be expected; there will be a higher pension charge next year. Much depends on how turnover will progress and to assess this, privileged information is required from the company.

15 **Borrowings:** leaving aside the fate of the facility due for renewal, the known facts indicate other worrying issues. All borrowings are unsecured, yet there are cross-guarantees only between the parent company and the UK

subsidiaries. Are the overseas companies ring-fenced? Is this due to possible litigation overseas from which the UK arms of the group are being protected? This may be why certain analyses of assets split geographically have not been shown.

16   **Risk exposure:** it is not stated that the 90% of floating rate borrowings are hedged against increases in interest rates. If not, the group can hardly afford any sizeable increase in borrowing costs, yet the company seems more concerned about matching balance sheet assets held in currencies (the translation risks) when the ratio of total borrowings to net worth is calculated as a modest 43% (28.7/66.0).

17   **Reflection:** the company management has clearly made significant strides to reorganize its group interests and it is easy to say that a loss-making division can be sold if there are no buyers around. At this juncture, the bank needs to know:

   ♦ future operating forecasts (including cash flow) by division or by subsidiary company;

   ♦ more details of the security aspect for potential borrowers;

   ♦ up-to-date comment on the outstanding exceptional items in train;

   ♦ more information about risk-averse policy through derivatives;

   ♦ what reward is there to lend to the group and over what period?

   ♦ if the bank is a new entrant, an appraisal of management capabilities should be made bearing in mind the past track record.

18   **The decision:** given suitably beneficial answers to the questions set in point 14, a modest lending facility should be considered.

What did happen?

Turnover for the following year proved to be identical to 2003. Profit before tax and exceptional items totalled £2.6 million. Exceptional items totalled £10.8 million. Share capital and reserves less goodwill were restated for 2003 at £26.5 million (this year £23.2 million) after the company adopted the FRS17 accounting recommendation on retirement benefits. The £30 million syndicated loan refinancing was successfully completed to last for three years. Total borrowings reduced to £23.5 million and net current assets amounted to £29.3 million.

The Chair stated: 'with the completion of our European reorganization, we are focusing on growing sales throughout our business from our lower and more efficient cost base and from continuing innovation in new products. The new financial year has started well and although there are signs of increased raw material pricing pressure, we expect to make further progress.'

Case two – a pharmaceutical and healthcare supplier

The company had a turnover from continuing operations for the year ended 31 March 2001 of £8.8 million with a profit before tax of £0.2 million. For the ensuing year the forecast is to achieve a turnover of £9.6 million and probably a further, modest, profit. The balance sheet for this lending exercise is as follows.

Balance sheet	Forecast at 31 March 2002 (£ million)
Intangible (goodwill etc)	0.8
Tangible	4.2
Fixed assets	**5.0**
Trade debtors	2.6
Less trade creditors	−1.4
	1.2
Stocks	2.1
Cash on deposit	1.4
Borrowings: short term	−0.2
Other balances (net)	−1.5
Net current assets	**3.0**
Provisions & liabilities	**−0.5**
Shareholders funds	**7.5**

The company has been granted the opportunity to acquire the rights to a number of brand names and increase its coverage in the sector. The purchase comprises a division of the vendor's operations and, as such, no separate profit and loss account and balance sheet are available, but it is estimated that for the first year the division may attain break-even point on trading, excluding any acquisition costs. The deal will therefore be the purchase of the relevant assets relating to the brands being sold. The agreed purchase price is £6.8 million, made up as goodwill £2 million, brand names £3 million, tangible fixed assets £1 million and stock £0.8 million. Deferred payment terms apply to £0.8 million of the purchase price, but cash of £6 million is required now to complete the deal.

As banker to the company you are asked to provide finance. Do you comply with this request, for what amount and on what terms? This is the first opportunity to offer a sizeable loan to the company.

Suggested comments

1. The acquisition will increase the balance sheet footings of the company by 90%. The greater part of the purchase price is not represented by tangible assets. The company's present management will be integrating the new business into the group and their skills to do this are as yet unproven. It is not known whether the change of owners (and sales force) will affect future sales of the brands. It is decided to enquire of the company the background to the deal; how the purchase price was calculated; what plan the company has to promote the new brands; what fallback scenario is ready should either the bank's decision be a refusal or, if the deal goes ahead, what if the trading returns that are forecast do not immediately materialize.

2. The meeting with the management proved enlightening: there has been something of a boardroom difference of opinion. Four key directors are retiring and redundancy compensation is due. The burden of financing the whole of the purchase price through debt will be prohibitive, at around £0.5 million, as it will push the borrowing ratio up to 82% (refer to point 4) of shareholders funds net of intangible assets and remove any interest cover on borrowings.

3. The management has already foreseen that the deal could not be financed solely by debt and is pursuing the option of raising further equity finance through a 'rights' issue to shareholders. Will the bank provide the balance of funding and how much will this be?

4. Adding the tangible new assets of £1.8 million to tangible net worth of £6.7 million gives a revised net worth of £8.5 million. Future borrowings will still be considerably below this figure (and the 'one-to-one gearing ratio).

5. Much will depend on what level of earnings can be achieved the following year. In view of the potential uncertainties, the bank may wish to run a liquidation exercise and to estimate asset values on this basis: reducing debtors by one-third, stocks by two-thirds and plant etc by three-quarters reveals a valuation figure of £3.8 million, including cash held of £1.4 million and freehold land and buildings (mostly based on a 1986 valuation) of £3.4 million. There would appear to be good security for the bank in this respect.

6. Presumably the company will utilize its cash deposit to part finance the acquisition and so reduce the cost of commercial borrowing.

What did happen?

Lower than expected initial sales of the newly acquired brands coincided with the writing off of their marketing expenditure and some exceptional costs relating to redundancy payments also arose. A group loss before tax of £1 million was reported for the year ended 31 March 2002. A bank loan was granted of £2.9 million partly to finance the acquisition at a variable interest cost of 1.375% pa over LIBOR, repayable over approximately seven years. The interest rate risk on the loan was hedged by use of an interest rate swap, converting the loan cost to a fixed rate of 6.95% pa. A fixed and floating debenture over all company assets was put in place as well as a first legal charge over the property and assignment of a life policy.

The balance of the purchase price was made up through a 'rights issue' to existing shareholders, raising £4.7 million net of expenses. This sum plus the bank loan aggregated £7.6 million, exceeding the acquisition cost of £6.8 million and effectively replenishing the cash flow lost through the year's trading loss. At 31 March 2002 overdraft and loan borrowings of £3 million amounted to 45% of tangible net worth.

Turnover improved the following year to £14.7 million and the gross profit return on turnover increased from 27.6% to 30.5%. Profit before interest and tax achieved was £0.47 million and the interest cover was 2.3 times. The deferred acquisition payment was made during the year and by the year-end surplus cash held had dropped to £0.1 million. It had been prudent to raise money in excess of the immediate acquisition price and to retain the money on deposit for use during the year. The bank had financed only 38% of the money raised for the deal and the company was recovering well from the previous year's setback.

Case three – a service company providing security to vacant properties

This example has been chosen to show how a company restructuring can be implemented after the breaking of banking covenants. The company has generated a turnover of c.£43 million for the past two years, 70% within the UK where the market has been declining and competition from smaller, local, firms has been increasing. Selected details from the financial statements are as follows.

Years ended 31 March (£'million)	2002	2003 before re-structuring	2003 after re-structuring
Interest payable in year	7.4	4.2	
Pretax profit/loss(-) before interest	1.3	–1.1	
& before exceptional items	–5.2	–2.0	
Group balance sheet			
Intangible assets (goodwill)	69.0	64.9	64.9
Tangible assets (moveable items)	14.4	10.6	10.6
Net current assets before	1.7	3.6	3.4
Short-term debt	–62.4	–63.3	–3.3
Provisions & term liabilities	–0.3	–0.8	–0.8
Bank loans	0	0	–44.8
Shareholders funds	22.4	15.0	30.0

The exceptional items in 2002 referred to a strategic review (£1.4 million), goodwill etc impairment (£0.9 million) and closing interest rate swaps and loan refinancing costs (£2.9 million). In 2003 there were business closure (£1.4 million) and reorganization (£0.6 million) costs.

Comment

The group is vastly under-capitalized with massive short-term debt mainly supported by long-term intangible assets. Despite the acquisitions made in earlier years, that were probably financed short-term as an interim measure, there has not been the generation of sufficient profits annually to support such expenditure. The breaking of the banking covenants (not stated which, but probably arising from an inadequate ratio of net worth to loans) put the company close to liquidation.

What did happen?

In the notes to the financial statements under 'post balance sheet events' it was disclosed that, following the approval of shareholders at an Extraordinary General Meeting, senior bank debt totalling £15 million was exchanged for £15 million of zero coupon convertible preference shares and the maturity of other bank loans was extended by five years. In addition, the banks agreed to a two-year period during which no principal debt repayments would be made. The bank interest saving was LIBOR + 2.5% pa on £15 million of loans.

Equity shareholders agreed to relinquish 92% of their holdings for repurchase by the company and the remaining 8% of their holdings were written down by a further 90%. Exercise of the preference shares would give the banks control of the company.

Why did the banks not put the company into liquidation? The answer probably is found in the lack of a sufficiently high realization value of the tangible assets and faith in the capabilities of the (new) management. To a lesser degree, the measures now adopted by management to enable the company to be profitable (potentially over the next two years) must have been acceptable to the banks, and profitable trading results from some European subsidiaries are already being shown.

Index